# The acts of the risen Lord Jesus

Titles in this series:

An index of Scripture references for all the volumes may be found at <http://www.thegospelcoalition.org/resources/nsbt>.

NEW STUDIES IN BIBLICAL THEOLOGY 27

*Series editor: D. A. Carson*

# The acts of the risen Lord Jesus

LUKE'S ACCOUNT OF GOD'S
UNFOLDING PLAN

*Alan J. Thompson*

APOLLOS

INTERVARSITY PRESS
DOWNERS GROVE, ILLINOIS 60515

APOLLOS
An imprint of Inter-Varsity Press, England
Norton Street
Nottingham NG7 3HR, England
Website: www.ivpbooks.com
Email: ivp@ivpbooks.com

InterVarsity Press, USA
P.O. Box 1400
Downers Grove, IL 60515-1426, USA
Website: www.ivpress.com
Email: email@ivpress.com

InterVarsity Press®, USA, is the book-publishing division of InterVarsity Christian Fellowship/ USA® <www.intervarsity.org> and a member movement of the International Fellowship of Evangelical Students.

Inter-Varsity Press, England, is closely linked with the Universities and Colleges Christian Fellowship, a student movement connecting Christian Unions throughout Great Britain, and a member movement of the International Fellowship of Evangelical Students. Website: www.uccf.org.uk

Unless stated otherwise, Scripture quotations are from the Holy Bible, New International Version. Copyright © 1973, 1978, 1984 by International Bible Society. First published in Great Britain in 1979. Used by permission of Hodder & Stoughton, a division of Hodder Headline Ltd. All rights reserved. 'NIV' is a trademark of International Bible Society. UK trademark number 1448790.

The map on p. 111 is from The NIV Study Bible, ed. K. Barker, Grand Rapids: Zondervan, 1985, p. 1646; used by permission.

First published 2011.

Set in Monotype Times New Roman
Typeset in Great Britain by Servis Filmsetting Ltd, Stockport, Cheshire
Printed and bound in Great Britain by 4edge Limited

USA ISBN 978-0-8308-2628-5
UK ISBN 978-1-84474-535-7

**British Library Cataloguing in Publication Data**
A catalog record for this book is available from the British Library.

**Library of Congress Cataloging-in-Publication Data**

Thompson, Alan J.
  The Acts of the risen Lord Jesus : Luke's account of God's unfolding plan / Alan J. Thompson.
     p. cm.—(New studies in biblical theology ; 27)
  Includes bibliographical references and index.
  ISBN 978-0-8308-2628-5 (pbk. : alk. paper)
  1. Bible. N.T. Acts—Criticism, interpretation, etc. I. Title.
  BS2625.52.T56 2011
  226'.06—dc22
                                                            2011006821

| P | 18 | 17 | 16 | 15 | 14 | 13 | 12 | 11 | 10 | 9 | 8 | 7 | 6 | 5 | 4 | 3 | 2 | 1 |
| Y | 26 | 25 | 24 | 23 | 22 | 21 | 20 | 19 | 18 | 17 | 16 | 15 | 14 | 13 | 12 | 11 |

In memory of Doug Hewlett

# Contents

# Series preface

*New Studies in Biblical Theology* is a series of monographs that address key issues in the discipline of biblical theology.

Contributions to the series focus on one or more of three areas: (1) the nature and status of biblical theology, including its relations with other disciplines (e.g. historical theology, exegesis, systematic theology, historical criticism, narrative theology); (2) the articulation and exposition of the structure of thought of a particular biblical writer or corpus; and (3) the delineation of a biblical theme across all or part of the biblical corpora.

Above all, these monographs are creative attempts to help thinking Christians understand their Bibles better. The series aims simultaneously to instruct and to edify, to interact with the current literature, and to point the way ahead. In God's universe, mind and heart should not be divorced: in this series we will try not to separate what God has joined together. While the notes interact with the best of scholarly literature, the text is uncluttered with untransliterated Greek and Hebrew, and tries to avoid too much technical jargon. The volumes are written within the framework of confessional evangelicalism, but there is always an attempt at thoughtful engagement with the sweep of the relevant literature.

Much contemporary theological reflection on Acts seeks primarily to answer questions arising from our own disputes: the role of the Spirit in Christian life, the continuity or otherwise of gifts like tongues, the place of prophecy in the life of the church, and so on. One must ask, of course, if those are the dominant concerns of Acts. True, Acts does in some ways address such questions, but the strength of Dr Thompson's book is that it uncovers the main theological emphases of the book of Acts on the book's own terms. Moreover, although this volume focuses on Acts, Dr Thompson wisely keeps an eye peeled for theological connections with Luke's

Gospel. This volume will be a treasure trove for all who seek to understand Acts better, not least those who teach and preach the book.

*D. A. Carson*
*Trinity Evangelical Divinity School*

# Author's preface

The richness of God's Word is amazing. The book of Acts, in particular, is full of challenge, encouragement and comfort. In studying Acts I have been amazed again at God's faithfulness, the kindness and power of the risen Lord Jesus, the enablement and transforming work of the Spirit sent by Jesus, and the privilege of receiving the good news of God's saving grace in Christ. Although I hope this book may make some contribution to the academic study of Acts, my main goal is to help believers who read, teach or preach through the book of Acts to see Luke's 'framework' of God's kingdom and the reign of Christ more clearly and to rejoice in, be encouraged and reassured by, and proclaim the good news of God's saving purposes in the death and resurrection of the Lord Jesus.

This book could not have been accomplished without the generosity and help of many. I wish to thank Geoff Harper, Michael Thate and especially my wife, Alayne, for reading through and offering helpful advice on earlier stages of this book, the Principal, David Cook, and Board of Sydney Missionary and Bible College for granting a sabbatical that enabled the book to be completed, the staff and research facilities at Tyndale House, Cambridge, for helping make the sabbatical both productive and enjoyable, and our girls, Deborah and Rebekah, for their joyful participation in our travels. I also wish to thank Don Carson for his advice and encouragement, and for accepting this book into the New Studies in Biblical Theology series, and Philip Duce and the staff at IVP for their help in the editorial process. This book is dedicated *in memorium* to Doug Hewlett in gratitude for his faithful teaching and godly example in bringing honour to the name of the Lord Jesus.

*Alan J. Thompson*

# Abbreviations

| | |
|---|---|
| *1 En.* | *1 Enoch* |
| 1 Macc. | 1 Maccabees |
| 2 Macc. | 2 Maccabees |
| AB | Anchor Bible |
| *Ant.* | *Jewish Antiquities* (Josephus) |
| AV | Authorized (King James) Version |
| BECNT | Baker Exegetical Commentary on the New Testament |
| *Bib* | *Biblica* |
| *BJRL* | *Bulletin of the John Rylands Library, University of Manchester* |
| BST | The Bible Speaks Today |
| CBET | Contributions to Biblical Exegesis and Theology |
| *EQ* | *Evangelical Quarterly* |
| ESV | English Standard Version |
| *ETL* | *Ephemerides theologicae lovanienses* |
| *ExpTim* | *Expository Times* |
| HCSB | Holman Christian Standard Bible |
| *HTR* | *Harvard Theological Review* |
| *IBS* | *Irish Biblical Studies* |
| ICC | International Critical Commentary |
| *Int* | *Interpretation* |
| *JBL* | *Journal of Biblical Literature* |
| *JETS* | *Journal of the Evangelical Theological Society* |
| JPTSup | Journal of Pentecostal Theology Supplement Series |
| JSJSup | Supplements to the Journal for the Study of Judaism |
| *JSNT* | *Journal for the Study of the New Testament* |
| JSNTSup | Journal for the Study of the New Testament Supplement Series |
| *J. W.* | *Jewish War* (Josephus) |

| | |
|---|---|
| lit. | literally |
| LNTS | Library of New Testament Studies |
| LXX | Septuagint |
| mg. | margin |
| NAC | New American Commentary |
| NASB | New American Standard Bible |
| NICNT | New International Commentary on the New Testament |
| NICOT | New International Commentary on the Old Testament |
| NIGTC | New International Greek Testament Commentary |
| NIV | New International Version |
| NKJV | New King James Version |
| NLT | New Living Translation |
| *NovT* | *Novum Testamentum* |
| NSBT | New Studies in Biblical Theology |
| NT | New Testament |
| *NTS* | *New Testament Studies* |
| OT | Old Testament |
| PNTC | Pillar New Testament Commentary |
| *Pss Sol.* | *Psalms of Solomon* |
| PTMS | Pittsburgh Theological Monograph Series |
| RSV | Revised Standard Version |
| *SBJT* | *Southern Baptist Journal of Theology* |
| SBLDS | Society of Biblical Literature Dissertation Series |
| *Sib. Or.* | *Sibylline Oracles* |
| SNTSMS | Society for New Testament Studies Monograph Series |
| SP | Sacra pagina |
| *Them* | *Themelios* |
| TNIV | Today's New International Version |
| tr. | translation |
| *TynBul* | *Tyndale Bulletin* |
| *TZ* | *Theologische Zeitschrift* |
| WBC | Word Biblical Commentary |
| *WTJ* | *Westminster Theological Journal* |
| WUNT | Wissenschaftliche Untersuchungen zum Neuen Testament |

# Introduction

What major themes, issues or debates come to mind when someone mentions 'the book of Acts' to you? The answer to this question in everyday conversations about Acts inevitably includes a cluster of issues related to anything from the charismatic movement (speaking in tongues as a sign of receiving the Spirit, baptism of the Holy Spirit as a second blessing), church government and practice (congregational versus presbyterian church government, the responsibilities of deacons, infant/household baptism versus baptism of believers, baptism as a condition of salvation) to missionary methods (whether or not we should follow the same strategies).[1] It seems that, at the popular level at least, Acts is still used more for answers to debates that were not necessarily prominent in Luke's aims than listened to for Luke's own emphases.

My aim in this work is not to address all of these debates but rather to offer a framework for interpreting the book of Acts so that the major themes highlighted by Luke may be identified and related to the book of Acts as a whole. One of the areas of focus for the New Studies in Biblical Theology series is 'the articulation and exposition of the structure of thought of a particular biblical writer or corpus'. It is within this area that I seek to make a contribution. This book will especially highlight Acts as an account of the 'continuing story' of God's saving purposes. Luke intends his work to be read in the light of OT promises and the continuing reign of Christ. Acts is best understood, therefore, in this 'biblical-theological' framework that highlights the move from the OT to what the kingdom of God looks like now that Christ has come, died, risen and ascended to the right hand of the Father.[2] It is in this light – the continuing reign of Christ in the inaugurated kingdom of God – that Luke's own emphases on themes such

---

[1] Cf. Fee and Stuart 2003: 108 for references to some of these.
[2] On biblical theology see Rosner 2000: 3–11, esp. p. 10.

as the saving purposes of God, suffering and opposition as the gospel spreads and local churches are established, the resurrection of Christ, Israel and the Gentiles, the Holy Spirit, the temple, law and apostolic authority are better understood and integrated.[3] Although various studies have drawn attention to these themes, my aim is to highlight the 'inaugurated kingdom of God' as the organizing framework for integrating Luke's overall emphases in Acts.[4]

This framework, however, is not merely of theoretical or antiquarian interest. Luke emphasizes the continued outworking of God's purposes for a reason. The rest of this chapter will show briefly that understanding Luke's stated purpose helps us to see how we should approach Acts. A brief excursus at the end of the chapter will summarize my assumptions in this book concerning matters of authorship, audience and interpreting Acts. Those familiar with these matters of standard NT introduction may skip the excursus at the end of this introduction and continue with the biblical-theological material in chapter 1.

---

[3] This book therefore obviously does not provide a commentary on all the passages in Acts nor does it summarize all the themes in Acts.

[4] In addition to the now flourishing amount of technical monographs on various aspects of Lukan theology (cf. Bovon 2006), the most comprehensive discussion of the theology of Acts as a whole is found in the book edited by Marshall and Peterson (1998). As a multi-author volume, however, that book did not seek to integrate substantially the findings of the individual chapters. Jacob Jervell's book on the theology of Acts (1996) is really the only book written in recent times on the theology of Acts by one author who integrates the theological themes treated. It is helpful in drawing attention to Jewish aspects of Acts, but his views are generally recognized to be rather idiosyncratic (e.g. that 'the church is Israel', 'Torah is the distinguishing mark' and the Gentiles are an 'associate people', 43, 61). The book by Dennis Johnson (1997) is the only book in recent times to look at the theological message of Acts at a level that is also accessible to the wider Christian public (he also manages to look at theological themes without neglecting the historical reliability of Acts). My own approach is closest to Johnson's understanding of the message of Acts. I would, however, like to highlight and integrate some other themes and develop further the reference to 'The History of Redemption' in his title. Chris Green's book (2005) is a readable, popular-level introduction to the layout of the book of Acts with helps for preachers (cf. Cook 2007). However, it is more of an introduction to the structure and flow of Acts. The best succinct study of the theology of Acts is now that of Peterson 2009: 53–97. Thus, while there continues to be a never-ending stream of books on Pauline theology, and a growing number of technical studies on Acts (which are often doctoral dissertations), there are still very few books at a more 'accessible' level on the theology of Acts. It seems as though there is still room for further discussion of the theology of a writer who wrote more than Paul in the NT!

# Reassurance concerning God's purposes: the purpose(s) of the book of Acts

Why did Luke write Acts? Luke's stated purpose in the preface to his Gospel, the language and style of his writing as 'biblical narrative' and his explicit links between the OT, Luke's Gospel and Acts all indicate that Luke is writing for a Christian audience familiar with the promises and language of the OT in order to provide assurance concerning the continued outworking of God's saving purposes.

First, regarding Luke's purpose, in the opening verse of his Gospel, Luke tells us he is joining others in compiling a narrative concerning 'the things that have been fulfilled among us' (Luke 1:1).[5] The passive voice of the verb 'fulfilled/accomplished' indicates that the events have been fulfilled/accomplished *by God*, and this is in keeping with Luke's emphasis throughout his Gospel and Acts on the fulfilment of God's plan.[6] In 1:4 of his Gospel Luke gives us the purpose of his writing project: he is writing in order that 'you may know the certainty of the things you have been taught'.[7] The indication here is that readers such as Theophilus had been taught or instructed about the faith.[8] What Luke's audience needed, however, was 'certainty' or 'assurance' about what they had been taught.[9] When Luke's Gospel and the book of Acts are read in the light of this preface, it appears that Luke is writing to provide reassurance to believers about the nature of the events surrounding Jesus' life, death, resurrection, the spread of the message about Jesus, and the nature of God's people following Jesus' ascension. He is providing

---

[5] *Peri tōn peplērophorēmenōn en ēmin pragmatōn.* Cf. Marshall (1993: 163–182) for a discussion concerning the importance of the prologue of Luke's Gospel for understanding both Luke's Gospel and Acts.

[6] Cf. Peterson 1993: 83–104. In Luke's Gospel see e.g. 1:20, 57; 2:6, 21–22; 4:21; 9:31; 21:22, 24; 24:44–47. In Acts see 1:4, 16; 2:1, 16, 23, 30–31; 3:18, 24; 4:25–28; 7:52; 8:35; 10:43; 13:23, 32–33; 15:15; 17:2–3; 24:14–15; 26:6–7, 22–23; 28:23. Cf. also Bock 1998: 41–62.

[7] *Hina epignōs . . . tēn asphaleian.*

[8] Bock (1994: 65–66) notes that *katēcheō* can refer to a report (Acts 21:24) or to receiving instruction (Acts 18:25); *logōn* can refer to events (Luke 7:17; Acts 8:21; 15:6) or instruction (Luke 4:32; 10:39) or to a 'message received' (Luke 1:20; 6:47). Together with the term 'assurance', the reference to 'instruction' here indicates that a believer is being addressed.

[9] The term *asphaleia* is used in Acts 5:23 to mean 'safe' (and elsewhere only in 1 Thess. 5:3). Bock (1994: 65) observes that the use of this term here 'with a verb of knowing points to a psychological goal. It refers to knowing the truth but doing so securely.' Related terms to *asphaleia* are used in Acts 2:36, 21:34, 22:30 and 25:26 to refer to assurance or 'determining the facts with certainty' (ibid).

assurance that these events really are the work of God, that God really has been accomplishing his purposes, that Jesus really is who he said he was, and that believers in Jesus really are the true people of God. All of this is especially important in the light of the rejection and persecution faced by these believers, not the least of which came from those who also claimed to belong to the heritage of God's people and who read the same Bible.

Secondly, this leads us to a further observation helpful for determining Luke's purposes – the genre of Acts. Vanhoozer describes a genre as a kind of literature that indicates 'literary practices' which bear 'family resemblances' to other kinds of literature.[10] Although a full discussion concerning the genre of Acts cannot be entered into here, the 'family resemblances' between the narrative of Acts and OT historical narrative indicate that Luke is not only writing history; he is writing 'biblical history'.[11] Rosner's evidence in support of this includes:

1. The imitation of LXX language and style in Acts, giving it a 'biblical atmosphere' (esp. in Acts 1 – 15).
2. The language of fulfilment in Acts that is prominent in a wide range of topics covered (Christology, mission to Gentiles, Holy Spirit) and the prominence of significant themes in Acts that are central OT themes (i.e. Jerusalem, temple and law).[12]
3. Similarities to the OT in the depiction of episodes.
4. Literary techniques in Acts that may also be found in OT narratives (e.g. set formulae or summary statements in Kings to move from one king to another; speeches and prayers that introduce, sum up and transition; periods of history marked out; the writing of narrative 'through a series of main characters' or 'biographical' sections such as with Abraham, Jacob and Joseph in Genesis).

[10] Vanhoozer 1998: 338, 340, citing Fowler 1982: 41.

[11] Rosner 1993: 65–82. Other similar phrases have also been used, such as 'theological history' (Maddox 1982: 16), 'sacred narrative' (Sterling 1992: 363) and 'biblical narrative' (Gasque 1989: 348). Rosner cites Sterling and Gasque on pp. 81–82 of his article. Cf. also the summary of Rosner's article in Peterson 2009: 13–14. The 'biographical' nature of OT historiography (mentioned in point 4) is also evident in the summaries of OT history in Acts 7 and 13 and reflects the way Luke himself is recounting the history of the church in Acts.

[12] In referring to Luke's use of the OT in Acts I will use the general distinction (following R. B. Hays 1989: 23, 29) between 'quotation' and 'allusion' where 'quotation' refers to an explicit citation and 'allusion' refers to an intended reference to the OT, which, although not an explicit citation, is more obvious than an 'echo' (which is more 'subtle'; I am not examining 'echoes' in this book).

5. A theological understanding of history in which God is in control and is fulfilling his covenant promises. In Acts this is highlighted by the prominence of key terms that indicate divine sovereignty (the most well known being *dei*, 'it is necessary') and the emphasis on God's actions, which lead the narrative events along).[13]

Thus 'the author is continuing the story of Israel where it left off. That is to say, he is intending to write *biblical narrative*.'[14] In addition to these observations concerning the language, style and themes of OT narrative, we may note Paul House's observations regarding narrative summaries of OT history in 'the narratives of Old Testament narrative', such as Deuteronomy 1 – 4; Joshua 23 – 24; Judges 1 – 2; 1 Samuel 12; 2 Kings 17; and Psalms 78, 89, 104 – 106.[15] One of the functions of these historical summaries, according to House, is that 'the writers place themselves and their audiences . . . into that story'.[16] In the context of the narrative of Acts the major speeches of Acts 7 and 13 are largely narrative accounts of OT history from different perspectives in order to highlight continuing participation in that history. In Acts 7 the pattern of rejecting and persecuting God's messengers is noted, and in Acts 13 the pattern of God's saving provision for his people, which finds fulfilment in the death and resurrection of Jesus and which now includes Gentiles, is emphasized.

Thirdly, three strategically placed texts (at the beginning and end of Luke's Gospel and then at the beginning of Acts) also indicate that Luke wants his readers to read along a historical line from the OT to the Gospel of Luke and on to the book of Acts to see the outworking of God's saving plan:

(1) Luke 1:1 'the things that have been *fulfilled* among us'
(2) Luke 24:44–47
    (a) 'everything must be *fulfilled* . . . written . . . in the Law . . . Prophets . . . Psalms'
    (b) 'the Christ will suffer and rise from the dead on the third day

---

[13] Other terms Rosner refers to include *hē boulē tou theou* (the will of God), *thelēma* (will), *horizō* (foreordain), *prooorizō* (predestine) and *prooraō* (foresee). For more on God's sovereignty in Acts see ch. 1.

[14] Gasque 1989: 348 (emphasis original), cited by Rosner (1993: 82). Note also the interesting suggestion of Barrett (1996: 94–104) that together Luke and Acts may be described as 'the first New Testament'.

[15] House 2005: 229–245.

[16] Ibid. 232.

      (c) and repentance and forgiveness of sins will be
           preached . . .'
(3) Acts 1:1 'in my former book . . .'

At the beginning of Luke's Gospel (1) the links between the OT
and Luke's writing are indicated ('the things that have been fulfilled
among us'). At the end of Luke's Gospel (2) the links between (a) the
OT ('everything must be fulfilled . . . Law . . . Prophets . . . Psalms')
and (b) the account of Jesus' life, death and resurrection in Luke's
Gospel ('about me . . . the Christ will suffer and rise') are confirmed,
*and* the links between (a) the OT and (c) the spread of the Gospel in
Acts are also identified ('everything must be fulfilled . . . *and* repentance and forgiveness . . . will be preached'). At the beginning of Acts
(3) the link between Luke's Gospel and Acts is highlighted ('in my
former book . . .'). These three texts indicate that Luke intends Acts
to be read as a continuation of this line as he recounts the continued
outworking of God's saving purposes (see the figure below).

| OT | Luke † | Acts |
|---|---|---|

The above observations concerning the purpose and genre of Acts
help us to see how we should approach Acts. Since Acts is written for
a Christian audience for the purpose of providing reassurance concerning God's actions, and since the narrative of Acts is patterned
after the style and features of OT narrative, which highlight the
accomplishment of God's purposes in history, then, as in OT narrative, the main character in the narrative of Acts is God. That is, Acts
is not merely 'objective history' to satisfy our curiosity about various
events. Nor is it necessarily prescriptive of everything it describes
(though it is not merely descriptive either). The main concern of the
author for his readers is that we look to see what *God* is doing in the
narrative, how God is accomplishing his purposes and how we may
embrace and identify with these purposes and so glorify the God of
the biblical narrative.[17]

Of course, the main salvation-historical development that has
taken place following the OT is the life, death, resurrection and
ascension of the Lord Jesus. In the following chapters we will see
that the focus of Acts is on the continued accomplishment of God's
saving purposes through the risen Lord Jesus. The kingdom has

---

[17] Cf. Hamilton 2008: 34–47; 2010: 419–440.

indeed been inaugurated in the life, death, resurrection and ascension of the Lord Jesus. The Lord Jesus is continuing to reign and all who come to him in repentance and faith are truly God's people and will receive the promised blessings of forgiveness and the Holy Spirit. God's people may be assured therefore that, because the Lord Jesus continues to reign, they will be enabled by the Holy Spirit to serve him and reflect his character, the word will continue to spread even in the midst of opposition, and local churches will be established and strengthened with the apostolic message about the Lord Jesus. Luke's emphasis on the nature of the kingdom of God, therefore, is as relevant for Christian readers today as it was for the first century. All who follow the Lord Jesus this side of the cross and resurrection need to know that God is continuing to accomplish his purposes even now through the reign of the Lord Jesus. It is to the theme of the inaugurated kingdom of God, therefore, that we turn in chapter 1.

# Excursus: assumptions concerning authorship, audience and interpreting Acts

## Authorship and audience

I am assuming throughout this study that the same author wrote both the Gospel of Luke and the book of Acts, that this author is Luke, the 'sometime companion of Paul', and that he probably wrote Acts sometime before AD 70.[18] Who was Luke writing for?[19] The attempt to locate a particular 'Lukan community' is fraught with difficulty and has now been largely abandoned.[20] The lack of any reference to a particular community, coupled with the general nature of the prologue of Luke's Gospel, makes any such historical reconstruction for a particular locality tentative at best.[21] Thus clues

---

[18] My own argumentation for this may be found in A. J. Thompson 2004. An accessible and recent defence of this view may be found in Peterson 2009: 1–5. The phrase 'sometime companion of Paul' is used by Witherington (1998: 59), among others, to indicate that Luke was not an 'inseparable' companion of Paul. Michael Thompson's forthcoming article 'Paul in the Book of Acts: Differences and Distance' (which will be published in *Expository Times*) is a recent re-examination of the 'we-passages' in Acts which argues that these are the work of Luke as an eyewitness to the events described in these passages.

[19] The following section borrows from my discussion in A. J. Thompson 2008a: 10–12.

[20] Cf. Allison 1988: 62–70; Moxnes 1994: 379–389; Barton 1998: 173–194.

[21] Allison 1988: 66, cited in Barton 1998: 187.

must be examined in the narrative itself for descriptions of who the readers implied by the narrative may be.[22]

The name of the addressee, Theophilus, mentioned in both prefaces, does not provide any further decisive evidence. A common Greek name, it was used by both Jews and Greeks.[23] The suggestion that Acts is intended solely for a readership outside the church (i.e. as a defence of Christianity to Roman readers), however, is the most unlikely option. In addition to the problem Roman officials would have had in understanding the relevance of much of the book[24] and the difficulty many would have had in noticing the many allusions to the LXX,[25] Luke's repeated use of the plural pronoun 'us' in his preface to the Gospel indicates an identification with the readership of his work. As Marguerat notes,

> the narrative which follows (the Gospel and Acts) takes place within a readership composed of a common faith in the saving events (the 'events . . . fulfilled among us') and a common adherence to a tradition ('handed on [to us] by those who from the beginning were eyewitnesses').[26]

Thus a Christian readership is most likely implied by the preface to Luke's Gospel.

Other clues in the narrative, however, have been the basis for conflicting claims for the readership of Acts. Many have focused on whether or not this Christian readership was primarily Gentile or Jewish. Those in favour of a Gentile-Christian readership point to (1) the emphasis on the Gentile mission, (2) the absence of primarily Jewish preoccupations (such as Matt. 5:21–48), (3) the use of the LXX and the absence of Hebrew and Aramaic terms, and (4) Luke's

---

[22] Kurz 1993: 13.

[23] Witherington 1998: 63. The term 'most excellent' is used only four times in the NT, all by Luke (Luke 1:1; Acts 23:26 [Felix]; 24:3 [Felix]; 26:25 [Festus]). Although it may indicate that Theophilus was an official or person of some rank, it was also a common term for polite address.

[24] Cassidy (1987: 148–155) argues contra the 'political apologetic' view of Haenchen 1971: 105; Conzelmann 1987: xlvii–xlviii; 1960: 138–144; Cadbury 1927: 308–313; Walaskay 1983: esp. 37, 50, 65–67. Note also the mixed portrayals of Roman officials (cf. Gallio, Acts 18:17; Felix, Acts 24:26–27). Cf. also Rowe: 2009: 3–4, 10–11.

[25] Ravens (1995:13) draws attention to 'Luke's allusive use of the LXX'. Cf. also Steyn 1995.

[26] Marguerat 2002: 23–24. Cf. also Kurz 1993: 14.

Greco-Roman preface.[27] Those in favour of a Jewish-Christian readership, however, respond by pointing out (1) that the emphasis on Gentile mission needs to be understood in the context of Israel's restoration and does not necessarily entail a complete rejection of the Jews, (2) Luke's many references to primarily Jewish concerns (e.g. the clean/unclean issue in Acts 10), (3) the fact that a Greek-speaking Jewish readership could explain Luke's use of the LXX and the absence of Hebrew and Aramaic terms, and (4) that many of the Gentile converts in Acts were God-fearers who had already attached themselves to Judaism (without undergoing circumcision).[28] It seems, therefore, that in the light of such seemingly conflicting claims for the audience of Luke-Acts, it would be wise to follow the course proposed by Marguerat, that 'the Lucan work implies a diversified readership'.[29] That is, the intended audience may include both Jewish and Gentile Christian readers. A Jewish or Gentile Christian audience familiar with the language and promises of the OT, however, appears to be the primary target.

## *Interpreting Acts*

My focus in this book will be on the text of Acts itself.[30] Although I am not arguing for Luke's reliability as a historian in this book, I do not assume there is a necessary disjunction between Luke's role as historian and theologian.[31] Since Luke's Gospel and the book of Acts cannot be dealt with entirely separately, there will be some reference at times to Luke's Gospel.[32] There are sufficient

---

[27] Cf. Fitzmyer 1981: 57–59; Kurz 1993: 13–14. These arguments are summarized in Ravens 1995: 14.

[28] Esler 1987: 24–26, 30–45; Jervell 1972: 175–177; Ravens 1995: 14–16.

[29] Marguerat 2002: 83.

[30] As noted above, in providing a biblical-theological 'framework' this book obviously does not cover all that should be said about Acts. For instance, although important for a full understanding of Acts, this book does not examine the ways in which these themes might be heard in a Greco-Roman world with imperial claims for authority (though I have examined aspects of this in A. J. Thompson 2008a; cf. Rowe 2009).

[31] The classic book which argued that Luke was both a historian and a theologian is that of Marshall 1970. See also the M. B. Thompson article 'Paul in the Book of Acts' (forthcoming), where he argues for a positive assessment of Luke's reliability in his portrait of Paul. On the question of idealization and the portrait of the church in Acts see A. J. Thompson 2008b: 523–542.

[32] Whether one thinks that Luke and Acts were written separately, with Luke's Gospel written before and independently of Acts, or if one thinks that Luke produced the two books as two parts of one work, readers of Acts cannot treat Acts as entirely independent from Luke's Gospel. This is especially so since in Acts 1:1 Luke himself

distinctives in style and focus, however, to warrant treating Acts independently.[33]

Although much has been written about interpreting biblical narrative in general and the narrative of Acts in particular, I have found it particularly helpful to look out for various forms of repetition in seeking to observe Luke's emphases.[34] This is sometimes the best way to determine the difference between what some call 'descriptive' and 'prescriptive' elements in the narrative of Acts. For example, the appointment of a leader (Matthias) by lot is unlikely to be 'prescriptive' for the appointment of all church leaders just because it has been 'described' once (Acts 1:23–26). The frequent references to the way material possessions are used, however, indicate that Luke is trying to make a point (i.e. that he is arguing for or 'prescribing' something). In the case of material possessions it appears that by both positive and negative portraits he shows that the reality of one's allegiance to the Lord Jesus is evidenced in the way one uses material possessions (Luke 16:13).[35] It seems that if Luke wants to make a point, he highlights something by repetition. This repetition may be seen in

- patterns (such as the parallels between Peter and Paul)[36]
- summary statements[37]
- narration of major events[38]

---

directs us to his Gospel. See the lengthy discussion of this in Verheyden 1999 and the recent summary in Bird 2007.

[33] Carson and Moo 2005: 203.

[34] For more information on interpreting Acts see the succinct summaries in C. Green 2005: 13–35 and Peterson 2009: 39–49. For an analysis of literary approaches to Acts see Spencer 1993: 381–414.

[35] Note the positive portraits in 2:44–45; 4:32, 34–35; 4:36–37; 6:1–7; 9:36, 39; 11:27–30; 16:15, 34; 20:35; and the contrasting negative portraits in 1:18; 5:1–11; 8:18–23; 16:16, 19; 19:23–27; 24:26. Cf. most recently C. Hays 2010.

[36] Cf. Moessner 1986. Note the helpful table in C. Green 2005: 25. I.e. both Peter and Paul heal a lame man (3:2–8; 14:8–10), do miracles at a distance (5:15; 19:12), exorcise demonic spirits (5:16; 16:16–18), confront sorcerers (8:18–24; 13:6–11), raise the dead (9:36–41; 20:9–12), have heavenly visions (10:9–16; 16:9; 18:9–10; 23:11), are miraculously released from prison (5:19; 12:7–11; 16:25–28) and preach to Jews using Ps. 16:10 (2:27; 13:35). Some parallels extend back to Jesus' activity in the Gospel of Luke as well (note the pattern at the outset of each person's ministry where a reference to the Holy Spirit's activity is followed by a major sermon and the healing of a paralytic in Luke 3 – 5, Acts 2 – 3, 13 – 14).

[37] 2:47; 6:7; 9:31; 12:24; 16:5; 19:20; 28:30–31.

[38] E.g. Cornelius' conversion (Acts 10 – 11; 15:7–9); Saul's conversion (Acts 9, 22, 26); sharing resources (Acts 2:42–47; 4:32–37).

- terms within individual accounts[39]
- 'frames' or 'inclusios'[40]
- themes in contrasting accounts[41]

It is not always easy to determine with certainty what Luke may be 'prescribing' in the narrative of Acts. In addition to the observations above concerning Luke's purposes and audience (assurance for believers concerning the outworking of God's purposes in Christ), however, keeping an eye out for these kinds of repetitions will at least help to alert us to the fact that something is being emphasized! Although much more could be said about Luke's narrative techniques, my aim here is merely to summarize briefly the approach taken in this book as I focus primarily on the text of Acts in order to highlight the biblical-theological framework of the inaugurated kingdom of God in Acts.

[39] E.g. 'temple' (Acts 3:1–3, 8, 10), 'name' (Acts 4:7, 10, 12, 17–18), 'teaching' (Acts 5:21, 25, 28, 34, 42), 'our fathers' (Acts 7:11–15) and 'eunuch' (Acts 8:27, 32, 34, 36, 38–39).

[40] E.g. Acts 6:1 and 7 (the increase of the disciples); 9:2 and 20 (Saul's actions in Damascus); 9:1 and 31 (from murderous threats to peace); 11:1 and 18 (a contrast concerning the acceptance of the Gentiles); 12:1–4 and 20–23 (the 'authority' of Herod, who is called a 'king' in 12:1 and 20–21).

[41] E.g. the use of money and material possessions mentioned above.

# Chapter One

# Living 'between the times': the kingdom of God

We have seen that Luke primarily wrote Acts to provide assurance to his readers concerning the purposes and plan of God. This, in addition to the likelihood that he is aiming to highlight the 'continuing story' of the fulfilment of God's promises for his people, indicates that we should look primarily for what Luke is saying about God and his purposes in Acts and how this may provide reassurance for his readers. Thus this chapter will continue the discussion of the last chapter by focusing on what Luke says about the outworking of God's purposes with a treatment of the sovereignty of God, the kingdom of God, the reign of Christ and the spread of the word in the midst of opposition. We will see that Luke is drawing attention to the continued outworking of God's saving purposes specifically in the inaugurated kingdom of God through the reign of the Lord Jesus. It is within this framework that Luke wants his readers to see his account of the unstoppable spread of the word and the strengthening of local churches in the midst of persecution and opposition.

## The sovereignty of God

Although many often approach the book of Acts by focusing primarily on the human participants in the narrative (such as Peter and the apostles, Paul, Stephen, Cornelius), the focus in the book of Acts is actually on God.[1] That Luke is highlighting the sovereignty of God in history is indicated by his use of key terms as well as the way in which he describes God's involvement in the history of Israel, the events surrounding the life, death and resurrection of Jesus, and the subsequent developments in the history of the church that he is recounting. We will examine this broad theme of the

[1] Cf. Squires 1993, Jervell 1996, Gaventa 2003 and esp. the summary in Walton 2008: 291–306.

accomplishment of God's purposes first before focusing attention on the kingdom of God and the continuing reign of the Lord Jesus.

## Key terms

As noted in the previous chapter, one of the ways the book of Acts evidences a theological understanding of history in which God is in control and fulfilling his covenant promises is in the prominence of terms that indicate divine sovereignty.[2] The most prominent term in Acts that draws attention to 'divine necessity' is *dei*, 'it is necessary'.[3] The term occurs 40 times in Luke-Acts (18 in Luke; 22 in Acts), which is almost twice as many times as in all 13 of Paul's letters (24 times in total), and significantly more than anywhere else in the NT (6 in Mark, 8 in Matthew, 10 in John).[4] Although the term does not always refer to divine necessity (i.e. Acts 15:5; 16:30; 19:36; 25:24), Luke particularly highlights divine necessity in the life, death, resurrection and ascension of Jesus (Luke 2:49; 4:43; 9:22; 13:33; 17:25; 22:37; 24:7, 26, 44; Acts 1:16; 3:21; 17:3), the calling, suffering and journeys of Paul (Acts 9:16; 19:21; 23:11; 27:24, 26) and suffering in the life of believers (14:22). As Walton correctly observes, 'This Lukan favourite term exposes his belief that God has a purpose which is being carried out through the stories which Luke tells in Acts.'[5]

## Israel's history

The narrative summaries of Israel's history given in the speeches of Stephen (Acts 7) and Paul (Acts 13) also draw attention to the view (which Luke adopts in his summary of these speeches) that God has directed Israel's history and that current events in Acts are a continuation of these histories.

### God's sovereignty in Israel's history in Acts 7

In Stephen's speech (Acts 7:2–46) the term *theos*, 'God', is mentioned sixteen times (the term *kyrios*, 'Lord', is also used twice with reference to God) and God is the subject of the action in the narrative. God appeared to, spoke to, gave promises to and sent Abraham (vv.

---

[2] Walton 2008: 295–296.
[3] Cf. Cosgrove 1984: 168–190.
[4] In addition to *dei*, Rosner (1993: 79) refers to *hē boulē tou theou* (the will of God), *thelēma* (will), *horizō* (foreordain), *proorizō* (predestine) and *prooraō* (foresee). Cf. also Conzelmann 1960: 151–154; Fitzmyer 1981: 170–181; Squires 1993: 1–3; 1998: 19–39; Marguerat 2002: 96–103; Walton 2008: 295–296.
[5] Walton 2008: 296.

2–8); he was with, rescued and gave wisdom to Joseph (vv. 9–10); he fulfilled his promise to Abraham in rescuing the people of Israel (vv. 5, 17); he appeared to, sent and used Moses to deliver the people of Israel (vv. 25, 31–35); he directed Moses concerning the construction of the tabernacle, drove out the nations before Israel and was favourable to David (vv. 44–46). Running throughout this narrative account of Israel's history is an undercurrent of the rejection of God's messengers (Joseph, v. 9; Moses, vv. 27, 35, 39).[6] This rejection and even resistance (v. 51) to God's messengers, however, does not leave God inactive. Despite the actions of the patriarchs, God accomplished his purposes through Joseph (vv. 9–10).[7] Although the Israelites worshipped 'what their hands had made', God turned away from Israel, handed them over to idol worship and sent them into exile as promised (vv. 41–43).[8] In fact, as Stephen nears the end of his speech he quotes Isaiah 66:1–2, which declares that heaven is God's throne, the earth his footstool and God has 'made all these things' (Acts 7:49–50).

This pattern comes to the fore in Stephen's conclusion, where he declares that his audience is following the pattern of those (their fathers) who persecuted the prophets. Even though their fathers killed those who predicted the coming of Jesus, and Stephen's audience followed suit in betraying and murdering this Righteous One, still the one predicted came just as God's messengers, the prophets, had predicted.[9] The appearance again of the glory of God (cf. vv.

---

[6] The primary significance of this speech in its narrative context will be examined further in the discussion of the temple on pp. 164–172.

[7] The contrast in 7:9–10 between the actions of the patriarchs and God ('they sold him . . . but God was with him . . . and rescued him . . . gave Joseph . . . and enabled him') is reminiscent of (though not identical in wording) to Joseph's assessment in Genesis 50:20 ('You intended to harm me, but God intended it for good to accomplish what is now being done, the saving of many lives').

[8] Spencer (2004: 87) notes that the relationship between Amos 5:25–27 in Acts 7:42–43 (idolatry that led to the exile) and the immediate context in Acts 7:40–41 (idolatry in worshipping the golden calf) seems to be that Amos identified Israel's wandering as God's judgment banishing them 'beyond Damascus' (i.e. to Assyria), and thus moves directly from the wilderness period to his own idolatrous age on the brink of deportation (i.e. he moves directly from exodus to exile). Stephen agrees with this assessment of Israel's history but extends it to his own day with the alteration to exile 'beyond *Babylon*' (instead of 'beyond *Damascus*'). Stephen therefore alerts these second-temple officials to the fact that they are in no more a privileged position than those being sent to exile before the temple was built.

[9] Note the similar summary of Israel's history given by Jesus in Luke 20:9–19 (and Matt. 21:33–46; Mark 12:1–12). Cf. also 2 Chron. 24:19; 36:15–16; Neh. 9:26; Jer. 44:4–6; and esp. Jer. 7:25–29.

2, 55), and now the person of Jesus at the right hand of God, clearly shows that God's purposes were not thwarted but accomplished through this rejected Righteous One. This reappearance together with the clear allusions to Jesus' own actions at his death (cf. vv. 59–60 with Luke 23:34, 46) as Stephen is murdered indicate that this pattern is continuing. Stephen is God's messenger, now not as a messenger anticipating the coming of the Lord Jesus, but as one who points to (vv. 55–56), even prays to (vv. 59–60), and reflects the character of the Lord Jesus (vv. 59–60).

### God's sovereignty in Israel's history in Acts 13

In Paul's speech in Acts 13:16–37 God is again the main character in the history of Israel and is again the subject of the main verbs. This time the emphasis is not so much on the rejection of God's messengers but the gracious provision of God for his people. The God of Israel chose their fathers, made the people prosper in Egypt, led them out, bore with them in the wilderness, overthrew the nations and gave them the land (vv. 17–20). Then God gave the people judges, installed and removed Saul as king, and made David king (vv. 20–22). In fact, it was only when David had served God's purposes in his own generation that he fell asleep (v. 36). Finally, it is from the descendants of David that God brings to Israel, as he promised (implying also a preservation of that promise through those descendants), the Saviour, Jesus (vv. 23–37). God's purposes were fulfilled in the condemnation and execution of Jesus (vv. 27–29) and God raised Jesus from the dead (vv. 30–37). The anticipation that God would do something incredible in their days (v. 41), the promise of light for the Gentiles and salvation for the ends of the earth (v. 47) and the granting of eternal life to 'all who were appointed' (v. 48) indicate that the culmination of God's sovereign and gracious provision for his people comes in the offer of salvation (v. 26), forgiveness of sins (v. 38), justification (v. 39) and eternal life (vv. 46, 48), by God's grace (v. 43), through the death and resurrection of the Lord Jesus to all who would believe, even Gentiles (v. 48).

## Jesus' life, death and resurrection

### Jesus' life

The surveys of God's actions in Israel's history given above have already indicated that part of Luke's purpose is to highlight the continued accomplishment of God's purposes in Jesus' ministry despite the rejection he faced from his own people. This is seen in his description of God's involvement in all aspects of Jesus' ministry: his life, death and resurrection. Regarding Jesus' life, Peter's summary in Acts 2:22 is that God accredited Jesus to the people of Israel by miracles, wonders and signs, which God did among them through Jesus. Similarly, in Acts 10:36–38 Peter states that God is the one who sent the word (*logos*) to Israel, 'telling the good news of peace through Jesus Christ'.[10] Furthermore, God anointed Jesus with the Holy Spirit and power and Jesus 'went around doing good and healing all who were under the power of the devil, because God was with him' (10:38). Again, in Acts 13:23 Paul states that God is the one who has 'brought to Israel the Saviour Jesus, as he promised'.

## *Jesus' death*

Regarding Jesus' death, Luke's Gospel emphasizes the accomplishment of God's purpose even if the wickedness and culpability of those involved in Jesus' death are also maintained.[11] Predicted by Jesus himself (Luke 9:22; 13:33) in keeping with the predictions of the Scriptures (Luke 18:31; 24:26–27, 44–46), it is clear that the Christ 'had to (*dei*) suffer' (24:26) because everything written about him 'must (*dei*) be fulfilled' (24:44). Even the betrayal by Judas, though deserving of judgment, is described in terms of the Son of Man going 'as it has been decreed' (22:22).

When we come to Acts, the same emphasis on the accomplishment of God's purposes remains, as does the accompanying responsibility of those involved. Between the ascension of Jesus 'into heaven' in Acts 1:11 and the descent of the sound like a violent wind 'from heaven' in Acts 2:1–4 there seems to be an unusual digression that focuses on Judas' death and his replacement (Acts 1:12–26). Part of the reason for this lengthy excursus is to highlight the restoration of the number of apostles to twelve in keeping with the promises of Jesus concerning the role the twelve would play over the people of Israel (cf. Luke 22:30).[12] The dominant feature of the passage, however, is that the sovereign plan of God has not been derailed by this most wicked of actions – a betrayal from among the ranks

---

[10] Gathercole (2006: 221–227) suggests that Luke 1:2, Acts 10:36, 13:26 and 20:32 indicate the possibility of 'an incipient logos Christology in Luke-Acts'.

[11] Cf. esp. Conzelmann 1960: 153, 200. Conzelmann mistakenly argued, however, that Luke sees no atoning value in the death of Jesus. Cf. Larkin 1977: 325–335.

[12] Pao 2000: 123–127.

of Jesus' own inner circle.[13] Far from discrediting the ministry of Jesus, this betrayal was anticipated. In verse 16 the language of 'had to' (*dei*), 'be fulfilled', 'which the Holy Spirit spoke . . . concerning Judas' and 'long ago' indicates that this betrayal ought to be no surprise and has long been anticipated.[14] Furthermore, the sovereign plan of God is continuing to be worked out in the provision of a replacement for Judas. This too Scripture anticipated (Acts 1:20, citing Ps. 109:8).[15] Following prayer to the Lord requesting that he show them whom he has chosen, the decision is made by casting lots.[16] Although there is no direct allusion to Proverbs 16:33 here, as Marshall correctly observes, 'it clearly was the basis of the method chosen here'.[17] That proverb, of course, attributes God's sovereignty even to the apparent randomness of casting lots as 'its every decision is from the Lord'. The point seems to be that God's plan and the role of Jesus' followers continue to be on track despite apparently disastrous circumstances.

A similar juxtaposition of the sovereign plan of God and the responsibility of those involved in Jesus' death is found in Acts 2:23 and 4:27–28. In 2:23, despite the fact that Peter's listeners, with the help of wicked men, were responsible for putting Jesus to death, Jesus is said to have been 'handed over' (*ekdoton*) by the 'predetermined' (*horizō*) 'plan' (*boulē*) and 'foreknowledge' (*prognōsis*) of God ('God's set purpose and foreknowledge' NIV). Similarly, in 4:27–28 Herod, Pilate, the Gentiles and the people of Israel conspire together in opposition to Jesus, the holy servant anointed by God. Nevertheless, they do what God's 'hand' (*cheir*)[18] and 'plan' (*boulē*) had 'predetermined' (*proōrisen*) to happen.[19] Likewise in 13:27–29 Paul states that although the people of Jerusalem and their rulers condemned Jesus and asked Pilate to have him executed, they nevertheless 'fulfilled the words of the prophets that are read every Sabbath' and 'carried out all that was written about him'. Thus

---

[13] Cf. Peterson 2009: 124 for the relationship between Matt. 27:5–8 and Acts 1:18.

[14] Cf. Marshall 2007: 530 regarding the use of Ps. 69 here. In the context of a 'Davidic typology' Jesus fulfils supremely the pattern of the betrayal of the Davidic King.

[15] Ps. 109, like Ps. 69, has to do with betrayal and opposition to David.

[16] See more on this later in this chapter in the section on the reign of the Lord Jesus.

[17] Marshall 2007: 531. Cf. also Luke 1:9.

[18] I.e. God's power. Cf. Bock 2007: 208.

[19] Cf. Carson 2000: 53–54 for a discussion of the implications of this text for 'compatibilism' between God's sovereignty and human responsibility.

repeatedly throughout Luke and Acts, although the wickedness and culpability of those involved in Jesus' death are not diminished, the purpose and plan of God are said to have been carried out.[20]

## Jesus' resurrection

A consistent feature of references to Jesus' resurrection in Acts is the statement that 'God raised him from the dead.'[21] Returning to passages mentioned above, just as God is the subject accomplishing his purposes in the summaries of Israel's history, so he is the subject accomplishing his purposes in the summaries of Jesus' 'history'. In Acts 2, following references to God's accreditation of Jesus, his accomplishment of miracles through Jesus and the outworking of his predetermined plan in the death of Jesus, Peter states that God is also the one who raised him from the dead (2:24 and again in 2:32).[22] Likewise in Acts 10, following an account of how God sent the 'word' to Israel, anointed Jesus and was with Jesus for him to do good and heal, Peter states that God raised him from the dead, caused him to be seen, chose those who would see him and appointed Jesus as judge (10:40–42). In Acts 13 Paul's speech combines these 'histories' of Israel and Jesus. He highlights God's actions in choosing the fathers, guiding Israel's history (13:17–22) and finally bringing to Israel Jesus as promised, whose death fulfils the words of the prophets and all that was written about him (13:23–29). Paul follows this summary of God's actions in the history of Israel and the life and death of Jesus with an emphasis on God's action in raising Jesus from the dead. That God is the one who raised Jesus from the dead is stated four times in the following eight verses (13:30, 33, 34, 37). Though more on the significance of Jesus' resurrection will be given in the following chapter, at this point we merely note that Luke is highlighting the continued accomplishment of God's sovereign purposes in the death of Jesus (even through the wicked actions of those who put Jesus to death) and in the resurrection of Jesus.[23]

---

[20] Texts such as Acts 2:23 and 4:27–28 also indicate that Luke does not limit those responsible for Jesus' death to the Jewish leaders, or the Jewish people in Jerusalem: he includes Herod, Gentiles and Pilate. Cf. Bock 1996: 1498; contra e.g. J. T. Sanders 1987.

[21] Hence the title of Anderson's 2006 book *'But God Raised Him from the Dead': The Theology of Jesus' Resurrection in Luke-Acts.*

[22] Cf. also 3:15; 4:10; 5:30; 17:31.

[23] Contra Cadbury (1927: 280), who argued that in Acts the death of Jesus is merely a prelude to the resurrection.

## Subsequent developments in the church

In Acts, Luke is, of course, writing an account that is subsequent to the events in the history of Israel and the events surrounding the life, death and resurrection of Jesus. Here too, however, Luke aims to show that God is continuing to accomplish his purposes. In addition to the language of fulfilment that is pervasive throughout Acts[24] and the specific interventions of angels or the Holy Spirit to direct the spread of the Gospel,[25] there are emphases on God's action in moving the events of the narrative along. Perhaps the most prominent aspect of God's action in Acts involves the inclusion of the Gentiles. This is seen especially in the conversion of Cornelius but also in later summaries of ministry among the Gentiles in Acts.

### The conversion of Cornelius and his household

In the account of Cornelius' conversion the action of God is highlighted in Cornelius' vision in which an angel instructs him concerning where and how to find Peter (10:3–6) and Peter's vision concerning God's declaration of what has been made clean followed by instruction from the Spirit about the men who were looking for Peter (10:9–20).[26] In addition to these obvious indications of specific divine guidance, what is striking about the account of these events is the stress on the 'coincidences' of timing throughout the narrative. It is as the three men were 'approaching the city' that 'Peter went up on the roof to pray' (v. 9). It is 'while Peter was wondering about the meaning of the vision' that 'the men sent by Cornelius found out where Simon's house was and stopped at the gate' (v. 17). It is then 'while Peter was still thinking about the vision' that the Spirit tells him about the three men looking for him and tells him to go downstairs and to go with them (vv. 19–20). The emphasis on God's timing reaches a climax when it was 'while Peter was still speaking' that 'the Holy Spirit came on all who heard the message' (v. 44).

---

[24] In addition to 1:16, 3:18, 13:27, 33, 17:2–3, 26:22–23, etc., with reference to Jesus' death, cf. 2:1, 16, 30–31, 3:24, 13:47, 15:15, 28:25 regarding events in the life of the church. Cf. Peterson 1993: 83–104.

[25] Cf. 8:26, 39; 10:3–6; 12:7–10, 23; 13:2–4; 16:6–10; 18:9–11; 20:22–23; 21:4, 10–11; 23:11; 27:23–26.

[26] As Spencer (2004: 121) correctly observes, the voice that declares 'Do not call anything impure that God has made clean' does 'not insist that Peter goes ahead and consumes unclean meat on this occasion, but it does demand that Peter acknowledges God's sovereignty in determining purity boundaries and, by implication, adjusting those boundaries if he so chooses'.

Peter's retelling of the account also highlights the amazing timing of the events when, after recounting the vision, he states that '*right then* (*kai idou exautēs*) three men who had been sent to me from Caesarea stopped at the house where I was staying' (11:11). Then Peter states that it was as he began to speak that the Holy Spirit came upon them (11:15), indicating again that he had more to say and that the Spirit came 'without any initiative on his part'.[27] That this is all meant to highlight the sovereign action of God in including Cornelius is emphasized at the conclusion to the account in 11:17–18. Peter concludes his summary of the events by stating that it was God who gave them the Holy Spirit and adding, 'who was I to think that I could oppose God?' The Jewish believers respond by praising God and marvelling that 'God has granted even the Gentiles repentance unto life'.

This same stress on God's action in including the Gentiles in Acts 10 – 11 is found in Peter's summary of these events before the Jerusalem Council in Acts 15. Peter states that *God* made the choice that Gentiles would hear the message of the gospel from his mouth and that they would believe (15:7).[28] Furthermore, God is the one who gave them the Holy Spirit, showing that he accepted them, that he made no distinction between the two groups and that he had purified their hearts by faith (vv. 8–9). James's summary at the conclusion of the Council looks back to Peter's account as a description of how God had 'showed his concern by taking from the Gentiles a people for himself', which is in agreement with the words of prophets (vv. 14–15).[29]

### Paul's ministry among Gentiles
In addition to this specific inclusion of the Gentile Cornelius and his household through faith, summaries of Gentile inclusion that frame the beginning and end of Paul's ministry to Gentiles in Acts also highlight God's sovereignty. These summaries attribute the whole of Paul's ministry among Gentiles and the response of Gentiles to the work of God. In the context leading up to the Jerusalem Council Paul and Barnabas have returned to Antioch, having completed 'the

---

[27] Bock 2007: 408.

[28] In Greek the verb for 'choose' is completed with the two infinitives 'to hear' and 'to believe' (*exelexato ho theos . . . akousai . . . kai pisteusai*).

[29] The phrase in Greek is *ho theos epeskepsato labein ex ethnōn laon tō onomati autou* (God visited to take out from the Gentiles a people for his name).

work' under the grace of God (14:26).[30] This was 'the work' to which they had been called, set apart and sent by the Holy Spirit (13:2–4). In Antioch they report to the church 'all that God had done through them and how he had opened the door of faith to the Gentiles' (14:27). On their way to the Jerusalem Council Paul and Barnabas travel through Phoenicia and Samaria telling how the Gentiles have been converted, and upon arrival in Jerusalem report to the welcoming church, apostles and elders 'everything God had done through them' (15:3–4). At the Jerusalem Council itself Paul and Barnabas tell about 'the miraculous signs and wonders God had done among the Gentiles through them' (v. 12). At the end of Paul's ministry as a free man in Acts, when he arrives in Jerusalem in Acts 21, he reports again to the welcoming brothers in Jerusalem, including James and the elders. Luke states that Paul recounted in detail (lit. 'each one of the things') 'what God had done among the Gentiles through his ministry', which elicits a response of praise to God from these church leaders in Jerusalem (21:19–20). Although more could be said,[31] it seems clear that one of Luke's aims is to reassure readers such as Theophilus that God is continuing to accomplish his purposes (as promised in the OT) in the life, death and resurrection of Jesus, and in the developments subsequent to Jesus' earthly ministry by the inclusion of Gentiles among the followers of Jesus. Luke's focus on the accomplishment of God's purposes, however, must also be understood in the context of his references to the kingdom of God. It is to this that we now turn.

## The kingdom of God

In the discussion that follows we will see that Luke's focus on the accomplishment of God's saving purposes is placed within the specific framework of the inauguration of God's kingdom in the ministry of Jesus. Although there are not a large number of references to the kingdom of God in Acts, their strategic placement and contexts indicate an importance that outweighs the number of occurrences of the phrase. Before looking at Acts, however, I will briefly clarify the relationship between the sovereignty of God and the phrase 'the

---

[30] This section is often described as Paul's 'first missionary journey'. The use of this designation may, however, neglect Paul's earlier ministry in Damascus (9:20–22), Jerusalem (9:28–29) and Antioch (11:25–26).

[31] Cf. also Acts 16:10, 14; 18:10–11.

kingdom of God' and summarize the use of the phrase in the Gospel of Luke.

## The kingdom of God and the sovereignty of God

There is a sense in which the phrase 'kingdom of God' refers to God's universal sovereignty.[32] God always rules over his creation, he is the sovereign King over all he has made and 'his kingdom rules over all'.[33] In this sense, given that all are under God's sovereign rule, all are in God's kingdom.[34] The OT, however, also anticipates a time when God's rule will be established in keeping with his saving promises. This will be a time when the enemies of God and the enemies of his people will be defeated and God's people will be blessed.[35] The arrival of the kingdom of God in this sense is something like 'the fulfilment of God's saving promises' or 'the saving rule of God' and one must 'receive' the kingdom or 'enter into' the kingdom (Luke 18:17) to participate in these saving promises.[36] It is the accomplishment of this saving rule already, in advance of the final consummation, even in the midst of continued opposition, that Luke particularly highlights.

## The kingdom of God in Luke's Gospel

### The arrival of the kingdom

The kingdom of God is of course a major aspect of Jesus' ministry in Luke's Gospel, as it is in each of the Synoptic Gospels.[37] The statements which summarize Jesus' ministry in Luke 4:43, 8:1, 9:2, 11, 16:16 and 18:29 indicate that 'preaching the kingdom

---

[32] Cf. the summary of the following texts in Schreiner 2008: 49–50, 53–54.

[33] Ps. 103:19; cf. also Pss 47:8; 93:1; 97:1; 99:1; Dan. 4:34–35; Matt. 13:41.

[34] Cf. Carson 2008: 104–107.

[35] Cf. Dan. 2:44; Isa. 9:7; 24:23; 25:6–9; Zech. 14:9; Obad. 21; Amos 9:11–15.

[36] The phrases 'saving promises' and 'saving rule' are taken from Schreiner 2008: 49, 54. Beasley-Murray (1986: 339) uses the phrase 'saving sovereignty'. Similarly, France (1990: 15) uses the phrase 'God in saving action'.

[37] Regarding the fact that some of the OT passages above speak of a new exodus, return from exile and new creation, Schreiner (2008: 48, n. 20) helpfully notes, 'We see from this that the Gospel writers did not typically refer to the fulfillment of God's promises in terms of return from exile or as a new exodus. Instead, they spoke of the coming of God's kingdom. It is important to see, however, that the coming of the kingdom means the fulfillment of God's promises regarding a new exodus and return from exile. Hence there is no need to drive a wedge between the notion of God's kingdom and new exodus and return from exile, though it is important for the sake of precision to note that the terminology typically used in the Gospels is not that of a new exodus or a return from exile but of the coming of the kingdom of God (but see Matt. 2:15, 18).'

of God' epitomizes Jesus' ministry.[38] Jesus' teaching about the
kingdom of God is best understood along the lines of 'inaugurated
eschatology', or, in the words of George Ladd, 'fulfilment without
consummation'.[39] That is, there is both an 'already' and a 'not yet'
aspect to the kingdom. Thus, in keeping with OT expectations, Jesus
expected a future consummation of the kingdom.[40] The more striking element of Jesus' teaching in the Gospels, however, is that he
did not just announce a future kingdom; he announced the present
arrival of that kingdom in his own ministry. In Luke's Gospel the
presence of the kingdom is especially emphasized in Luke 10:9, 11;
11:20; and 17:21.[41] In Luke 10:9, 11 Jesus tells his disciples to go
into the towns ahead of him and announce that 'the kingdom of
God is near' (with the sense of arrival), and Luke 10:9 adds that the
kingdom has come 'upon you' (*eph hymas*).[42] In 11:20 exorcisms by
Jesus are tied to the presence of the kingdom, which is said to have
'come to you'.[43] In 17:21, a passage unique to Luke's Gospel, Jesus
answers a question about the kingdom's presence by stating that
the kingdom of God is 'among you' (NIV mg.). Given that this is a
response to the Pharisees, it is unlikely to be a statement about a
spiritual internalization of the kingdom in their hearts but is rather
a declaration that the kingdom of God is 'in their presence'. That is,
in the context of the previous verses, the point is that the kingdom
has come with the coming of the King, and the Pharisees should
not miss the presence of the kingdom right before their eyes.[44]

[38] Regarding these references to the kingdom in the Synoptic parallel passages, it
should be noted that Luke 4:43 is not found in Mark 1:38; Luke 8:1 is not found in
Matt. 13 and Mark 4; the phrase 'kingdom of God' in Luke 9:11 is not found in the
equivalent sections of Matt. 14:14 and Mark 6:34.

[39] Ladd 1993: 63. Cf. Seccombe (2002: 166–199) for a summary of recent
interpretations of the kingdom of God.

[40] In addition to references to a future second coming in passages such as Luke
12:40–46, 17:22–37, 18:8 and 21:27–28, see also references to a future kingdom of
God in 13:23–30; 14:14, 15–24; 19:11–27 (12, 14–15, 27); 21:5–38 (esp. v. 31); 22:18. In
these passages it appears that Jesus anticipated a period of time between his first and
second coming but emphasizes the certainty and suddenness of the future kingdom's
arrival.

[41] See also Luke 7:28; 8:10; 9:27; and 16:16. On this last verse see Marshall 1978:
629 and Schreiner 2008: 58–59.

[42] Cf. the use of *engizō* (come near) in Luke 12:33; 15:1; 18:40; 22:47; 24:15, 28;
Acts 21:33 ('the commander came up and arrested' Paul).

[43] In this verse the verb *phthanō* is used with the prepositional phrase 'upon you'
(*eph hymas*). Cf. also the sense of 'attain' in Rom. 9:31; Phil. 3:16; even 'overtaken' in
1 Thess. 4:15. Bock 1996: 1080.

[44] Bock (1996: 1416–1417) notes that the prepositional phrase used here, *entos
hymōn*, is often synonymous with *en mesō*, which a number of versions of the Greek

Entrance to the kingdom, therefore, is possible already and requires a response to Jesus.

## Entrance into the kingdom

Although space prevents a full discussion of the importance of the kingdom of God throughout Luke's Gospel, we will focus on one particular narrative unit, Luke 18:9 – 19:10, which is the concluding part of the long journey section (Luke 9 – 19) in Luke's Gospel before Jesus' arrival in Jerusalem. We will focus on this unit primarily because of its important narrative location (at the culmination of Jesus' journey to Jerusalem) and its emphasis on the kingdom.[45] Broadly speaking, Luke 18:9 – 19:10 includes the parable of the Pharisee and the tax collector, children being brought to Jesus, the rich ruler, a prediction of Jesus' death and resurrection, a blind beggar receiving sight, and culminates in the account of Zacchaeus the tax collector. Rather than being an arbitrary collection of events from Jesus' life, however, this section particularly stresses the response of those who will enter the kingdom of God.[46] A variety of expressions are used to describe the result of this response: justification (18:14), receiving or entering the kingdom of God (18:16–17, 24–25), eternal life (18:18, 29), receiving mercy (18:13, 38–39) and salvation (18:26, 42; 19:9–10).[47] As with the descriptions of the result, there are also a variety of ways of expressing the required response of those who will enter the kingdom. This response is to be characterized by a humble acknowledgment of one's sinfulness (18:14), dependent trust in Jesus alone (18:16–17, 37–42), and an abandonment of any other source of confidence (18:11–12, 18–30; 19:1–10).[48] In each case Jesus is the one who determines what this response should be and is the one to whom the response must be made. Thus those who respond are described as those who come

OT indicate when they translate Exod. 34:9 in either way (see also Exod. 17:7). Note also the present tense 'is'.

[45] Cf. Bock (1996: 957–964) and J. B. Green (1997: 394–399) for summaries of the structure and importance of the 'journey section' of Luke's Gospel.

[46] Cf. J. B. Green 1997: 643; Nolland 1993: 872.

[47] Note that Jesus' discussion with the ruler and the follow-up discussion with his disciples in 18:18–30 incorporate many of these expressions. The parallels between the humility described in 18:14 and in 18:15–17 seem to warrant the inclusion of the language of justification here too.

[48] The parallels between 19:1–10 and 18:18–30 ('wealth' in 18:23–25 and 19:2, 8; 'salvation', 18:26; 19:9–10) indicate that Zacchaeus is a 'rich man who enters the kingdom of God' (18:25). Allusions to Luke 3:8–14 indicate also that Zacchaeus is a 'child of Abraham' who 'produces fruit in keeping with repentance'.

to him (18:16), follow him (18:22, 28, 43), have faith in him (18:42) or welcome him gladly (19:6). Tucked away in the middle of this section is Jesus' final and most detailed prediction of his impending suffering, death and resurrection in Jerusalem (18:31–33).[49] The conclusion to this long journey anticipated since 9:51 and referred to regularly along the way is now imminent. Thus this detailed description of what Jesus is about to face indicates again that the Jesus to whom response must be made in order to enter the kingdom of God is the soon-to-be rejected, suffering, dying and resurrected Jesus.

### The departure and return of the king

Luke 19:11–27 is a concluding parable to the journey section that continues this focus on the kingdom of God (19:11) before the transitional section in 19:28–44 describing the approach of 'the king' to Jerusalem (note 19:38).[50] This parable is another clue that Luke connects the kingship of Jesus with the kingdom of God.[51] Luke tells us that Jesus told this parable 'because he was near Jerusalem and the people thought that the kingdom of God was going to appear at once' (19:11).[52] The concluding parable in 19:11–27 therefore comes in the context of Jesus' imminent arrival in Jerusalem and deals with false expectations concerning Jerusalem and the kingdom of God.[53] The parable focuses on a man who is appointed king and the responses to his kingdom (19:12, 14–15, 27).[54] In particular, even though the reign of this king is rejected (19:14, 27) he nevertheless departs and receives a kingdom (19:12, 15) and returns to call his servants to account for their service (19:15–27). In view of the impending arrival in Jerusalem, the response of the

[49] Earlier predictions in Luke 9:22, 44, 12:49–50, 13:32–33, 17:25 did not contain the specific details found in these verses regarding handing over to Gentiles, mocking, insulting, spitting and flogging.

[50] Cf. Bock 1996: 957–959 concerning this aspect of the structure of the 'journey section'. It seems that the journey section does not officially end till 19:44, as Jesus is still approaching Jerusalem in 19:41; but in 19:54 he is clearly in the city (in the temple area).

[51] Ziccardi 2008: 460–473.

[52] Note this association between Jerusalem and the rule of God in Pss 2:6; 110:2; and Isa. 52:7–8.

[53] Cf. Bock 1996: 1526–1529 on the differences between this parable and the similar one in Matt. 25:14–30.

[54] Note that the rationale given for the parable in Luke 19:11 is not in the introduction to the parable in Matt. 25:14; the references to receiving a kingdom in Luke 19:12 and 15 are not found in Matt. 25 (Matt. 25 just has a man going on a journey with no reference to kingdom); and references to rejecting the reign of the king in Luke 19:14 and 27 are also not found in Matt. 25.

rulers and crowds, and the betrayal by Judas, the parable seems to indicate again (i.e. as with 18:31–33) that Jesus' death and rejection in Jerusalem are integral to the kingdom and must come first. Furthermore, Jesus' disciples must be prepared for a period of faithful service before the king returns; judgment of the king's enemies is still to come.[55] Following the unfolding of the events in Jerusalem in Luke 20 – 23, Jesus provides clarification in Luke 24 regarding the promises of the Scriptures for Israel (24:21), the death and resurrection of the Messiah (24:25–27, 44–46), and the role of Jerusalem (24:47, 52) and the nations (24:47) in the light of his resurrection (24:31, 36–43) and in ways that recall hopes for Israel and the nations in the opening chapters of Luke's Gospel.[56] The stage is set for further clarification concerning the next stage in the kingdom between the king's departure and return.

## The kingdom of God in Acts

Having surveyed briefly some of the emphases concerning the kingdom of God in Luke's Gospel, we are now better prepared to understand the significance of Luke's strategic placement of references to the kingdom of God in Acts. Announcing the arrival of the kingdom of God was a major aspect of Jesus' ministry. Now that Jesus has suffered, died, risen and ascended as he said he would, what happens next? As Jesus' teaching indicated, the kingdom has come 'already'; nevertheless, the kingdom has 'not yet' been consummated in fullness and there will be a period in-between. So what does the kingdom of God look like now in this period of the 'now and not yet'? Jesus himself stressed that people enter the kingdom as they humbly trust in him. How do people enter the kingdom now that he has departed? What is the 'king' of the kingdom doing now? How will God's saving purposes be carried out now? What about the promises of the OT regarding the blessings of the kingdom age?

---

[55] Cf. Seccombe 2002: 493–499 for a discussion of the second coming of Jesus in this parable (contra Wright 1996: 632–639).

[56] The hope that Jesus would 'redeem Israel' in 24:21 recalls Zechariah's praise that the God of Israel has come 'and has redeemed his people' (1:68), Simeon's hope for 'the consolation of Israel' (2:25) and Anna's address to 'all who were looking forward to the redemption of Jerusalem' (2:38). Forgiveness of sins for the nations in 24:47 recalls expectations raised in Simeon's praise for God's salvation in Jesus, 'a light for revelation to the Gentiles and for glory to your people Israel' (2:32), expectations that have largely gone unfulfilled in Luke's narrative so far. The significance of the opening and closing chapters of Luke's Gospel will be discussed further on pp. 75–76 with reference to the resurrection.

What about the institutions of Israel and the leadership of Israel? Who are God's people now and who leads them? If followers of Jesus are 'in the kingdom of God', why do they face suffering and why are they opposed? Questions such as these are what the book of Acts addresses within the 'framework' of 'the kingdom of God' between the 'now' and the 'not yet'.

## Luke's 'framing' references to the kingdom in Acts 1 and 28

Although there are eight references to the specific phrases 'the kingdom of God' or 'the kingdom' in Acts,[57] the particular location and contexts of two references to the kingdom of God at the beginning and another two at the end of Acts (1:3, 6; 28:23, 31) indicate that Luke is 'framing' his work with these references and that readers are meant to read the material between chapters 1 and 28 within this 'frame'.[58] In addition to the observation that two references to the kingdom of God introduce and another two conclude the book of Acts, the contexts of these references indicate that Luke is referring to the concept of the kingdom in the narrative of Acts more often than just where the specific phrase occurs.[59] In these contexts there is an emphasis on comprehensive teaching about the kingdom of God and an association of the kingdom of God with major themes found elsewhere in Acts.

At the beginning of Acts the kingdom of God is presented in 1:3 as the one topic of conversation during Jesus' forty-day instruction of his disciples before his ascension. Then in 1:6 the question about the restoration of the kingdom to Israel is raised in the context of this forty-day instruction concerning the kingdom of God in 1:2–5.[60]

[57] Cf. 'The kingdom of God': Acts 1:3; 8:12; 14:22; 19:8; 28:23, 31. 'The kingdom': 1:6; 20:25.

[58] Cf. Tannehill 1990: 352; Marguerat 2002: 207; C. Green 2005: 17–19.

[59] Study of the kingdom of God and eschatology in Acts is often done in the shadow of Conzelmann's arguments (1960: 95–97, 123). Conzelmann assumed that the early Christians expected the end of the world immediately or at least within their lifetimes, the earlier tradition of the teaching of Jesus was that the kingdom was exclusively future and immediate, and that this fervent expectation prevented them from writing a history recording Jesus' place within what would be world history. Therefore, according to Conzelmann, Luke's writing is out of place and must be written to correct a crisis; in particular the crisis that the end and Jesus' return had not happened. Thus he argued that Luke downplays all reference to the future (placing the kingdom in the very distant future) and emphasizes history (he also argued that Luke distinguished between the message of the kingdom and the kingdom itself). Marshall (1970) responded to these arguments and noted that although Luke is interested in salvation history, the evidence for a supposed 'crisis' and downplaying of the future is lacking.

[60] Note the *oun* ('so' NIV) at the beginning of v. 6.

Acts 1:8 is clearly 'programmatic' for the geographical spread of the gospel in Acts. It should also be noted, however, that Jesus' answer to the disciples' question about the kingdom relates to Israel, promises of restoration, Jesus' own role in that restoration, the role of the Holy Spirit, the role of the apostles as witnesses of Jesus, and the place of Jerusalem, Judea, Samaria and 'the ends of the earth' in this restoration. The significance of this question concerning the kingdom in the context of Acts 1:1–8 is such that we will examine it in more detail in chapter 3 (on Israel and the kingdom) and chapter 4 (on the Holy Spirit and the kingdom). At this stage we are merely noting that Jesus' teaching to the disciples and Jesus' answer to the disciples' question are obviously foundational for what the rest of the book is about: the kingdom!

At the end of Acts, in 28:23, the context is a climactic meeting between Paul and 'large numbers' of the Jewish leaders in Rome, and again the emphasis is on extensive instruction. This time, although the time mentioned is just one day, Luke states that Paul explained and declared to them the kingdom of God 'from morning till evening'.[61] In this context Paul has just stated that he is in chains because of 'the hope of Israel' (28:20) and, along with explaining the kingdom of God, he 'tried to convince them about Jesus from the Law of Moses and from the Prophets' (28:23). Thus comprehensiveness is emphasized in both the extended amount of time and in the extensive amount of content referred to. The last reference to the kingdom of God in Acts is also the final verse of the book of Acts. Once again the kingdom is mentioned in the context of comprehensive explanation. In Acts 28:31 we are told that Paul 'preached the kingdom of God and taught about the Lord Jesus Christ'. There appears to be a certain extensiveness of teaching implied in the association of 'the things about the Lord Jesus Christ' and the full title given to Jesus here.[62] The context of this final summary statement of Paul's teaching, however, is given in Acts 28:30 where we are told that Paul stayed for 'two whole years' in his rented house preaching the kingdom of God and teaching about the Lord Jesus Christ. Thus the final note sounded in Acts is the bold proclamation of 'the kingdom of God'.[63]

---

[61] Contra Fitzmyer 1998: 794–795, Luke's point is not that Paul was long-winded!

[62] Note that in Greek the phrase 'the things about' (*ta peri*) Jesus implies broad instruction about Jesus and is similar to what is found at the conclusion of Luke's Gospel in 24:27, 44.

[63] It should be noted that a number of narrative indicators in Acts show that the conclusion to Acts was deliberate and is not 'abrupt' or due simply to the fact that

It has sometimes been noted that references to the kingdom of God in Acts are shorthand summaries for apostolic preaching.[64] The fact that 8:12, 28:23 and 31 also identify Jesus as the subject of this preaching indicates, as Dodd notes, that

> the kingdom of God is conceived as coming in the events of the life, death, and resurrection of Jesus, and to proclaim these facts, in their proper setting [i.e. in the light of the promises of the OT], is to preach the gospel of the Kingdom of God.[65]

Peterson also correctly observes that, in the light of Luke 24:44–47 and Acts 1:3, Jesus was showing the apostles 'how to proclaim the kingdom appropriately, in light of "the things which have been accomplished among us" '.[66] Although there is an emphasis on how the kingdom is proclaimed, it appears that Luke has more in mind than that. As noted above, the opening references to the kingdom of God in Acts 1:3 and 6 are set in contexts where Jesus is explaining the *nature* of the kingdom of God, not just how to proclaim the kingdom of God. Although more detailed attention will be given to 1:6–8 in chapters 3 and 4, we have already noted here that Jesus' answer addresses not only the content of the proclamation (they will be witnesses *of Jesus*) but also the unfolding of events significant for understanding the nature of the kingdom after his ascension (i.e. the place of Israel, the eschatological promise of the Spirit, the fulfilment of God's saving promises). As noted above, this teaching on the kingdom in the opening verses of Acts is obviously foundational for what the rest of the book is about.[67]

Luke had run out of room on his scroll or that Paul had died and Luke had now run out of material! For further discussion see Troftgruben 2010. Cf. A. J. Thompson 2008a: 165–169 and Rowe 2009: 99–102 for the significance of these verses in the context of imperial claims for authority.

[64] Cf. 8:12; 19:8; 20:25; 28:23, 31; cf. also 14:22.

[65] Dodd 1944: 24, cited by Peterson 1993: 94, n. 27.

[66] Peterson 1993: 94–95, n. 27. See also the discussion on preaching the gospel on pp. 88–101.

[67] Note also that in Acts 20:25 Paul refers to 'preaching the kingdom' in the same context as referring to proclaiming 'the whole will (or 'plan', *boulē*) of God'. The kingdom, therefore, may be viewed broadly as the 'plan of God' through Jesus, something Luke is drawing attention to in the wider narrative of Acts (cf. 2:23; 4:28; 5:38–39; 13:36). C. Green (2005: 17–18) helpfully observes also that inside these four 'framing' references at the beginning and end of Acts two references are located in the context of evangelism (8:12; 19:8) and two are located in the context of strengthening churches and leadership in the context of suffering (14:22; 20:25).

An indication that Luke is drawing our attention to the setting of this period of the kingdom before the 'not yet' consummation of the kingdom is found in 1:10–11, immediately after Jesus' answer to the disciples' question about the kingdom.[68] This is now Luke's third reference to Jesus' ascension.[69] Although attention has rightly been paid to the importance of the ascension in Acts 1 (see below on the reign of the Lord Jesus), one feature of this particular reference to the ascension appears to be the fact that 'this same Jesus, who has been taken from you into heaven, *will come back* in the same way you have seen him go into heaven'.[70] That is, just as Jesus taught in the Gospel of Luke (see above), there is going to be an interim period, there is a 'not yet' aspect to the kingdom even if the times and dates of God's schedule are not for the disciples to know (1:7).

To summarize: in the light of the double references to the kingdom in the introduction and conclusion of Acts, the emphasis on comprehensive teaching on the kingdom associated with these references, the explanation given by Jesus about the kingdom in the opening verses of Acts, and the fact that Luke chooses to end his work on the subject of the kingdom of God in the last verse, it seems that these are important 'framing' verses for understanding Luke's focus in the book of Acts. The book of Acts, therefore, is not just a sequel to the Gospel of Luke in the sense that it describes the spread of the gospel, or in the sense that it describes the growth of the church, or in the way it describes the inclusion of Gentiles. Though the book of Acts includes all of these elements, this 'frame' for the book indicates that the book of Acts is a sequel to the Gospel of Luke in the sense that all of these elements are placed within the 'framework' of Luke's explanation of what the kingdom of God looks like now that Jesus has come, announced the arrival of the kingdom, died, risen and ascended to the right hand of the Father. Readers such as Theophilus may be reassured that God's saving plan, his kingdom, is continuing to be worked out through the crucified and risen Lord Jesus in keeping with Jesus' own teaching. The continuing role of

[68] See also Acts 14:22, which is discussed further below (pp. 63–65) in the context of suffering and opposition.

[69] Luke 24:50–51; Acts 1:2; and now here Acts 1:10–11.

[70] Cf. also the references to a future return of Jesus (3:20) or a future role for Jesus as Judge (10:42; 17:31) indicating that, contra Conzelmann 1960: 95–97, Luke has not eliminated the expectation of an imminent parousia due to some supposed 'crisis' brought about by its delay.

the Lord Jesus in the kingdom, therefore, must also be examined in this context.

## The continuing reign of the Lord Jesus

As noted above, a major emphasis of Jesus' teaching was that the kingdom of God had already arrived. The kingdom of God had arrived, said Jesus, because the kingdom of God was present in *his* ministry. Because he, the King of the kingdom was here, entrance to the kingdom was through response to *him*. The actions of Jesus presented further evidence for his claims concerning the arrival of God's kingdom. The natural question after Jesus' departure then would be, 'What about the kingdom now?' Luke tells Theophilus in the first verse in Acts that his first book was all about what Jesus began to do and teach. The implication of these opening words in Acts is that he is now going to write about all that Jesus *continues* to do and teach. Thus we may now get even more specific about what the book of Acts is about. Luke's Gospel was written to provide assurance to Theophilus about the person and work of Jesus, that God's purposes were accomplished through him, that Jesus' suffering and death were anticipated in Scripture, and that Jesus brought about the inauguration of God's kingdom, the fulfilment of God's saving promises. The book of Acts, therefore, is about the continuation of those saving promises, the kingdom of God, through the Lord Jesus. Jesus is still the mediator of that kingdom, the one who administers those saving promises and the one who carries out God's saving plan.

Luke's statement in the first verse of Acts that his first book was about all that Jesus began to do and teach and therefore that his second book will be about what Jesus is continuing to do and teach is already a corrective to some popular approaches to Acts. Strictly speaking then the book is not primarily about the 'Acts of the Apostles'. After Acts 1, of the twelve apostles named in 1:13 and 26, only the names of Peter and John appear again.[71] Some have correctly noted the importance of the Holy Spirit in Acts and

---

[71] Incidentally, this is therefore not a reason to think that Matthias was the 'wrong choice' or that they should have waited for Paul, who was supposedly 'God's choice'. This view is not advocated today by many but was held e.g. by G. Campbell Morgan (1924: 19–20). It should be noted, of course, that generic references to 'the apostles' occur throughout Acts (e.g. 2:42–43; 4:33, 35–37; 5:12; etc.) and James's death is mentioned in 12:2.

have suggested that the book should be called the 'Acts of the Holy Spirit'.[72] As important as the Holy Spirit is in Acts, it should be noted that even this designation does not quite capture the emphasis of Luke in Acts. Acts 1:1 indicates that the book is going to be about what Jesus is continuing to do and teach; therefore, the 'Acts of the Risen Lord Jesus' would be a better title. It must be said, though, that this could also be understood as a shorthand expression for something like 'the Acts of the Lord Jesus, through his people, by the Holy Spirit, for the accomplishment of God's purposes'! Some have thought that Acts exhibits an 'absentee Christology' in which Christ has departed and is now 'absent'.[73] Zwiep even claims that Luke's Christology 'is dominated by the (physical) absence *and present inactivity* of the exalted Lord'.[74] This is the exact opposite of what Luke is advocating in Acts. In what follows we will see that, according to Luke, Jesus is very much active: he is continuing to reign.

## *The ascended Lord Jesus reigns from heaven*

Acts 1 sets the stage for the rest of Acts with a focus on 'the day' of the ascension of the Lord Jesus. In fact Luke 'frames' this chapter with references to Jesus' ascension in the almost identical phrase 'until the day he was taken up' in 1:2 and again in 1:22.[75] In between these verses we have, as noted above, another reference to Jesus' ascension in 1:10–11, where Luke refers four times in the space of these two verses to the fact that Jesus is in 'heaven'. The focus here is not on his 'absence' and consequent 'inactivity', but rather on the 'place' from which Jesus rules for the rest of Acts. The reason for the emphasis on this location here will be clarified in Acts 2:33–36, where this place is associated with Jesus' supreme authority over all. Initial evidence for this rule is seen already towards the end of Acts 1 as well as in the following account of Pentecost.

In Acts 1:24–26 the believers choose two men who meet the

---

[72] Bruce 1988: 31 (following J. A. Bengel and A. T. Pierson). Bruce does, however, argue that Acts 1:1 suggests that Acts is about all that Jesus *continued* to do and teach (30).

[73] The phrase 'absentee Christology' was coined by Moule 1966: 165, 179–180. Cf. also Conzelmann 1960: 186, 206. Sleeman (2009: 13), however, has shown that Moule's position was more nuanced than that of Conzelmann's. Cf. also Buckwalter 1996: 174.

[74] Zwiep 1997: 182 (emphasis original), cited by Sleeman 2009: 15.

[75] *Achri hēs hēmeras . . . anelēmphthē*, 1:2; *heōs tēs hēmeras hēs anelēmphthē*, 1:22. Cf. Spencer 2004: 33.

qualifications for being a replacement apostle for Judas. Then, before they cast lots, they pray to the Lord who knows 'everyone's heart' (1:24). Some have suggested that because the language of knowing hearts is used in Acts 15:8 to refer to the Father, this must be prayer to the Father too.[76] However, the prayer here to 'the Lord' to show them which apostle he 'has chosen' is also identical to language used at the beginning of the chapter, where Luke tells us about the instruction Jesus gave to his apostles whom 'he had chosen'.[77] This opening and closing 'frame' in Acts 1 regarding the apostles 'chosen' by Jesus, and the 'frame' regarding 'the day he was taken up', together with the immediately preceding reference to 'the Lord' Jesus in this context (1:21), all indicate that 'the Lord' who is being prayed to in 1:24 is the Lord Jesus. Luke shows then that Jesus not only has such authority that he may be prayed to,[78] but Jesus is also continuing to direct affairs from 'heaven'. The Lord Jesus is still ruling over his people, choosing which disciple will join the ranks of the other eleven apostles he has chosen, and controlling the outcome of the lot to bring about this appointment.

## The reigning Lord Jesus pours out the Spirit

Following the focus on '*the day* he was taken up' in Acts 1, Acts 2 begins with a reference to the arrival of '*the day* of Pentecost' (2:1).[79] Furthermore, following the emphasis on the ascension of the Lord Jesus 'into heaven' (1:10–11), the mention in 2:2 of a sound coming 'from heaven' alerts us to the possibility that the Lord Jesus is continuing to act and that he is behind the events of Pentecost too. This is in fact what Peter argues in response to questions concerning the declaration of the wonders of God in a variety of languages. What this means, argues Peter, is that God's promise to pour out the Holy Spirit in the last days has been fulfilled (2:16–17). The reason for this is that the promised Davidic King has come and has been raised for ever to sit on David's throne (2:30–31).[80] The use of 'therefore' (*oun*) in verse 33 (omitted in the NIV) shows that the pouring out of the Holy Spirit on the day of Pentecost is evidence of the reign of

[76] Conzelmann 1987: 12, 25; Fitzmyer 1998: 227; Pervo 2009: 55.
[77] *Hous exelexato*, 1:2; *hon exelexō*, 1:24.
[78] For other references to prayer to Jesus in Acts see 7:59–60; 9:10–16 (note also Luke 6:13).
[79] Spencer 2004: 33.
[80] Cf. Hahn 2005: 294–321 for a discussion of the relationship between the kingdom of God and the kingdom of David.

the Lord Jesus from the throne of David. Here we need to note the parallelism in the words Peter uses in 2:17 (quoting Joel 2:28) and in 2:33:

2:17 'God says, *I will pour out* my Spirit'
2:33 'Exalted . . . he has received . . . and *has poured out* what you now see and hear'

Jesus is the Lord who sits 'at the right hand' of the Father, a position of power and authority and the place from which blessing and deliverance come for God's people.[81] Now he is the bestower of God's blessing for God's people, sending the Holy Spirit, God's enabling presence for his people. Thus in Acts 16:7 the Holy Spirit (who is mentioned in 16:6) is referred to as 'the Spirit of Jesus'. It is most likely that this phrase is used in the light of the declaration in 2:33 that the Lord Jesus received and poured out the Holy Spirit. In the light of Acts 2, therefore, this phrase, 'the Spirit of Jesus', highlights Jesus' 'lordship of the Spirit' as he is the one who sent the Holy Spirit.[82] As important as Pentecost is for the narrative of Acts, and as important as the Holy Spirit is for the transformation and enabling of God's people in Acts, Luke shows in Acts 1 and 2 that it is the ascension of the Lord Jesus that is determinative for the events of the rest of the narrative of Acts. Luke's opening of the narrative of Acts with reference to two 'days', the 'day he was taken up into heaven' and the 'day of Pentecost' when the Holy Spirit was poured out 'from heaven', are designed to show that it is the Lord Jesus who rules and directs affairs in this period of the kingdom of God.[83]

## *The reigning Lord Jesus adds to the church*

When we continue reading through the narrative of Acts, we find ongoing references to Jesus' activity. In Acts 2:47 'the Lord added to their number daily those who were being saved'. In view of the overwhelming emphasis throughout Acts 2 that Jesus is 'the Lord' upon whom we must call (cf. 2:21 and 34–36), the 'Lord' at the end

---

[81] Cf. Exod. 15:6; Pss 18:35; 44:3; 60:5; 98:1.

[82] Buckwalter 1996: 180–182; Turner 1996: 304–305.

[83] Furthermore, according to Acts 2:34–35 (citing Ps. 110:1), he will reign from God's right hand until the Father makes his enemies a footstool for his feet. Again this indicates a period of time between the ascension and return, and that during this period of time there will be opposition to his rule, but he nevertheless rules from a position of power and authority.

of Acts 2 who is adding believers to the church is Jesus who has been made 'Lord and Christ'.[84] Thus not only is the Lord Jesus the one who is responsible for the pouring out of the Holy Spirit and the events of Pentecost; he is the one who is adding believers to the number of those who are saved. Similarly, in 5:32 Peter and the apostles declare that he has been exalted to the right hand of God in order to give 'repentance and forgiveness of sins to Israel'. Thus he is the one who not only grants forgiveness in response to repentance, but is even said to grant the required response of repentance itself.

We will break the narrative sequence here and come back to Acts 9 and Saul's conversion below, where it will be placed in the context of the rest of Paul's ministry in Acts. In Acts 11 – 12 the Lord Jesus is again highlighted as the one responsible for the growth of the church. Those scattered because of the persecution in Jerusalem began to tell 'the good news about the Lord Jesus' to Greeks as well as Jews (11:20). Then we read that 'a great number of people believed and turned to the Lord'. The reason given for this large response is that 'the Lord's hand was with them' (11:21). The references to the message about the 'Lord Jesus' and the number turning to 'the Lord', in this context indicate that 'the Lord' whose hand is with them is the Lord Jesus again. This is a crucial narrative setting, as we read not only of the introduction of Gentiles to the church following the major narrative focus on the conversion of Cornelius (and in keeping with what the Lord Jesus had said in 1:6–8), but also of the establishment of the church at Antioch, which will go on to become the next major sending church in the book of Acts (13:1 – 14:28).[85] The Lord Jesus is here again continuing to rule according to his promise, enabling the disciples in their ministry and adding to the growth of the church.

When we come to Saul's conversion in Acts 9 (and the references to this event again in Acts 22 and 26), we find that the greatest threat

---

[84] This statement is not a contradiction of Luke 2:11, nor does it advocate 'adoptionist Christology'. Acts 2:31 speaks of the resurrection of the Christ (i.e. he already was the Christ) and 2:34 speaks of the exaltation of the Lord (i.e. he already was Lord). Acts 2:36 indicates that Jesus' resurrection and exaltation declare the inauguration of his reign in full authority and power. Cf. Strauss 1995: 144–145.

[85] Note also the discussion of Acts 26:23 on pp. 80–81. In the narrative of Acts this verse comes at a climactic moment in Paul's climactic defence. The statement here that Jesus 'as the first to rise from the dead, would proclaim light to his own people and to the Gentiles' must refer to the preaching of Jesus' people (including Paul) to the Gentiles in Acts. This verse indicates, however, that Jesus himself does this preaching (through his people).

to the life of the church up to this point is not only stopped but turned around by none other than the Lord Jesus himself.[86] The description of Saul in Acts 8:3 as one who is destroying the church and going from house to house and dragging off men and women to prison, and in 9:1 as still 'breathing out murderous threats', highlights the severity of this threat. The contrast, however, between his approach to the synagogues of Damascus in 9:2 in order to drag men and women off to prison and his activity in the synagogues of Damascus in 9:19–20 proclaiming that Jesus is the Son of God shows the power of the Lord Jesus not only to overcome this threat but to enlist Saul as his own most devoted follower. In the narrative of Acts 9 the persecutor of 9:1–2 becomes the bold proclaimer in 9:19–20, even under threat of persecution himself, and this is all due to the work of the Lord Jesus.

In 9:15–16 the rest of Paul's ministry is outlined under the authority of the Lord Jesus. Paul's ministry before the Gentiles and their kings and the people of Israel will be developed from Acts 13 through to the end of the book. This ministry is said to take place, however, because Paul is Jesus' 'chosen instrument'. It is as Jesus' representative, bearing his name and suffering for his name, that Paul will minister, and it is Jesus himself who outlines the course of his ministry.[87]

At a major turning point in the narrative of Acts (16:6–10) we find the directing activity of 'the Spirit of Jesus' as Paul crosses from 'Asia to Europe'. After much is made of the prevention of Paul and his companions from preaching in the province of Asia and Bithynia at the border of Mysia, and the vision of a man from Macedonia urging them to come over to Macedonia, they conclude that 'God had called us to preach the gospel' to the Macedonians (16:10). It is significant, therefore, that in the very next incident in Philippi of Macedonia Lydia responds to Paul's message, because 'the Lord opened her heart' (16:14). The immediately following statement that she is now a 'believer in the Lord' (16:15) indicates that 'the Lord' here is the Lord Jesus. Thus we see that following the directing activity of 'the Spirit of Jesus', the goal of 'God's call' was the conversion of Lydia, whose heart the Lord Jesus himself opened.[88]

---

[86] The transformation of Saul described here indicates that this is a 'conversion' and not a 'call' only. Cf. Kern 2003: 63–80.

[87] Sleeman 2009: 205–208.

[88] Cf. the discussion of the significance of bridging this divide in discussions of ancient rulers in A. J. Thompson 2008a: 74–79.

It is in the light of the authority of the Lord Jesus over Paul's ministry then that we read of reassurances given to Paul along the way that the Lord Jesus is continuing to guide his mission and Paul's ministry. In 18:9–11, in the context of opposition, 'the Lord' speaks to Paul in a vision encouraging him not to be afraid and to keep on speaking, 'for I am with you'. In view of Paul's conversion and call to ministry in Acts 9 'the Lord' here is the Lord Jesus. Paul's ministry will not come to an end here (in Corinth) because, the Lord says, 'I have many people in this city'. Here again the Lord Jesus is responsible for the outcome of and response to Paul's ministry.

The final phase of Paul's ministry in Acts is also carried out under the direction of the Lord Jesus. In 23:11, in the midst of opposition, Paul receives further reassurance from the Lord to 'take courage'. The reason for this courage is the promise that 'as you have testified about me in Jerusalem, so you must also testify in Rome'. The previous chapter, where Paul refers to his 'testimony' about Jesus in Jerusalem (22:18–19), indicates that 'the Lord' here is again the Lord Jesus. Thus the subsequent events where Paul is rescued from a plot to take his life (23:12–35), sent to Caesar in the midst of false charges and corrupt rulers (24:1 – 26:32), marvellously protected through storm, shipwreck and snakebite (27:1 – 28:10) and arrives safely in Rome (28:11–16) are all meant to be read in the light of this promise from the Lord Jesus in 23:11.[89] It is under Jesus' care and as his representative that Paul travels to Rome. Paul's conversion and ministry may be made much of in the narrative of Acts. For Luke, however, this is all the more occasion for marvelling at the transforming power of the Lord Jesus.

# Suffering: the fullness of the kingdom has yet to come

As Paul House has correctly observed, 'Acts has no purpose, no plot, no structure, and no history without suffering. Therefore, proper interpretation of Acts depends in part on the commentator's grasp of suffering's importance in Acts.'[90] This is all the more important

---

[89] It is interesting that the only use of the term *tharsos*, 'courage', in Acts is found in 28:15, and the only use of the cognate verb *tharseō*, 'take courage', in Acts is found in 23:11. In the light of the Lord's command to take courage, for he will testify about him in Rome (23:11), Paul indeed 'takes courage' when he reaches Rome (28:15).

[90] House 1990: 321.

in view of the words of Paul and Barnabas to the believers in Acts 14:22, 'We must go through many hardships to enter the kingdom of God.'[91] In the light of the emphasis in Acts on the continued accomplishment of God's saving purposes through the risen and reigning Lord Jesus within the framework of the inaugurated kingdom of God, this verse is a significant statement about this interim period. The reference to the 'kingdom of God' here clearly has a future orientation; it has yet to be entered and there must (*dei*, 'it is necessary') be suffering beforehand. The Lord reigns and is accomplishing his saving purposes, yet his reign remains contested, the fullness of the kingdom is still 'not yet'. The accomplishment of God's saving purposes in this 'not yet' period of the kingdom therefore helps to explain why suffering is intimately related to two of the dominant themes of Acts: the spread of the word and the establishment and strengthening of local churches.

## Suffering and the spread of the word

Luke punctuates his narrative at regular intervals with statements about the continued progress of the word, indicating that the spread of the word is a major theme in Acts.[92] As Luke's Gospel highlighted the journey of the Lord Jesus to Jerusalem, so Acts highlights the journey of the word about Jesus away from Jerusalem.[93] The association of active verbs with the growth and spread of the word in the summary statements of Acts (cf. also Acts 20:32) together with the recurring descriptions of suffering and persecution experienced by the Christian community in the narrative of Acts indicate that this theme should not be understood as evidence for an 'over-realized' eschatology in a triumphalistic church. It is the *word* that grows 'with power' (Acts 19:20), often in the midst of the persecution of

---

[91] Cf. Cunningham 1997. This verse will be treated in more detail below.

[92] Acts 4:4, 29, 31; 6:7; 12:24; 13:5–12, 46–48; 14:3; 17:13; 18:5; 19:20. On the importance of the spread of the word in Acts see Kodell 1974: 505–519; O'Reilly 1987: esp. 91–121; Rosner 1998: 215–233; Bovon 2006: 272, 457; and esp. Pao 2000: 147–180. Pao relates the theme of the word to the creation of the community of the word in the midst of opposition within the framework of the Isaianic New Exodus (i.e. Isa. 2:3, 'the word of the Lord [will go out] from Jerusalem', and Isa. 40 – 55). Cf. A. J. Thompson 2008a: 135–170 for reference to ancient literary discussions concerning the destructive effects of division and strife and a comparison with the contexts of Luke's statements concerning the spread of the word in the midst of opposition and cities in states of division, conflict and confusion.

[93] Pao (2000: 150–156) notes the locations of references to 'the word' in the narrative of Acts and observes that 'the word' never visits a geographical location twice.

*believers.*[94] The spread of the word, however, is not hindered by the persecution and suffering of believers. In fact, sometimes the persecution of believers is even the means for the continued spread of the word.

## Suffering and the spread of the word in Jerusalem and beyond Jerusalem

Luke draws particular attention to the inability of those opposed to believers to stop the progress of the word. In Acts 4:4 Peter and John are placed in jail. In the very next verse, however, Luke states, 'But many who heard the message ['word'] believed, and the number of men grew to about five thousand' (4:5). Similarly, in Acts 5:18 all the apostles are placed in jail. Once again Luke begins the very next verse with 'but'. In this instance, he states, 'But during the night an angel of the Lord opened the doors of the jail and brought them out' (5:19). The reason for this miraculous escape was so that the apostles could 'tell the people the full message of this new life' (5:20). Likewise, in 5:40–41 the apostles are flogged and ordered not to speak in the name of Jesus. The very next verse, however, highlights the continued ('day after day') proclamation of the good news that the Christ is Jesus (5:42). Thus the summary statement in 6:7 concerning the spread of the word is a summary of this spread in Acts 3 – 7 in the midst of both internal threats and rising external opposition to the Christian community, which culminates in the death of Stephen.[95]

The death of Stephen brings about the greatest persecution the church has faced to that point. So great is the persecution that 'all except the apostles were scattered throughout Judea and Samaria' (Acts 8:1).[96] The description of Saul destroying the church and going from house to house dragging off men and women and putting them in prison (8:3) accentuates even further the severity of this opposition. Once again, however, in the very next verse Luke states that 'those who had been scattered preached the word wherever they went' (8:4). In this instance Luke is not only placing side-by-side

[94] Pao (2000: 160, 162–163, 167–169) discusses the summary statements in Acts 6:7, 12:24, 19:20 (and the verbs used) in the context of Exod. 1:7, 20.

[95] See ch. 5.

[96] In this context the decision of the apostles to remain in Jerusalem is not a sign of their reluctance to take the gospel to the nations or that they somehow escaped the persecution, but of their bravery in remaining in Jerusalem in the midst of severe persecution. Cf. Schnabel 2004, 1: 670–673.

statements about opposition and the inability of that opposition to stop the spread of the word (as he has done in 4:3–4; 5:18–20, 40–42); he is stating this time that the opposition was the very means for the continued spread of the word. This is picked up again in Acts 11:19–21, where Luke describes the spread of the word to Jews (11:19) and to Greeks (11:20), with the result that 'a great number of people believed and turned to the Lord' (11:21). This great number, as observed above, was due to the fact that 'the Lord's hand' was with those who preached the word as they were scattered.

### Suffering and Peter's rescue

The accounts in Acts 12 of Peter's escape from prison and Herod's death dramatically highlight this theme of the inability of those opposed to God's people to halt the spread of the word. The purpose of Acts 12 has been much debated and the ending of Acts 12 (vv. 20–23) has been a particular cause of difficulty due to its apparent disconnection from the account of Peter's release.[97] At least part of the reason for the inclusion of this chapter, however, lies in the contrast between Herod as a powerful 'king' in violent opposition to the Christian community, and 'the Lord' who is able to overcome this threat and enable the word to continue to spread.[98] The whole account is framed with references to the kingship of Herod.[99] The account opens with a description of Herod as 'King Herod' (*hērōdēs ho basileus*, 12:1). At the conclusion of the chapter Herod's kingship is again emphasized (12:20–21) with references to the 'servant of the king' (*tou basileōs*), 'the king's country' (*apo tēs basilikēs*), Herod's 'royal robes' (*esthēta basilikēn*), and Herod's 'throne' (*kathisas epi tou bēmatos*).[100] His powerful opposition against the church is particularly stressed in verses 1–6: he acts violently against some in the church (v. 1), kills James the brother of John with the sword (v. 2), sees that this pleases the Jews and so proceeds to arrest Peter also

---

[97] The following summarizes A. J. Thompson 2008a: 141–143. Cf. the discussions in Witherington 1998: 382–383; Barrett 1994: 569–573; Allen 1997: 5–24, 93–98. Witherington states that 12:20–23 should be seen as a 'separate tradition from Luke's Herodian source, referring to an event that transpired somewhat later' (389).

[98] Tannehill 1990: 152. Contra Barrett 1994: 570, who states that Herod 'is peripheral to the story'.

[99] Haenchen 1971: 388.

[100] His title 'king' was bestowed on him by the emperor Gaius and his realm included Galilee, Perea and, later, under the reign of Claudius, Judea (cf. Josephus, *Ant.* 19.292, 351–352; *J. W.* 2.215–217). Thus at this time Agrippa had received 'the whole of his grandfather's kingdom' (*tē patrōa basileia pasē*, Josephus, *J. W.* 2.215).

(v. 3, with the implication that Peter's life is also in danger)[101] and has Peter placed in prison guarded by four squads of soldiers and bound with chains (vv. 4, 6). The reference to the earnest prayer of the church in verse 5 indicates, however, that one more powerful than Herod is able to be called upon.

Subsequent events do not encourage us to place confidence in the human participants in this account. Peter is portrayed as helpless, asleep when the rescue began, oblivious to the events of his rescue, and comes to his senses only when he is outside (vv. 6, 9, 11–12). Rhoda, although she is at least excited that Peter is out and recognizes Peter, nevertheless is not portrayed in the most flattering light as she leaves Peter (whose life is surely in danger) outside still knocking at the door (vv. 13–14). The believers (who, we are reminded in v. 12, were still praying for Peter) then hear that Peter is at the door and respond that Rhoda must be crazy! After further insistence from Rhoda, they conclude that it must be his angel instead.[102] Finally, when they open the door and see Peter, they are astonished (v. 16). In this context this does not appear to be a release that has been brought about by the great faith of a praying church.[103] What then is the emphasis of this account?

In spite of the great lengths 'King' Herod goes to in securing Peter in prison (12:4), 'an angel of the Lord' struck Peter on the side, woke him up, and led him out of the prison effortlessly (vv. 7–10). The agent of this deliverance, however, is further clarified throughout the narrative. In 12:11 Peter states that 'the Lord' (*ho kyrios*) had sent his angel to rescue him. Then in the concluding summary before Peter leaves, Luke declares simply that 'the Lord' (*ho kyrios*) had brought Peter out of prison (12:17). Thus the focus of the account of Peter's rescue is on the power of 'the Lord' to overcome the violent opposition of 'King Herod'.[104] At the conclusion of the account in

---

[101] Cf. Cunningham 1997: 236.

[102] Peterson (2009: 365–366) suggests that since the term *angelos* can mean 'messenger' it could be that the church thinks he has just sent them a message. The other alternative is that they thought this was his 'guardian angel'. Either way, the point is that they think it cannot be Peter himself!

[103] Although Cunningham (1997: 241) correctly identifies the references to prayer in Acts 12, it appears that the emphasis in 12:12–17 is more on the irony of the situation than on the community's prayer as such.

[104] In the context of an emphasis on the 'lordship of Jesus' in Acts 10 – 11, it is possible that this account contrasts the 'kingship' of Herod with the true King, the Lord Jesus. The word (*logos*) that God sent to Israel is the good news of peace (*eirēnē*) through Jesus Christ, 'who is Lord of all' (10:36). It is this 'Lord of all' who brings peace in contrast to the absence of peace in the realm of this 'king' (12:20; cf. also

the midst of the emphasis on the 'kingship' of Herod noted above, Herod's refusal to give praise to God leads to his downfall as 'an angel of the Lord' strikes again. This time it is Herod who is 'struck' down, and he dies (12:22).[105] It is in this context of defeated opposition that another summary statement records the continued progress of the word (12:24). Despite the efforts of Herod the tyrant who opposed and persecuted the believers, 'the word of God continued to increase and spread' (12:24).[106] Thus, although it is correct to see the description in 12:24 of the continued growth and increase of the word as one of the summary statements that contribute towards the portrait of the spread of the word in the face of opposition in Acts, it is the power of the Lord that enables the deliverance of his people, the defeat of opposition and the continued spread of the word.

## Suffering and Paul's ministry

As noted above, at the heart of Saul's conversion and call is the statement from the Lord Jesus summarizing two aspects of his future ministry: he will both 'bear' the Lord's name before Gentiles, kings and the people of Israel and 'suffer' for the Lord's name (9:15–16). These twin features of Paul's ministry are then immediately demonstrated in his preaching in Damascus (9:20–22) and Jerusalem (9:28) and also in the persecution he faces in Damascus (9:23–25) and Jerusalem (9:29–30). On numerous occasions throughout his ministry, persecution against Paul (like the persecution he himself inflicted on believers before his conversion, 8:3–4) was often the reason for his movement and continued ministry in other places (cf. 9:25, 30; 13:50; 14:6; cf. also 17:10, 14). On other occasions, however, Paul remained to proclaim the gospel in the face of persecution and opposition (cf. 14:2–3, 19–20; 20:22–24; 21:13). Either way, persecution and opposition continued to accompany, but not thwart, the spread of the word in Paul's ministry as he faced opposition from Jew and Gentile alike.[107]

The whole final section of Acts, which describes Paul's arrest

---

9:31). In contrast to the tyrannical rule of 'King' Herod (12:20), belief in 'the Lord' Jesus results in the gifts of forgiveness of sins and the Holy Spirit (10:43; 11:17) and the presence of his 'hand' with them as they proclaim the good news about him in the midst of persecution (11:21).

[105] Cf. Pao 2000: 199–201 for the placement of this passage within the 'anti-idol' theme in Acts. Cf. also Allen 1997: 89–90, 104–107.

[106] Pao 2000: 152. Cf. also Cunningham 1997: 241–242.

[107] Note the Gentile opposition also in 14:5; 16:20–21; 17:32; 19:25–41. Cf. Rapske 1998: 235–256; Cunningham 1997: 186–294.

in Jerusalem and defences before various audiences on his way to Rome, is also placed within the context of ongoing suffering and persecution. A preview of what is ahead is given in Paul's speech to the Ephesian elders, where he declares that he is compelled to go to Jerusalem and that the Holy Spirit has warned him of continued persecution and hardships, but that he is determined to persevere in the task of 'testifying to the gospel of God's grace' (20:22–24).[108] This is confirmed by Agabus in 21:11 where Paul again affirms his commitment to persevere and even die for 'the name of the Lord Jesus' (21:13).[109]

## A suffering Saviour

The suffering of believers in Acts is, of course, consistent with the fact that they follow a suffering Saviour. A major feature of Luke and Acts is that the suffering of the Lord Jesus was integral to the accomplishment of God's saving purposes. Thus, as observed above, it is regularly stated that 'the Christ had to suffer' (Luke 24:26, 46; Acts 3:18; 17:3; 26:23). Similarly, the Lord Jesus is regularly identified as the (suffering) 'Servant' of Isaiah (Acts 3:13, 18, 26; 4:27; 8:32–33). This pattern of suffering, where believers follow their Lord in experiencing rejection and suffering, is indicated by Luke in parallels between Jesus, Stephen and Paul.[110] Thus, like Jesus, Stephen commits his spirit to the Lord and prays for the forgiveness of his attackers after his speech (7:59–60), and, like Jesus, Saul is told that he too 'must suffer' (*dei*, 9:16).[111] When Paul arrives in Jerusalem, it

---

[108] Some have thought that there is a contradiction between 20:22, where the Spirit compels Paul to go to Jerusalem, and 21:4, where it appears that the Spirit (the disciples 'through the Spirit') urges Paul *not* to go to Jerusalem. In the light of the statement in 20:22 concerning the Spirit's role in urging Paul to go to Jerusalem and 21:12, where it is clear that it is the believers who are urging Paul not to go to Jerusalem, it is better to see in 21:4 a combination of these two emphases. The Spirit has warned again (as in 20:23) of impending suffering and it is the believers, acting out of human concern, who are urging Paul not to go to Jerusalem. Cf. Bovon 1995: 34 (who cites Chrysostom); cf. also Barrett 1998: 990–991; Fitzmyer 1998: 688; Hur 2001: 264–266.

[109] Agabus' prophecy ('the Holy Spirit says') in 21:10–11 (that the Jews will bind and hand Paul over to Gentiles) is confirmed by Paul's statement in 28:17 that he was 'handed over to the Romans' (and appears therefore to have been fulfilled in 21:30 when the Jews seized Paul and dragged him from the temple, which then led to the commander of the Roman troops coming in 21:31 and ordering in 21:33 that Paul be bound in chains).

[110] Cf. Moessner 1986: 220–256.

[111] For Acts 7:59 see Luke 23:46, and for Acts 7:60 see Luke 23:34. Cf. the discussion on pp. 167–172 (which also indicates the differences between Stephen and Jesus at this point).

looks very much like he will follow in Jesus' footsteps as the repeated cries of the crowd 'Away with him!' (21:36) and 'Rid the earth of him! He's not fit to live!' (22:22), which 'frame' Paul's defence in Jerusalem, are much like the cries from the crowd against Jesus before his death in Jerusalem (Luke 23:18).[112]

## Suffering for some and deliverance for others

The sometimes contrasting outcomes for God's people found side by side caution against simplistic answers concerning the reasons why in the book of Acts some suffer and others are delivered. In the same context as Peter's miraculous escape from the power of King Herod we have an account of the death of James, the brother of John, who was 'put to death with the sword'.[113] Similarly, the Hellenistic Jews so opposed to Stephen that they stoned him to death in a fit of rage (6:9; 7:57–60) opposed Paul and tried to kill him in Jerusalem (9:29). Paul, however, managed to escape, as the believers found a way to send him off to Tarsus safely (9:30). It should also be noted that Luke writes of the spread of the gospel in the midst of a world where there is famine (11:27–30), injustice (24:27), storm (27:7–38) and shipwreck (27:39–44). Nevertheless, Luke's emphasis on the spread of the word in the midst of opposition indicates that one of the ways in which he seeks to 'reassure' readers such as Theophilus concerning the things they have been taught (Luke 1:1–4) is to highlight the sobering truth concerning the inevitability of suffering in this 'not yet' phase of the kingdom. Although the kingdom has been inaugurated and the risen and ascended Lord Jesus is reigning at the right hand of the Father, nevertheless, in this interim period, before the Lord Jesus returns (Acts 1:11), 'we must go through many hardships to enter the kingdom of God' in its fullness (14:22). Believers may also be reassured, however, that despite opposition, the risen Lord Jesus is reigning and continuing to accomplish God's saving purposes through the spread of the gospel to the nations.

---

[112] The cry 'Away with this man!' in Luke 23:18 is unique to Luke's Gospel. It should be noted that the repeated statements of Jesus' innocence in Luke 23 are also similar to the repeated claims to innocence for Paul in Acts 21 – 28. The close identification of the Lord Jesus with his people in Acts indicates that there is also a sense in which as they are persecuted he continues to experience rejection (Acts 9:4–5; 22:7–8; 26:14–15).

[113] This is the James who was one of Jesus' own 'inner circle' with John and Peter, who witnessed Jesus' transfiguration, and was with Jesus in the garden of Gethsemane.

## Suffering and the strengthening of local churches

The statement in Acts 14:22 concerning suffering during this 'interim' period of the kingdom is also a significant pointer to another major theme in Acts. Just as the spread of the word in the midst of opposition is a major theme, so the strengthening and establishment of local churches to remain faithful in the midst of opposition is a major theme. This was the reason why Paul set out on the so-called second missionary journey in Acts 15:36: Paul said to Barnabas, 'Let us go *back* and visit the brothers in all the towns where we preached the word of the Lord and see how they are doing.' Thus, after Paul and Barnabas' disagreement, Paul and Silas went through Syria and Cilicia 'strengthening the churches' (15:41). Likewise, the summary statement in 16:5 states that 'the churches were strengthened in the faith and grew daily in numbers'.[114] We will look at just three passages here due to their significance for this theme of strengthening churches in their narrative contexts: Acts 11:19–30; 14:21–23; and 20:17–38.

### Strengthening the church in Antioch

Acts 11:19–30 focuses on both the growth *and* the establishment of the church in Antioch. This account is placed in the centre of a section that runs from the summary statement in 9:31 through to the summary statement in 12:24–25 and is therefore set between two sections that focus on Peter (i.e. God's sovereign inclusion of the Gentiles through Peter in 9:32 – 11:18, and the Lord's powerful rescue of Peter in 12:1–25). This new church arises through the spread of the word in the context of persecution (11:19); it is the first church in Acts where Jew and Gentile fellowship together (11:19–20); it is where the disciples were first called Christians (11:26); and it will become the next major sending church in Acts (cf. Acts 13 – 14). In this significant section then, the growth of the church in Antioch is described three times in terms of its 'great numbers'. In 11:21 'the Lord's hand' was with those who spread the word such that 'a great number of people believed and turned to the Lord'. In 11:22–24 after Barnabas arrived from Jerusalem, he saw 'evidence of the grace of God' and 'a great number of people were brought to the Lord'. In 11:25–26 Barnabas and Saul 'taught great numbers of

---

[114] The summary statement in Acts 9:31 also highlights the role of the Holy Spirit in strengthening the church.

people'. Thus one of the themes of this account is that, although persecution brought the believers there, as a result of 'the hand' of the Lord Jesus, the word continued to grow and the church increased in numbers.

In addition to this emphasis on the growth of the church in numbers, however, this section particularly stresses the 'establishment' or 'strengthening' of the church in Antioch. Thus, in the light of Acts 4:36, Barnabas was sent from Jerusalem because he was 'Mr Encouragement'. So, true to his name, when he saw evidence of God's grace he was glad and 'encouraged them' (11:23). More specifically, in the context of persecution (11:19), 'Mr Encouragement' encouraged them in wholehearted perseverance 'to remain true to the Lord with all their hearts'. Furthermore, Barnabas travels over a hundred miles to Tarsus so that Saul can help him in this task of nurturing this church. Thus the reference to Paul and Barnabas remaining in Antioch for 'a whole year' meeting with the church and teaching 'great numbers of people' is meant, in this context, to highlight a period of sustained strengthening (in contrast to the constant movement in 9:32 – 11:18 between Lydda, Joppa, Caesarea and Jerusalem). The establishment of the church in Antioch is complete in 11:29–30 when, after an emphasis on movement 'to Antioch' (11:19–20, 22b, 26–27), this narrative section concludes with movement from Antioch to Jerusalem.[115] The church in Antioch is established such that it is now able to provide assistance to the believers in Jerusalem.

*Strengthening the churches in Lystra, Iconium and Antioch*
Before we look at Acts 14:21–23 and 20:17–38, it will help us to see the significance of these passages in the narrative of Acts better if we grasp the broad outline of this section as a whole. The next major section in Acts after Acts 12 is the 'first missionary journey' in Acts 13 – 14, followed by the Jerusalem Council in 15:1 – 16:5.[116] Spencer helpfully lays out the general outline of this section:[117]

---

[115] C. Green 2005: 82.

[116] As mentioned above (in the discussion on pp. 37–38 concerning God's accomplishment of his purposes in 'subsequent developments in the church'), note the 'framing' reference to 'the work' in 13:2 and 14:26. See ch. 6 for an explanation for the continuation of the themes in Acts 15 through to 16:5.

[117] The following two outlines are simplified adaptations from Spencer 2004: 141.

| | |
|---|---|
| 13:1–3 | Commission in Antioch |
| 13:4 – 14:20 | Ministry in Cyprus, Pisidia, Lycaonia |
| 14:21–28 | Nurturing the churches |
| 15:1 – 16:5 | Evaluation in Jerusalem |

Given that Acts 15:1 – 16:5 is an examination of issues raised in Acts 13 – 14, it is best to group Acts 13:1 – 16:5 as one complete literary unit. At this point it is also helpful to note that Acts 16 – 21 follows a similar outline:

| | |
|---|---|
| 16:6–10 | Commission in Troas |
| 16:11 – 19:41 | Ministry in Philippi, Thessalonica, Berea, Athens, Corinth, Ephesus |
| 20:1 – 21:14 | Nurturing the churches |
| 21:15–36 | Evaluation in Jerusalem |

This appears to be the best way to outline this major section of Acts because (1) it fits better than the commonly adopted 'missionary journey' outline of Acts,[118] and (2) it fits better than the other commonly adopted outline for this section, which places a break at the summary statement in 19:20.[119]

What is noticeable from these broad outlines for the second half of Acts is the repeated pattern towards the end of each section that emphasizes extensive nurturing of the churches. Thus in Acts 14:21, following ministry in Antioch, Iconium, Lystra and Derbe characterized by persecution and opposition, Paul and Barnabas 'returned to Lystra, Iconium and Antioch'. Luke states that the aim of this 'return' in spite of the opposition they had faced in

---

[118] As ch. 6 will indicate, 16:1–5 (marked off by the 'summary statement' in 16:5) is best kept with Acts 15 rather than as part of another major literary unit that supposedly begins in 15:36. Also, within the narrative of Acts there does not appear to be another major literary break in the narrative between 18:22 and 18:23 (supposedly the end of the 'second missionary journey' and the beginning of the 'third missionary journey'). The focus on Ephesus in 18:19 and 21 continues in 18:24 and into Acts 19.

[119] I agree that the summary statements are significant narrative markers throughout Acts (hence my divisions already at 9:32 and 12:24–25). These summary statements that plot the growth of the word are, however, occasionally placed at the heart of narrative units rather than necessarily marking the end of narrative units. We will see in ch. 5 that this is the case with Acts 6:7 in the flow of Acts 3 – 7. Here it is perhaps enough to observe that Acts 19 focuses on Ephesus, and the statement of the growth of the word in 19:20 is placed in the middle of that section. The section is concluded, however, with Paul's sermon to the 'Ephesian' elders in Acts 20 (see A. J. Thompson 2008a: 151–159 for a discussion of the significance of Ephesus in Acts 19 – 20).

these cities is 'strengthening the disciples' and, similar to Barnabas in 11:23, 'encouraging them to remain true to the faith'.[120] It is in this context then, of strengthening the churches in the midst of opposition, that we find the one-sentence summary of what Paul and Barnabas said to encourage them to remain true to the faith: 'We must go through many hardships to enter the kingdom of God' (14:22). The implication is that the persecutions recounted in Acts 14 are not to be thought of as unique to Paul and Barnabas. Rather, this is part and parcel of the Christian life this side of the consummated kingdom. In addition to this sober assessment of the Christian life, Paul and Barnabas 'appointed elders' in each church. In this context of Paul and Barnabas' travels from city to city, they provide these churches with stability for the future by appointing leaders who will stay and further contribute to the strengthening of these churches.

### Strengthening the church in Ephesus

These themes of perseverance, faithful ministry in the face of persecution, strengthening the church, and the provision of elders to assist in this strengthening of the church become a major focus in Acts 20.[121] In this climactic speech – the only lengthy record in Acts of a speech of Paul's to Christians – Paul addresses Christian leaders.[122] In looking back over his ministry, Paul summarizes it under the twin themes that characterized his commission in 9:15–16: (1) suffering for Christ's name, and (2) bearing (or proclaiming) Christ's name before Jews and Gentiles. Thus (1) he emphasizes his commitment to the comprehensive proclamation of God's word with a range of terms for the activity of proclamation,[123] a range of comprehensive descriptions of the content of that preaching,[124] a reference to a

---

[120] Cf. also 13:43 ('continue in the grace of God').

[121] Cf. Kilgallen 1994: 112–121; Cunningham 1997: 267–270.

[122] The term 'elders' (*presbyteros*, 20:17; cf. Acts 11:30; 14:23; 15:2, 22; 1 Tim. 5:17; Titus 1:5–6; 1 Pet. 5:1; Jas 5:14) is used interchangeably with the term 'overseers' (*episkopos*, 20:28; cf. Phil. 1:1; 1 Tim. 3:1–2; Titus 1:7) and the task of being 'shepherds/pastors' (*poimainō*, 20:28; cf. 1 Pet. 5:2) in the sense that the same group of people are being addressed in these three ways. Each term, however, has different nuances to the task of leadership.

[123] *Anangelō* ('proclaim', vv. 20, 27), *didaskō* ('teach', v. 20), *diamartyromai* ('declare', vv. 21, 24), *kēryssō* ('preach', v. 25).

[124] 'Anything that would be helpful' (v. 20), 'Jews and Greeks . . . must turn to God in repentance and have faith in our Lord Jesus' (v. 21), 'testifying to the gospel of God's grace' (v. 24), 'preaching the kingdom' (v. 25), 'proclaim . . . the whole will of God' (v. 27).

variety of times and places for that proclamation,[125] and a reference
to the widespread audience to whom Paul proclaimed the gospel.[126]
(2) This commitment to the proclamation of God's word, however,
is expressed in the context of suffering and opposition as Paul looks
back on his ministry (vv. 18–21) and also as he looks ahead to future
ministry (vv. 22–24). Paul reminds the Ephesian elders of *his* pattern
of ministry in the face of opposition as something they have already
seen and 'know' (vv. 18, 20) because it is a model for *their* ministry
of caring for the flock (cf. vv. 34–35). Thus when Paul moves to
direct exhortation in verse 28, he urges the elders to 'keep watch'
over themselves and the flock, to 'be shepherds' over the flock and to
'be on your guard' (v. 31) because of the severe dangers to the flock
(vv. 29–30). Ultimately, however, Paul's confidence is in God and
'the word of his grace'. This is the same 'word' that 'spread widely'
and 'grew in power', which gave rise to the church in Ephesus (Acts
19:20). It is this 'word of his grace' that Paul commits these elders
to in order for them to be built up. This 'word of grace' is able to
bring them safe through to their inheritance (v. 32) and therefore
Paul appropriately concludes his time with these elders on his knees
in prayer (v. 36).

The last section of this chapter has drawn attention to the integral nature of the theme of suffering and opposition to the themes
of the spread of the word and the establishment and strengthening
of local churches. In the light of the 'framework' Luke provides
for this book concerning the continuing reign of the Lord Jesus
in the inaugurated kingdom of God, and the significant statement
concerning the strengthening of churches in the midst of suffering
in anticipation of the final kingdom in Acts 14:22, it seems Luke
intends readers to see the theme of suffering in Acts within this
broad framework of the inaugurated kingdom of God. Luke wants
readers such as Theophilus to be reassured concerning God's saving
purposes. Yes, God's kingdom has been inaugurated. The Lord
Jesus is continuing to reign at the right hand of the Father and is
building his church through the spread of the word. Nevertheless,
because the kingdom is still 'not yet' consummated, the spread of
the word and the establishing of churches will take place in the midst

---

[125] 'The whole time I was with you' (v. 18), 'from the first day I came into the
province of Asia' (v. 18), 'publically', 'house to house' (v. 20).
[126] 'To both Jews and Greeks' (v. 21), 'innocent of the blood of all men' (v. 26; cf.
Ezek. 3:18–19; 33:1–9).

of suffering. God's people will be strengthened, therefore, with the awareness that suffering remains a part of the Christian life this side of the consummated kingdom, and through elders in the context of local churches who will faithfully proclaim and teach God's word in the midst of suffering. It is this word, after all, that God in his grace uses to strengthen his people.

# Conclusion

Luke is showing that the kingdom of God, inaugurated in the person of the Lord Jesus, is continuing to be administered through him. In this sense his book is about 'the acts of the Lord Jesus'. The departure of the Lord Jesus does not mean the departure of the kingdom. In this period between the 'now' and the 'not yet' of the kingdom he is continuing to reign from the right hand of the Father, as seen in the pouring out of the Spirit and the spread of the good news about him. The suffering and opposition that believers continue to face is because the kingdom has 'not yet' come in fullness. Nevertheless, the word will continue to spread and in this 'inaugurated kingdom' God's people are strengthened in the context of local churches. This 'inaugurated kingdom' then is still to be understood as the fulfilment of God's saving promises and plan. God's eschatological (kingdom) promises for his people are continuing to be fulfilled through the Lord Jesus. According to the OT, however, the end-time promises of blessing were closely associated with the resurrection. The resurrection of Jesus, therefore, is the subject of the next chapter.

# Excursus: an expositional outline of Acts

As indicated above, my own analysis of the structure of Acts, particularly the second half of Acts, slightly differs from two other major approaches. On the one hand, many opt for a 'Pauline Missionary Journey' structure of Acts 13 – 21. This is commonly outlined in something like the following:[127]

|  |  |
|---|---|
| 13:1 – 14:28 | First missionary journey |
| 15:1–35 | Jerusalem Council |
| 15:36 – 18:22 | Second missionary journey |

---

[127] Cf. e.g. modified versions of this in Witherington (1998: vii–viii) and Bock (2007: viii, 47–48).

18:23 – 21:16  Third missionary journey
21:17 – 28:31  Trials of Paul and journey to Rome

The main difficulties with this approach are that (1) it tends to focus more on Paul than on the reign of the Lord Jesus and the purposes of God, which better capture Luke's emphasis, (2) it tends to have more of a focus on a circular motion of Paul's leaving from particular places and returning to particular places than on the continuing spread of the word moving further and further out, which the 'summary statement' outline (below) captures better, (3) more specifically, this structure does not do justice to the narrative flow at 15:36 and 18:22.[128]

A second approach to outlining Acts focuses on the major summary statements that, as noted in the discussion above, are found throughout the narrative of Acts:

6:7     'So the *word* of God spread. The number of disciples in Jerusalem increased rapidly, and a large number of priests became obedient to the faith.'

9:31     'Then the church throughout Judea, Galilee and Samaria enjoyed a time of peace. It was strengthened; and encouraged by the Holy Spirit, it grew in numbers, living in the fear of the Lord.'

12:24   'But the *word* of God continued to increase and spread.'

16:5    'So the churches were strengthened in the faith and grew daily in numbers.'

19:20  'In this way the *word* of the Lord spread widely and grew in power.'

Thus an outline that reflects these summary statements looks similar to the following:[129]

1:1 – 2:41     Prologue: Foundations for the church and its mission

2:42 – 6:7     The church in Jerusalem

6:8 – 9:31     Wider horizons for the church: Stephen, Samaria and Saul

---

[128] Cf. n. 118 above.
[129] Cf. e.g. modified versions of this in Carson and Moo 2005: 286–290 and Köstenberger, Kellum and Quarles 2009: 350–351.

| 9:32 – 12:24 | Peter and the first Gentile convert |
| 12:25 – 16:5 | Paul turns to the Gentiles |
| 16:6 – 19:20 | Further expansion into the Gentile world |
| 19:21 – 28:31 | To Jerusalem and then to Rome |

This outline better reflects a literary approach which recognizes where Luke appears to pause and comment on the previous section (or the section he is in the middle of), it places the emphasis on the purposes of God and the spread of his word as marking off these sections, and this reflects Luke's overall emphases in Acts better. A slight modification of the 'summary statement' outline of Acts, however, is needed. The main reasons for this 'modified summary statement' approach are primarily that (1) Acts 6:7 does not bring about a major shift from Jerusalem as is often reflected in these outlines; this shift comes after Acts 7. For reasons which chapter 5 of this book will develop, 6:1–7 is better seen as a transition to Acts 6 – 7, which brings a climax to themes that have been developing throughout Acts 3 – 5. Similarly (2), it is unlikely that Acts 19:20 should be taken as a major literary break in Acts 19. It is better to see this as a statement concerning the power of the word in the midst of the wider narrative focus on Ephesus in Acts 19 – 20.[130] Thus, in keeping with Luke's introduction in Acts 1 – 2 that the major theme of Acts is the reign of the Lord Jesus who enables the spread of the word, my own, very general, 'expositional outline' of Acts is as follows:

| Acts 1:1 – 2:47 | *The reign of Christ the Lord and the Holy Spirit* |
| Acts 3:1 – 8:3 | *The reign of Christ the Lord over rising opposition*<br>Internal and external |
| Acts 8:4 – 9:31 | *The reign of Christ the Lord over outcasts and enemies* |

[130] Cf. n. 119 above. As Spencer (2004: 141) suggests, the discussion in Jerusalem in 21:17–26 is best seen as a concluding 'wrap-up' to the previous section in Acts. The closing of the temple in 21:27–36 is therefore a fitting conclusion and a transition to the final chapters of Acts. There is also a slight variation among some outlines at 12:25. This verse is better translated as 'Barnabas and Saul returned [i.e. to Antioch], after they had completed their mission *in Jerusalem*' (i.e. 'returned from Jerusalem' NIV, rather than 'returned to Jerusalem' HCSB). This mission refers to the famine relief visit mentioned in 11:27–30 and provides a conclusion to this section rather than an introduction to the following section. Cf. Witherington 1998: 374–375.

Chapter Two

# The hope of Israel: the resurrection and the arrival of the last days

The last chapter drew attention to the inaugurated kingdom of God as Luke's framework for his demonstration of the continued outworking of God's saving promises through the ongoing reign of the Lord Jesus. In Acts, Luke shows that the inaugurated kingdom of God is still very much a reality even though Jesus, the one who announced the arrival of the kingdom, has ascended to heaven. He is continuing to be active and is continuing to rule from the right hand of the Father. In this chapter we will see that Luke's emphasis on the inauguration of the kingdom by Jesus and his continuing rule is the reason why the resurrection of Jesus features so prominently in Acts. The chapter will begin with a brief introduction to the significance of the resurrection in the OT and Luke's Gospel as an orientation to the discussion in Acts. Then some of the main features of the references to the resurrection of Jesus in Acts will be identified, and Luke's emphasis on the resurrection in Acts will be related to the theme of God's saving promises in Acts. The importance of the resurrection in Acts is closely related, however, to two other important issues in the theology of Acts: the significance of the death of Christ in Acts, and the nature of evangelistic preaching in Acts. Thus the chapter will conclude with an examination of these two issues. The following chapter will further examine the fulfilment of God's promises of blessing for the age to come.

## Resurrection hope

The teaching of the OT is especially important for understanding the significance of the resurrection in early Christianity and NT theology in general,[1] and the book of Acts in particular.[2]

---

[1] Wright 2003; Schreiner 2008: 104–105.
[2] Anderson 2006: 52–61.

In Ezekiel 37 a day is anticipated when God's people will have God's Spirit (37:14), return from exile (37:21), be united again (37:22), experience cleansing from sin and enablement to keep God's commands (37:23–24), and live under the reign of a new David (37:24–25). This is a time when God will fulfil the goal of his covenant promises to his people: he will dwell among them and be their God and they will be his people (37:23, 26–27).[3] This ultimate restoration of God's people and fulfilment of God's promises is characterized as nothing less than a resurrection from the dead. The dry bones represent the people of Israel and the departure of their 'hope' (37:11). Corpses rise, new life is breathed in and God's people will know that the Lord has spoken and that he has done it (37:13–14). As Schreiner observes, although there are complex issues in Ezekiel 37, it is clear that 'resurrection signifies the fulfillment of God's promises, the inauguration of the age to come – the restoration of exile and the return of Israel'.[4] Likewise, Isaiah 26 anticipates a time when the proud city of those who do evil will be levelled to the ground in judgment (26:5); in fact this judgment will come to the whole earth (26:9, 21).[5] In contrast to this, the city of salvation for those who trust in the Lord will be strong and characterized by peace (26:1–4, 12), for the Lord himself will bring it about and this brings glory to God (26:1–5, 12–15). The language of 'your zeal for your people' and 'you have enlarged the nation' (26:11, 15) indicates that God's covenant promises are also in view here.[6] Those who take part in this city of salvation, however, include the dead, as corpses will rise and shout for joy (26:19).[7] Similarly, Daniel 12 looks ahead to the time when some will rise to everlasting life and others to shame and everlasting contempt. There will be judgment for some; while others, like Daniel, 'at the end of the days', will rise to receive their

---

[3] Note this 'covenant formula' in similar language in Gen. 17:7 (in the Abrahamic covenant); Exod. 6:7; 19:5; 29:45–46; Lev. 26:12; Deut. 29:13 (in the Mosaic covenant); 2 Sam. 7:14 (in the Davidic covenant); and Jer. 30:22; 31:33; 32:38; Ezek. 14:11; 34:30; 36:28; 37:23, 27 (in the new covenant).

[4] Schreiner 2008: 105. Anderson (2006: 55, 61) prefers to see more explicit physical resurrection language in Isa. 26:19 and Dan. 12:1–3 than in Hos. 6:1–3 and Ezek. 37:1–14.

[5] Anderson 2006: 57–58.

[6] Ibid.

[7] Again Schreiner (2008: 105), in agreement with Childs 2001: 191–192 (and Wright 2003: 116–118; Motyer 1993: 218–220), notes that in this context 'it is a false dichotomy to ask whether the promise is for restoration of the nation or a future resurrection'. Anderson (2006: 58) also uses the language of 'false dichotomy'.

allotted inheritance (Dan. 12:1–3, 13).[8] Those who will be delivered are those whose names are in 'the book'; that is, those who are in a covenant relationship with God (11:32; 12:1).[9]

In each case the resurrection is bodily, is clearly God's doing, is reserved for the end of the age and is associated with the onset of the age to come, the culmination of the promises of blessing for God's people. Israel will be reunited, restored, forgiven and blessed with God's presence. There was not, of course, an expectation that there would be any overlap of the ages. It was expected that, with the resurrection at the end and the onset of blessing for God's people, there will be judgment for the wicked and the end of 'the old age'. This, we could say, was 'the hope of Israel'.

# Resurrection in Luke's Gospel

We will focus here on Luke 24 since this final chapter in Luke's Gospel emphasizes the significance of the resurrection as both a clarification of themes raised at the beginning of Luke's Gospel (concerning God's saving purposes for his people) and an anticipation of major emphases to follow in the book of Acts (concerning God's saving purposes through the Lord Jesus).[10] Luke 24, in three scenes (vv. 1–12, 13–35 and 36–53), much of which is unique to Luke's Gospel, emphasizes the physical reality as well as the meaning or significance of the resurrection.[11] We will see both of these aspects in Luke 24 before observing their continued development in the book of Acts.

The physical reality of the resurrection is repeatedly highlighted throughout Luke 24 in the following ways: (1) the confusion and despair of the disciples in each of the three scenes indicates that they were not naive or ready to believe anything and were not expecting a resurrection (scene 1, vv. 3–4, 11–12; scene 2, vv. 23–24; scene 3, vv. 37–39, 41; cf. also 23:55 – 24:1); (2) the emphasis on the empty tomb, particularly in the first scene (23:55; 24:3, 6, 12; cf. also 24:22–24) emphasizes that 'he is not here'; (3) the appearances of

---

[8] Anderson (2006: 58–61) highlights numerous parallels between Dan. 12:1–3 and Isa. 26:19 relating to the rising of bodies from the dust of the earth (i.e. a bodily resurrection) and 'the interrelated motifs of resurrection, covenant-loyalty, and enthronement/exaltation' (61).

[9] Ibid. 58.

[10] Peterson 1998: 30–32; Anderson 2006: 146–196.

[11] Cf. J. B. Green 1998: 227–246; Peterson 1998: 29–57.

Jesus (24:15, 24, 29, 31, 34–35, 36–43); (4) the physical, bodily (even if transformed) resurrection of Jesus (cf. references to 'the body', and particularly the placement of 'the body', in 23:52, 55; 24:3; i.e. the same body that went into the tomb was raised; the meal in 24:30; and almost every line, even word, of 24:36–43), which stresses that this was not a vision. Jesus was able to be touched and this was a unique event.

Luke not only affirms the physical reality of the resurrection, but also highlights its meaning and significance. As indicated above, there is considerable emphasis in each of the three scenes on the confusion of the disciples. Correspondingly, there is a focus on the explanations provided for the disciples. In 24:6–8 (from the first scene) the extended explanation given by angels is unique to Luke's Gospel and is particularly related to Jesus' own words. In 24:13–32 (from the second scene) the whole journey along the road with Jesus (also unique to Luke's Gospel) is about the journey to understanding of these two disciples. In 24:44–47 (from the third scene) the second half of the meeting and appearance with the disciples that began in 24:36 is all about reminding them of what Jesus had told them and their understanding of the Scriptures.

A key feature of this explanation concerns the accomplishment of God's purposes. This is highlighted through the use of *dei* (it is necessary) and the emphasis on the fulfilment of Jesus' words and especially the Scriptures. As noted above, 24:7–8 (which is unique to Luke's Gospel) particularly highlights the fulfilment of Jesus' words that the Son of Man 'must' (*dei*) be crucified and then be raised. In the second scene (24:26) Jesus states that the Christ had to suffer and enter into his glory. In this second scene the focus is now on the fulfilment of the Scriptures. In the third scene (24:44) Jesus states that 'this is what I told you' and that everything 'must' be fulfilled. This third scene now combines the fulfilment of Jesus' words and God's plan in the Scriptures.

When the Scriptures are referred to in Luke 24, the emphasis is not on a particular verse or two. Rather, the emphasis is repeatedly on the totality of Scripture. Thus in 24:25 Jesus refers to '*all* that the prophets have spoken' and then 'beginning with Moses and *all* the Prophets' he proceeds to explain what was said in '*all* the Scriptures' concerning himself (24:27). The disciples look back to that time on the road and refer to Jesus' opening of 'the Scriptures' to them (24:32). Similarly, in the third scene Jesus reminds them that he had told them '*everything*' must be fulfilled that is written about him, and then proceeds to give the most comprehensive summary of the totality of the OT Scriptures, 'the Law of Moses, the Prophets and the Psalms' (24:44). The disciples are then enabled to understand 'the Scriptures' (24:45). Thus the language of 'fulfilment' as it relates to the totality of Scripture indicates that the Scriptures were 'pointing forward to' or 'anticipating' the death and resurrection of Jesus and therefore that his death and resurrection are the realization of this hope. In these scenes then Jesus is the teacher. On the one hand, it appears that the OT is required to understand the significance of the resurrection and that the OT and Jesus' words are in harmony with each other. Yet, on the other hand, Jesus himself and his resurrection are required in order for the OT hope to be understood.[12]

Regular 'retrospective summaries' that look back to the Gospel accounts of Jesus' ministry in general and the events surrounding the crucifixion in particular are also characteristic of Luke 24 (cf. vv. 6–7, 14, 18–21, 44).[13] Thus, looking back now, readers of Luke's Gospel are meant to see that Jesus' ministry and the cross were an integral part of God's purposes. In addition to these general 'retrospective summaries', Luke 23:50 – 24:53 also points readers back to the opening chapters of Luke's Gospel. The final verses of Luke 24 return to the temple, where Luke's Gospel began (1:5; 2:37; 24:52–53). Furthermore, references to Joseph, who is 'righteous' ('upright' NIV) and 'waiting for the kingdom of God' (23:50–51), and the two disciples who 'had hoped' that Jesus would be the one 'to redeem Israel' point back to the opening chapters. The description of Joseph as righteous recalls the descriptions in the infancy narratives of Zechariah and Elizabeth (1:6–7, both 'righteous/upright'), Simeon (2:25–27, 'righteous') and Anna (2:36–38, though the exact term is not used). Similarly, the language of 'waiting for the kingdom of God' and hoping for one 'to redeem Israel' recalls language in the opening chapters. Zechariah praises the God of Israel because 'he

---

[12] Luke also highlights a spiritual dimension to grasping the reality and significance of the resurrection. In 24:16 the two disciples are 'kept from recognizing' Jesus. When Jesus rebukes the two disciples in 24:25 about their grasp of Scripture, he describes them as 'foolish' and 'slow of heart to believe all that the prophets have spoken'. So, corresponding with v. 16 (where 'their eyes' were kept from recognizing him), in v. 31 'their eyes were opened and they recognized him'. Similarly, in the third scene, after eyewitness testimony (vv. 33–35), physical appearances and a meal with Jesus (vv. 36–43), a reminder of Jesus' own words and the teaching of all Scripture (v. 44), it was not until Jesus himself 'opened their minds' that they were able to 'understand the Scriptures' (v. 45).

[13] J. B. Green 1997: 833.

has come and has redeemed his people' (1:68). Simeon was 'waiting for the consolation of Israel' (2:25), and Anna 'gave thanks to God and spoke about the child to all who were looking forward to ('waiting for') the redemption of Jerusalem' (2:38).[14]

In this way then Jesus' death and resurrection help us to understand the Scriptures in the sense that they now help to explain how the OT hope for the 'redemption' or 'consolation' of God's people is fulfilled. These hopes were raised in the opening chapters of Luke's Gospel but awaited clarification as to how they would be fulfilled. In the context of Luke 24:21 the now abandoned 'hope' (they 'had hoped') of the two disciples in the face of Jesus' death probably still referred to their hope for political deliverance from Rome.[15] Thus the clarification in Luke 24 concerning the relationship between the OT and Jesus' death and resurrection may more specifically be described as clarification concerning the fulfilment of this hope for Israel. With the resurrection of Jesus, the hoped-for kingdom of God, or promises of blessing for God's people, may now be received. The blessings associated with the age to come, the resurrection age, may now be received from the resurrected Jesus himself. Therefore, with this inauguration of the resurrection age to come, the blessings of the age to come are emphasized in the final verses of Luke's Gospel in anticipation of what is to follow in the book of Acts: repentance . . . forgiveness of sins . . . all nations . . . in the name of Jesus . . . Jerusalem . . . the Father's promise . . . power from on high (24:47–49). These links between the name of Jesus and the resurrection, the blessings of the age to come and the 'hope of Israel' are then developed further in Acts.

## Resurrection in Acts

The proclamation of Jesus' resurrection is one of the most prominent themes in Acts.[16] The resurrection of Jesus is the climax and focus of the sermons in Acts (see esp. Acts 2:24–32 and 13:30–37). Even Paul's defence before the Areopagus in Acts 17 was prompted by his earlier preaching concerning 'the good news about Jesus and the resurrection' (17:18–19). Paul's reference to the resurrection

[14] Note also the declaration to Mary in 1:33 that Jesus will 'reign over the house of Jacob for ever; his kingdom will never end'.
[15] Bock 1996: 1913–1914; cf. Isa. 41:14; 43:14; 44:22–24; 1 Macc. 4.11; *Pss Sol.* 9.1.
[16] Cf. Acts 2:24, 31–32; 3:15; 4:2, 10, 33; 5:30–31; 10:40–41; 13:30, 32–37; 17:3, 18, 31. Cf. Anderson 2006.

brought the sermon to a conclusion and the subject of the resurrection was what some wanted to hear about again (17:31–32). In the light of 17:18–19, therefore, it is likely that the resurrection of Jesus was the goal of Paul's sermon in Acts 17 from the beginning. Thus, whether for Jewish or Gentile audiences, it may be said that apostolic preaching in Acts is 'resurrection preaching' (Acts 4:2; 17:18–19).[17] In his summary in 4:33 Luke states that 'with great power the apostles continued to testify to the resurrection of the Lord Jesus'. The emphases found in Luke 24 on the physical reality (it is not enough to say 'he lives in my heart' only) as well as the meaning or significance of the resurrection are also seen in the preaching of the resurrection in Acts. The significance of the resurrection for the fulfilment of God's promises for his people, however, receives more detailed treatment in Acts.

As in Luke 24, the sermons in Acts (following a recounting of the events of Jesus' life and death by crucifixion) stress the historical reality of the resurrection with an emphasis on the physical, bodily resurrection of Jesus. The body put to death was the body raised (cf. Acts 2:23–24, 27, 31; 3:15; 5:30; 10:39–40; 13:29–31) and (as in Luke 24) Jesus' disciples saw him. The reality of Jesus' appearances, however, becomes dominant in Acts as the proclamation of Jesus repeatedly refers to eyewitness testimony. The term 'witness/testify' in Acts frequently has to do not with what we might describe as personal 'testimony' of what God has done in our lives, but with actual 'witness' or 'sight' of the risen Lord Jesus. Note the repetition of the theme of witness in association with the proclamation of the resurrection in the verses below:

| | |
|---|---|
| 2:32 | 'we are all witnesses of the fact' |
| 3:15 | 'we are witnesses of this' |
| 4:33 | 'the apostles continued to testify to the resurrection' |
| 5:32 | 'we are witnesses of these things' |
| 10:39, 41 | 'we are witnesses' '(he was seen) by witnesses' |
| 13:31 | 'he was seen . . . they are now his witnesses' |
| 22:15; 26:16 | Paul will be a witness of what he has seen[18] |

---

[17] Wagner 2004: 119.
[18] Cf. also references to Paul's 'testimony' about the Lord Jesus in these contexts: Acts 22:18; 23:11; 26:22.

Thus the resurrection is frequently spoken of in terms of 'eyewitness' testimony of the risen Christ.[19] So important is this 'eyewitness' testimony of the risen Christ that it is made one of the requirements for the replacement apostle in 1:22. That is, the addition of eyewitness testimony is frequently at the heart of the proclamation and indicates that the historical reality of the resurrection is crucial. For Luke (and for the proclamation of the early Christians) it was not enough only to speak of personal moral transformation, personal existential experience of the risen Christ or the philosophical superiority of Christianity; rather, the authentic apostolic *eyewitness* testimony of the historical reality was fundamental.[20]

Luke emphasizes more, however, than the historical reality of the resurrection of Jesus in Acts. The meaning or significance of the resurrection is especially developed in Acts. As we observed in the introductory chapter, Luke stresses the accomplishment of God's purposes in the death and resurrection of Christ. Thus Jesus' death, even though it was brought about by the actions of evil men, is attributed to God's 'set purpose and foreknowledge' (Acts 2:23). Similarly, in Acts 4:27–28 the actions of Herod, Pilate, the Gentiles and the people of Israel accomplished 'what your power and will had decided beforehand should happen'. The accomplishment of God's purposes in the death of Christ is also highlighted in the way Christ's death is said to conform to what God said would happen in OT Scripture. Thus the actions of handing Jesus over to be killed, disowning Jesus before Pilate (even though Pilate had decided to let Jesus go) and having the 'author of life' killed (3:13–14), though described as ignorant actions (3:17), are said to be 'how *God fulfilled* what he had foretold through all the prophets, saying that his Christ would suffer' (3:18). Likewise, the actions of the people of Jerusalem and their rulers in condemning Jesus 'fulfilled the words of the prophets' (Acts 13:27).

It is also in these contexts that we find the repeated emphasis in Acts that 'God raised him from the dead'.[21] This is the consistent refrain when the resurrection of Jesus is proclaimed, whether before a Jewish audience (2:24; 3:15; 4:10; 5:30), a Gentile audience familiar with the Scriptures and the life of Jesus (10:40), a Jewish and Gentile 'God-fearing' synagogue audience (13:30, 33–34, 37)

---

[19] Cf. J. B. Green 1998: 227–246.
[20] Cf. Peterson 1998: 32; 1 Cor. 15:14.
[21] Acts 2:24; 3:15; 4:10; 5:30; 10:40; 13:32–37; 17:31.

or a Gentile audience unfamiliar with the Scriptures of Israel but who have had a framework provided for them concerning the God of the Bible (17:31). In keeping with the corresponding emphasis on the accomplishment of God's actions in the death of Jesus mentioned above, the resurrection of Jesus is also then an outworking or accomplishment of God's action.

In Acts the resurrection is the climax of God's saving purposes, and it is on the basis of the resurrection that the blessings of salvation may be offered. The reason for this appears to be that in the resurrection of Jesus, the hoped-for resurrection age to come has arrived already, and it is because of the arrival of the age to come that the blessings of that age may now be received. This is stated in the narrative climax of Luke's references to Jesus' resurrection in Acts 26:23. Before examining that text, however, we can see that Luke is providing hints of this in the way in which Jesus' resurrection is associated with the resurrection of 'the dead' in general (i.e. in the plural, 'the dead ones'); that is, the resurrection of the dead expected to take place at the end of the age.[22] Thus in Acts 4:2 what disturbs the temple leadership is the apostles' proclamation of 'the resurrection of the dead' (plural) in Jesus. It appears that the general resurrection of all people at the end is in view and it is this resurrection that is being proclaimed 'in Jesus' (cf. also 17:31 and then 32). That is, in the context of Acts 3 – 4, Jesus' resurrection anticipates the general resurrection at the end of the age and makes available now, for all those who place their faith in him, the blessings of the 'last days'.[23] A general reference to 'the resurrection of the dead' (plural) is also what Paul says he is on trial for in 23:6 and 24:21. After the discussion below, it will become clearer that when Paul stands up before the Sanhedrin in Acts 23:6 and announces that he is on trial because of his hope in the resurrection of the dead, he is doing more than throwing a strategic grenade into the proceedings. In his proclamation of Jesus' resurrection he is announcing the fulfilment of God's promises that were anticipated to arrive in the age to come, the resurrection age. Thus he *is* on trial for his 'hope in the resurrection of the dead'.

In order to appreciate Paul's emphasis on the significance of the resurrection in his defences in Acts 24 and 26, it will be helpful to

---

[22] Acts 4:2; 17:31–32; 23:6; 24:15, 21; 26:6–7; 26:23.
[23] Cf. Anderson 2006: 281–284. See ch. 5 for the significance of Peter's sermon in Acts 3.

see the flow of argument in these two defences. Spencer's outline helpfully identifies the similarity in structure and perspective in these speeches of Paul in Acts 24 and 26:[24]

*Paul's trial before Felix: Acts 24*
Introduction:  opening comments to the judge (24:2–4 [Tertullus]; 24:10 [Paul])
Narration:  review of temple incident (24:11–13)
Declaration:  hope of resurrection (24:15–16)
Narration:  review of temple incident (24:17–20)
Declaration:  hope of resurrection (24:21)

*Paul's trial before Agrippa: Acts 26*
Introduction:  opening comments to the judge (26:2–3)
Narration:  review of Jerusalem upbringing (26:4–5)
Declaration:  hope of resurrection (26:6–8)
Narration:  review of conversion/call (26:9–21)
Declaration:  hope of resurrection (26:22–23)

Spencer helpfully highlights the centrality of the resurrection in Paul's defences, where it is raised both early as well as climactically. In Acts 24 the statements in verses 15 and 21 refer to the general resurrection of the dead at the end of the age.[25] Thus it is left to Paul's final and climactic trial in Acts to clarify what he means when he declares that he is on trial for his belief in the final resurrection of the dead.

Paul's final trial in Acts begins with all the pomp and ceremony appropriate to this climactic statement concerning this long trial section that concludes Acts. In 25:23 this is highlighted by Luke's introduction to the proceedings: 'Agrippa and Bernice came with great pomp and entered the audience room with the high ranking officers and the leading men of the city. At the command of Festus, Paul was brought in.' Then, following a summary of events that have led to this moment, Luke provides us with Paul's longest defence in this trial section (following the shortest one before Festus in Acts 25) and Paul's longest speech in Acts. It is in this speech

---

[24] The following two outlines are slightly adapted from Spencer 2004: 227–228, 236, 238.
[25] 'There will be a resurrection of both the righteous and the wicked' (24:15); 'it is concerning the resurrection of the dead (plural) that I am on trial' (24:21).

that the resurrection is again central. As Spencer's analysis of the structure indicates, the resurrection is again mentioned early in the defence in a general fashion and assumes a belief that God is able to 'raise the dead' (plural). It is then in Acts 26:22–23, in Paul's final words before being interrupted, that Paul declares that he is saying 'nothing beyond what the prophets and Moses said would happen – that the Christ would suffer and, as *the first to rise from the dead*, would proclaim light to his own people and to the Gentiles'.[26] Here, finally and climactically, Luke includes Paul's clarification of what he has meant throughout his earlier defences by stating that he is on trial for 'the resurrection of the dead' (plural). Jesus' resurrection is an end-time eschatological event that has already taken place in this age. As in Acts 4:2, to proclaim Jesus' resurrection was to proclaim the introduction (already in this age) of the eschatological blessings reserved for the resurrection age (at the end of this age) for all those who belong to Jesus.[27]

A further indication that Luke understands Jesus' resurrection to be the introduction of God's promises for the age to come is found in these final chapters of Acts in Paul's trial scenes when Paul refers to the resurrection as the 'hope of Israel'.[28] As in the opening and concluding chapters of Luke's Gospel, so here in these concluding chapters of Acts there are repeated references to the hopes of the people of Israel. Paul repeatedly states that being on trial for his proclamation of the resurrection of Jesus is in fact being on trial for the 'hope of Israel'. Notice the recurring reference to 'hope' in the summary of statements below concerning why Paul was on trial:

| | |
|---|---|
| 23:6 | 'I stand on trial because of my *hope* in the resurrection of the dead' |
| 24:14–15, 21 | 'I believe everything that agrees with the Law and that is written in the Prophets, and I have the same *hope* in God as these men, that there will be a resurrection . . . it is concerning the |

---

[26] *Prōtos ex anastaseōs nekrōn* (first to rise from the dead). This phrase reflects the terminology of *ek nekrōn* in Acts 3:15; 4:2, 10; 10:41; 13:30, 34; 17:3, 31. Anderson (2006: 282–283) notes that this phrase means that Jesus is the 'first from the resurrection of the dead' in the sense of 'the first to take part in the eschatological resurrection of the dead'.

[27] The eschatological nature of Jesus' resurrection is also evident in Acts 17:31, where Jesus' resurrection is given as proof of the final judgment that will be administered by Christ with justice.

[28] Cf. Kepple 1977: 231–241; Anderson 2006: 266–269, 286–291.

|              | resurrection of the dead that I am on trial before you today' |
|--------------|--------------------------------------------------------------|
| 26:6–8, 22–23 | 'it is because of my *hope* in what God has promised our fathers that I am on trial today . . . why should any of you consider it incredible that God raises the dead? . . . I am saying nothing beyond what the prophets and Moses said would happen – that the Christ would suffer and, as the first to rise from the dead would proclaim light . . .' |
| 28:20        | 'it is because of the *hope* of Israel that I am bound with this chain' |

Paul repeatedly declares that what he believes is consistent with the Scriptures ('the Law and the prophets', 'the prophets and Moses') and the promise of God to 'our fathers'.[29] This is the same 'hope' as his accusers have of a future resurrection (24:15), the 'hope' in God's promise that 'the twelve tribes' (i.e. the people of Israel) are 'hoping to see fulfilled' (26:6–8), and it is therefore 'the hope of Israel' (28:20). This is why Paul states that he is on trial because of his 'hope in the resurrection of the dead' (23:6 and again in 24:21). As Paul's final trial in 26:6–8 and 22–23 makes clear, the resurrection is the essence of the hope of Israel and the Scriptures. This 'hope' is the longed-for 'age-to-come' of the last days characterized by resurrection, the blessings of that age, the Holy Spirit and the return and restoration to God of God's people. It is this hope that Paul claims has been fulfilled and made available already in Jesus' resurrection from the dead. Thus Jesus' resurrection is tied to the heart of the fulfilment of God's promises and the outworking of his plans in salvation history. The resurrection of Jesus is 'first' and brings the eschatological resurrection into this age so that the blessings of that age are now available for all those who belong to him.

It is because of this connection between Jesus' resurrection and the resurrection at the end of the age, therefore, that Jesus' resurrection is also intimately tied to the offer of the blessings of salvation in Acts. It is the resurrected Jesus who pours out the Holy Spirit (Acts 2:33).[30] It is the resurrected Jesus who grants 'salvation' to

---

[29] 24:14; 26:6–7, 22; 28:17.

[30] As we noted in ch. 1, Acts 2:33 follows the declaration of Jesus' resurrection in 2:32 with *therefore* being exalted to the right hand of God 'he has received from the Father the promised Holy Spirit and has poured out what you now see and hear'.

the beggar – a healing in anticipation of the wholeness of the new creation (4:10–12).[31] Likewise, it is the resurrected Jesus who gives 'repentance and forgiveness of sins to Israel' (5:30–31). The link between the resurrection and the offer of the blessings of salvation is especially seen in Paul's synagogue sermon in Acts 13. Paul declares in 13:32–33 that 'what God promised our fathers he has fulfilled for us, their children, *by* raising up Jesus'. As indicated above in the repeated references in Paul's trials to the resurrection and God's promise, the resurrection of Jesus is here again the fulfilment of God's promise to his people. Then, following references to the Davidic promises and concluding again in 13:37 that God raised him from the dead, Paul states '*therefore* . . . through Jesus the forgiveness of sins is proclaimed to you'. It is because the resurrection of Jesus is the inauguration of the age to come that the blessings of that age such as the Holy Spirit, salvation, repentance and forgiveness may now be received. Schreiner correctly observes therefore that 'Luke concentrates on the resurrection of Jesus in Acts because it is the emblem of the new age, the signature of God's promises'.[32] The importance of the resurrection in Acts is closely related, however, to two other important issues in the theology of Acts: the significance of the death of Christ in Acts, and the nature of evangelistic preaching in Acts. Thus the following sections will examine these two issues before we move to the following chapter.

## Jesus' death and the resurrection in Acts

Some have observed this emphasis on the resurrection in Acts and have concluded that Luke denies any atoning significance to Jesus' death in both his Gospel and in the book of Acts.[33] Although, as we have seen in this chapter, the book of Acts certainly emphasizes the resurrection of Jesus, Luke does not deny the significance of Jesus' death for dealing with sin. Two features of Luke's writing need to be kept in mind here. First, Luke is selective in what he includes, and he summarizes what he records (cf. Acts 2:40). Thus Luke does not necessarily repeat information again if he has already drawn attention to a particular theme. Secondly, he also expects readers to keep in mind his first volume, the Gospel of Luke, when reading his

---

[31] Peterson 1998: 40.
[32] Schreiner 2008: 105.
[33] This view is especially associated with Conzelmann (cf. 1960: 200–202).

second volume, the book of Acts. This is indicated in the first verse of Acts, where he points us back to his first volume and reminds us of what he has already written about in anticipation of what he is going to go on and write about. Thus I will first summarize the main features of Jesus' death in Luke's Gospel before turning to the main features of Jesus' death in the book of Acts.

## Jesus' death in Luke's Gospel

What then needs to be kept in mind from Luke's first volume before we assess the importance of the resurrection in his second volume? One obvious observation to keep in mind is the fact that an account of Jesus' death has already been told in great detail. Some deny, however, that Luke has a theology of the atonement in his Gospel.[34] Although space prevents a detailed discussion here, this claim is usually based on the arguments that (1) Luke has omitted Mark 10:45 in the equivalent discussion in Luke 22:27, and (2) that Luke 22:19b–20 (concerning the body 'given for you' and the blood 'poured out for you') was not original to Luke's Gospel.[35] The first argument, however, requires a view of literary dependence among the Synoptic Gospels that is less certain these days.[36] Furthermore, the whole discussion in Luke 22:24–30 (i.e. the context for 22:27) takes place at the last supper and is unique to Luke's Gospel in this setting (thus to claim that Luke has consciously 'omitted' Mark 10:45, a saying from a different context and setting, neglects the uniqueness of this setting in Luke 22 as a whole). The second argument has been rejected by many, as the textual evidence supports the longer reading in 22:19b–20.[37]

Moving to more substantive observations concerning Luke's view of Jesus' death in his Gospel, we can note the following: (1) The structure of Luke's Gospel particularly highlights Jesus' 'journey' to Jerusalem from Luke 9:51. In this way Luke indicates that the whole of Jesus' ministry must be understood in the light of the cross with the goal of Jerusalem as the context for all that Jesus does 'on the way'. (2) Luke repeatedly emphasizes that Jesus' death was the plan and will of God (Luke 18:31; 22:22; 24:7, 25–27, 44–46). (3) In fact,

---

[34] Cf. the brief summary of this view in Doble 1996: 3–9. Cf. also Larkin 1977: 325–329.

[35] Franklin 1975: 65–67; Ehrman 1991: 576–591.

[36] Cf. France 2002: 41–45 for a succinct summary of the difficulties surrounding the 'simple literary dependence of one writer on another' (43).

[37] Cf. Bock 1996: 1721–1723.

as with the other Gospels, by including Jesus' concern for the 'cup' he was about to drink, Luke includes the fact that Jesus would drink the 'cup' of God's wrath (Luke 22:42–44; cf. Mark 14:32–42; Isa. 51:17, 19, 22; Jer. 25:15–29; 49:12).[38] Other indications that Jesus' death was wrath-bearing include the emphasis on the Passover in the last supper in association with Jesus' own suffering (Luke 22:1, 7–15) and thus the presentation of Jesus as the lamb for God's people; the sacrificial language of Jesus' body 'given' for his disciples and his blood 'poured out' for his disciples (Luke 22:19–20); and the darkness at noon while Jesus is on the cross as indicative of the 'day of the Lord' judgment (Luke 23:44–45; cf. Joel 2:10, 30–31; Amos 8:9; Zeph. 1:15; Jer. 15:9; Deut. 28:29; Job 5:14).[39] (4) Alongside this repeated stress on the will, plan and purpose of God in Jesus' death, however, is another emphasis in Luke's account of Jesus' death: Jesus was innocent and righteous, as seen in (a) the repeated statements concerning his innocence throughout Luke 23 (cf. 23:4, 14–15, 22, 41, 47), and (b) the allusions to the righteous sufferer of the Psalms (Pss 22:6–7, 18 and 69:21–22 in Luke 23:34–36; Ps. 31:5 in Luke 23:46; Ps. 31:18 in Luke 23:47; and Ps. 38:11 in Luke 23:49). He did not die for his own sins since he was righteous. (5) Luke also portrays Jesus as the Suffering Servant of Isaiah. Very broad allusions to this *may* be found in Luke 23:9 (Isa. 53:7–8 and Jesus' silence; cf. also Acts 8:32); Luke 23:34 (Isa. 53:12 and Jesus' intercession for the transgressors); Luke 23:35 (Isa. 42:1 and Jesus as 'the Chosen One'; cf. also Luke 9:35); and Luke 23:47 (Isa. 53:11 and Jesus as 'righteous'). More explicitly, however, a quotation of Isaiah 53:12 concerning the Suffering Servant of Isaiah is cited by Jesus in Luke 22:37 (in a passage unique to Luke's Gospel). In the context of Isaiah 52:13 – 53:12, Isaiah 53:12 sums up and concludes the whole 'Servant Song'.[40] This song, it must be remembered, refers to a Servant who was despised, rejected, stricken by God, pierced for our transgressions, bore the iniquity of us all, though he had done no violence, nor was any deceit in his mouth, he was crushed and suffered according to the Lord's will, but was a guilt offering and bore the sin of many. Furthermore, not only is Isaiah 53:12 found in a crucial setting for the whole of the Servant Song in Isaiah 53 as a summary verse, but the quotation of this verse by Jesus in Luke

---

[38] Marshall 1978: 831.
[39] Bolt 2004: 125–126; Bock 1996: 1858–1861.
[40] Larkin 1977: 329–335. Cf. also Mallen 2008: 120–125.

22:37 is also found in a prominent place in the narrative of Luke's Gospel. It comes at the end of the farewell discourse and right before the action that leads to the passion narrative. Thus it virtually stands as a heading for all that is to follow as Jesus then prepares in prayer for the ordeal of bearing God's wrath (22:39–46), faces his betrayer and accusers (22:47–71), and dies unjustly as one who is righteous and yet goes willingly to death by God's plan and purpose (23:1–46). (6) Luke explicitly and uniquely includes the statement from the Lord Jesus at the last supper that the cup which represents Jesus' blood is the inauguration of the new covenant (Luke 22:20). This new covenant in Jesus' blood of course ought to remind readers of the promises of Jeremiah and Ezekiel of forgiveness of sins, the Holy Spirit and a renewed/transformed people of God. (7) The outcome of all this is that 'forgiveness of sins', a prominent theme throughout Luke's Gospel (Luke 1:77; 3:3; 5:20–21, 23–24; 6:37; 7:42–43, 47–49; 11:4; 12:10; 17:3–4; 23:34), is therefore commanded (by Jesus himself) to be preached in his name to all nations (Luke 24:47).

In summary: as readers of Acts, if we keep in mind the dominant focus of Luke's first book as Luke expects us to (Acts 1:1), we will recognize, in narrative form, the main lines of a theology of the atonement anticipated in the OT and articulated in the NT letters. Jesus' death was God's will, purpose and judgment. Yet Jesus did not deserve to die, as he was righteous and innocent of all crime, perfectly obeying the will of God. The answer to this dilemma that Jesus did not deserve death and yet his death was God's judgment is found in the statements of the Lord Jesus himself, who pointed to the sacrificial nature of his death as a representative and substitutionary sacrifice for his people. Therefore the new-covenant blessings of forgiveness of sins and the presence of God among a transformed people may now be proclaimed, and must be proclaimed, to all nations.

## Jesus' death in the book of Acts

Teaching about Jesus' death in the book of Acts includes the following: (1) Jesus' death is the plan and will of God (Acts 1:16; 2:23; 3:18; 4:28; 13:27, 29; 17:3) – enough has been said about this in the introductory chapter and again in this chapter, so I will not develop the point again here. (2) Jesus died as one who bore the curse of God (Acts 5:30; 10:39; 13:29; cf. also Deut. 21:23; Gal. 3:13). In these verses Peter and Paul state that Jesus was killed by being hung 'on a tree'. This way of describing Jesus' death is most likely an allusion to the phrase found in Deuteronomy 21:23, where it is stated that anyone who is hung on a tree is 'cursed by God'.[41] As with many of Luke's allusions to the OT, he appears to be writing for an audience familiar with the OT and who would thus have been familiar with the significance of stating that someone was put to death 'on a tree' (something noted in the introductory chapter and evident in the many OT quotations and allusions in Acts).[42] (3) Nevertheless, even though Jesus' death is repeatedly stated to be God's plan and even though there are allusions to Jesus' death as the death of one 'cursed' by God, Acts (as with Luke's Gospel) repeatedly states that Jesus was an innocent, holy and righteous sufferer (Acts 3:14; 4:27; 7:52; 10:38; 13:28). (4) In this vein Luke continues his emphasis on Jesus as the Suffering Servant (Acts 3:13, 18, 26; 4:27; 8:32–33). (5) Likewise, in keeping with the emphasis in Luke's Gospel and in obedience to the command of Jesus himself, the new-covenant blessing of 'forgiveness of sins' is proclaimed 'through Jesus' in Acts (Acts 2:38; 3:19; 5:31; 8:22; 10:43; 13:38; 26:18). (6) Luke includes the words of Paul to the Ephesian elders that the church is bought with 'the blood of his own (Son)' (Acts 20:28) – a statement that further highlights the sacrificial nature of Christ's death and the costly price paid to redeem God's people.[43]

In summary: it is clear that Luke especially emphasizes the proclamation of Jesus' resurrection in Acts. These same messages, however, also highlight Jesus' death (reminding readers of all that Luke has said in his first volume), allude to his death as a curse (again keeping in mind what he has already said in his first volume) and then these messages proclaim the forgiveness of sins, calling for faith and repentance (as Jesus commanded his disciples to do in Luke 24). Having written a first volume, however, which elaborated in great detail the significance of Jesus' death (in view since at least Luke 9:51), Luke (understandably) summarizes aspects of Jesus' death in his second volume and develops more fully the event that

[41] Peterson 2009: 221–222.

[42] Note too that the same point is made by Paul in Gal. 3:13, where he elaborates on the significance of Jesus' death on a tree and states that Jesus bore God's curse or punishment in our place. The audience in Acts 13 is possibly the same (south) Galatian audience to whom Paul writes the letter to the Galatians (perhaps soon after he visited there in Acts 13 but before the Jerusalem Council in Acts 15). For this early dating of Galatians and provenance of the letter to south Galatia see Hemer 1989: 247–251, 277–307 and M. B. Thompson forthcoming.

[43] Cf. Witherington 1998: 623–624 and Peterson 2009: 570 for the translation of Acts 20:28 as 'the blood of his own (Son)'.

especially highlights Jesus' lordship and the arrival of the age to come. He expects his readers to remember that when the apostles preached Christ's death and resurrection, the death and resurrection are inseparable and are the basis for the resulting offer of forgiveness of sins. Christ's undeserved death was according to God's plan and purpose, and in this death he even bore God's wrath and punishment. The judgment he bore was therefore for his people (Luke 22) and it is because of this death and defeat of death that forgiveness of sins is offered to all who turn to the crucified and risen Saviour in repentance and faith.

## Preaching the gospel in Acts

As noted above, the emphasis on the resurrection of Jesus in Acts is found particularly in the speeches in Acts. Because many of these speeches are evangelistic sermons, this raises some questions concerning the content of evangelistic preaching in the book of Acts. Thus in this section the resurrection of Jesus in Acts will be discussed in the context of the broad features of evangelistic preaching in Acts more generally.

We have observed that Luke both begins and ends the book of Acts with two references to the kingdom of God (1:3, 6; 28:23, 31) and that part of Luke's purpose is to teach his Christian readers about the nature of the inaugurated kingdom of God in this new era, 'between the times' in the overlap of the ages. So what happens between the inauguration and consummation of the kingdom? Luke shows that God's people are no longer restricted to national Israel but includes all who repent and trust in the Lord Jesus. God's people will face opposition and suffering (this is what life will be like in this overlap of the ages), but they are nevertheless, by God's grace, characterized by a corresponding active movement *both* to proclaim the word – the message of the gospel – to all, *and* to establish and strengthen local churches. The spread of the word through proclamation, planting and strengthening local churches, in the midst of suffering, therefore, dominates Luke's instruction for Christian readers like Theophilus about what is to characterize the people of God in this new stage in salvation history.

It appears likely that Luke also intends to teach something about the nature of this proclamation, or what this proclamation is to be characterized by. In assessing whether or not Luke is trying to make a point (i.e. being 'prescriptive') we observed (in the introductory chapter) that one way of identifying this is to look for emphasis or repetition. In the case of preaching the gospel in Acts there is surely a case that Luke is trying to make a point. Not only do regular 'summary statements' plot the progress of the word throughout the narrative of Acts, but much of what Luke writes is in the form of speeches proclaiming and defending the gospel. For a book called 'acts' much of it is 'teaching'. Although calculations vary depending on how much speech one requires before something is labelled a 'speech', of approximately 1,000 verses in Acts, at least 365 are found in major and minor speeches and dialogues.[44] The main speeches of believers in Acts include Peter (eight), Stephen (one), James (one) and Paul (nine).[45] If we focus attention on the evangelistic speeches of Christians in Acts, it certainly seems that Luke is interested in showing how the gospel is proclaimed as well as documenting the spread of the gospel.

## Abbreviation and selection in Luke's account of apostolic preaching

Many have noted that Luke has provided us with carefully selected representative speeches – the point of which appears to be to provide us with models/patterns/examples for how the gospel was proclaimed and defended among the various audiences that Christians met as the gospel spread.[46] Thus, for example, in Paul's major speeches we have one each for Jews (13:16–41), Gentiles (17:22–31; cf. also 14:14–17) and Christian leaders (20:18–35). These speeches, in keeping with Luke's practice of selectivity, are *typical* of more general accounts and thus we are to read these as *typical* of the way Paul would present the gospel to a synagogue audience and *typical* of the way he would present the gospel to a Gentile audience with no background knowledge of God's special revelation.[47]

Furthermore, it appears that Luke has abbreviated these carefully selected representative speeches, given that what we have as even the longest speech would take only a few minutes to read (cf. also

---

[44] Soards 1994: 1.

[45] Peter: 1:16–25; 2:14–26; 3:12–26; 4:8–12; 5:29–32; 10:34–43; 11:5–17; 15:7–11. Stephen: 7:2–56. James: 15:13–21. Paul: 13:16–41; 14:15–17; 17:22–31; 20:17–35; 22:3–21; 24:10–21; 26:2–29; 27:21–26; 28:17–20. Padilla (2008) has also recently drawn attention to the importance of the speeches of 'outsiders' in Acts.

[46] Cf. accessible summaries in D. E. Johnson 1997: 141–165 and Wagner 2004: 15–37.

[47] C. Green 2005: 27.

Acts 2:40). It also seems that sometimes Luke abbreviates further as he progresses in the narrative. Thus Green has observed, for example, in Peter's evangelistic speeches of Acts 2 – 5, that we move from 23 verses in his first evangelistic speech (Acts 2:14–36), to 15 verses in his second (Acts 3:12–26), to 5 verses in his third (Acts 4:8–12), and to 4 verses in Peter's fourth evangelistic speech in these chapters (Acts 5:29–32).[48] Green is probably correct to suggest that we are meant to see in the smaller summaries allusions to the larger accounts that do not need constant repeating. When we focus on the evangelistic speeches in Acts, we find that although each speech suits its context and reflects the distinctive elements of each speaker, certain patterns begin to emerge. In the discussion below, following a table that provides a broad summary, we will examine the main features of the evangelistic speeches of Peter and Paul in Acts 2 – 5, 10, 13 and 17.[49] Consistent patterns emerge concerning their focus on God's saving purposes in Christ's death and resurrection so that forgiveness of sins may be offered to all who respond in repentance and faith.[50]

## Repeated features of evangelistic speeches in Acts[51]

### God-centred

One of the most striking features of these sermons is that, although they are clearly designed to proclaim Christ, they all begin with *God*. As we have already seen (in ch. 1), the focus is on *God's* actions in history and the fulfilment of *his* purposes and promises given in Scripture. This is the case whether the audience has a biblical background (e.g. Acts 2 – 5, 13 and Acts 10, even though, as 10:36–38 indicates, they knew about Jesus' ministry) or not, such as in Acts

[48] Ibid. 26–28, 59–60. The numbering here differs from Green's.

[49] I have omitted Acts 7 – 8, 14, 17, 15, 20 and 21 – 28 in the following discussion because Acts 7 (Stephen) is more of a defence against specific charges regarding law/temple (see ch. 5); Acts 8 (Philip to the Ethiopian) is a particular response to an individual's reading/question (see ch. 3); Acts 14 (Paul at Lystra) is a brief and particular response to the attempt to worship Paul and Barnabas (though similar main themes are developed in Acts 17); Acts 15 (Jerusalem Council) is a meeting with a number of speakers and not an 'evangelistic speech' (see ch. 6); Acts 20 (Paul to Ephesian elders) is to Christian leaders (see ch. 1); Paul's speeches in Acts 21 – 28, like Stephen's, are more 'defence' speeches against charges than primarily 'mission' speeches (though similar themes emerge and Paul seeks to shift his defence to evangelistic appeal when he can; cf. Acts 24:24–25; 26:27–29; see above on the resurrection in Acts).

[50] The role of the Holy Spirit in enabling this proclamation will be discussed in ch. 4.

[51] Cf. also D. E. Johnson 1997: 143, who adapts Dodd's outline (1944: 21–23).

Table 1: Major evangelistic speeches in Acts

| | Acts 2 | Acts 3 | Acts 4 | Acts 5 | Acts 10 | Acts 13 | Acts 17 |
|---|---|---|---|---|---|---|---|
| The speaker | Peter (with the eleven, 2:14) | Peter (with John, 3:11) | Peter (with John, 4:1, 7) | Peter and the other apostles (5:29) | Peter (10:34) | Paul (with his companions, 13:13–15) | Paul (17:22) |
| The audience | Jews from every nation (2:5) | The crowd in Solomon's portico (3:11) | The rulers, elders, scribes (4:5–6) | The Sanhedrin (5:27) | Cornelius and household (10:27) | Israel and Gentiles in a synagogue (13:16) | The Areopagus (17:22) |
| Occasion | Pentecost (2:12) | Healing and gathered crowd (3:12) | By what power or name? (4:7) | Escape, arrest, prohibition (5:27) | Messengers from Cornelius (10:33) | Invitation to speak (13:16) | 'Jesus and the resurrection' (17:18–20) |
| Introduction | Joel, fulfilment, God's action (2:16–17) | The God of Abraham, Isaac, Jacob, our fathers (3:13) | An act of kindness (4:8–9) (obedience to God, 4:19) | We must obey God . . . The God of our fathers . . . (5:29–30) | God shows no favouritism, God sent the message (10:34, 36) | God's action in Israel's history to David (13:16–23) | altar, worship, God, creation, humanity (17:22–29) |
| The events | 2:22–32 | 3:13–15 | 4:10–11 (4:20) | 5:30–31 | 10:36–42 | 13:23–37 | 17:31 |
| Jesus' life | Jesus' ministry | | | | Jesus' ministry | John's ministry | |
| Jesus' death | you killed him | you killed him | you killed him | you killed him | they killed him | they killed him | |
| Jesus' resurrection | God raised him we saw him | God raised him we saw him | God raised him we saw him | God raised him we saw him | God raised him we saw him | God raised him they saw him | God raised him from the dead |
| The offer | 2:38 (2:21, 40) | 3:16, 19, 21, 25–26 | 4:12 | 5:31–32 | 10:42–43 (10:44; 11:15–18) | 13:38–39, 46, 48 | 17:30–31 |
| Forgiveness of sins | forgiveness, Holy Spirit, saved from the 'day of the Lord' | sins wiped out, refreshing, blessing | (salvation) | (repentance and forgiveness of sins granted) | (judge), forgiveness, Holy Spirit, life | forgiveness of sins, justification (eternal life) | judgment is coming |
| The Holy Spirit | | | | | | | |
| The required response | 2:38, 41 | 3:16–26 | | (repentance) | 10:43, 47–48 (11:17–18) | 13:39, 48 | 17:30 (17:34) |
| Repentance, faith (baptism) | repent, be baptized, ('accepted the message') | repent and turn to God, 'listen', turn | | | believe (repentance granted, baptism) | believe | repent (some believed) |

17. There is either an assumption or reminder of God's purposes and action in Scripture, or, if there is not (as in Acts 17), then a biblical framework for understanding God and his purposes in the world is made known and explained first.[52] The emphasis is on God's initiative; he is active and personal and we are accountable to him. Thus, whether the audience is Jewish or Gentile, Jesus is not presented in abstraction or isolation from a broader understanding of God and God's purposes in the world. A 'world view' is painted (i.e. who God is, what he is like and how he relates to the world) and then the situation of the audience and what they need to know about Jesus are explained so that they grasp the biblical framework of God's sovereign purposes and salvation history.

*Audience-conscious*

In addition to this observation about the God-centredness of these speeches, however, it should also be noted that what is said about God varies from context to context. There is a sensitivity to and awareness of the audience and what they need to know. This 'audience adaptation' is evidenced in the following ways.[53] (1) Audience adaptation is evident in the various ways in which the speeches describe God and his purposes. Thus in Acts 2 God's promise concerning the Spirit in the last days is the obvious starting point; in Acts 10 the sermon begins with the fact that God does not show favouritism; in Acts 13 the focus is on God's gracious actions throughout Israel's history; and in Acts 17 God's sovereignty over and distinction from creation and therefore humanity's accountability to him are highlighted. In other words, the speeches do not just begin with 'here are some things you should know about God'. Although they all do begin with God and his purposes, they all focus on context-specific aspects of God's purposes. (2) Related to this, the speeches are preceded by some 'occasion' and are responses to that particular 'occasion'. Thus, whether the occasion is Pentecost, a healing, an arrest, or an enquiry, the speeches are all related to those particular occasions (i.e. explaining the pouring out of the

---

[52] Pao (2000: 193–197; cf. also Schnabel 2004, 2: 1399–1403) notes the following biblical allusions to Isaiah's polemic against idols in Acts 17: God is the creator of heaven and earth and gives life to all (Isa. 42:5; 45:18; and is therefore not dependent on his creatures; cf. also Ps. 50:10–12); he does not live in temples built by hands (Isa. 66:1–2); he is not like gold, silver, stone, an image made by man's skill (Isa. 40:18–20); he is near and must be sought (Isa. 55:6).

[53] Cf. Wagner 2004: 87–96.

Holy Spirit, explaining the significance of the healing, explaining the authority of Jesus). (3) Similarly, the speeches are often tied to specific opportunities by questions or invitations. Thus speeches in response to questions occur in Acts 2:12 ('What does this mean?'); 4:7 ('By what power or what name?'); 5:27–28 ('questioned by the high priest'); 17:18–20 ('May we know what this new teaching is?'); and in 3:12 an implied question is assumed as Peter 'answered ('said to' NIV) them . . .' (perhaps in response to the implied question 'How did these men make this beggar walk?').[54] Specific invitations to speak are found in 10:33 ('we are all here . . . to listen to everything the Lord has commanded you to tell us') and 13:15 ('if you have a message of encouragement for the people, please speak'). (4) The 'audience-conscious' nature of the speeches in Acts is further indicated in the way Jesus' death and resurrection are spoken of.[55] Not all Jews are blamed for Christ's death, as the summary on the table above indicates. There is a shift from 'you killed him' when audiences in Jerusalem are addressed (Acts 2 – 5) to 'they killed him' when audiences outside Jerusalem are addressed (Acts 10, 13). Likewise, not everyone was present for Jesus' resurrection appearances after he rose from the dead, as there is a shift from 'we saw him' when Peter and the apostles are speaking (Acts 2 – 5, 10) to 'they saw him' when Paul refers to these early resurrection appearances (Acts 13). The core elements remain the same concerning God's saving purposes and Christ's death and resurrection despite the variety of audiences. Finally (5), the variety of verbs used (see table 2 at the end of this chapter) also implies that various levels of interaction were expected from the audiences. Verbs of teaching, proclaiming, refuting, reasoning and persuading require hearers to understand, think, reason, consider and examine. The sheer variety of terms used for this preaching of the gospel cautions against reductionistic approaches to engaging with non-Christian audiences.

## Christ-focused

As with the observations above concerning the emphasis on God's purposes, the focus on Christ is also found in all of the evangelistic speeches, whether the speech is for those with or without a biblical

---

[54] Ibid. 150–151.
[55] The observations concerning 'you/they killed him', 'we/they saw him' and 'God raised him' in the table above and in this section are borrowed from C. Green 2005: 27–28.

background. In each instance, even Acts 17 (cf. 17:18, 31–32), the goal of the speech is to present Christ to the audience. In this sense there are a few key features we have already seen in this chapter. (1) The sermons are historically grounded accounts of the events of Jesus' life, death and resurrection. The speeches focus on what Christ did, what happened and the reality of apostolic eyewitnesses. This is especially prominent in the emphasis on phrases such as 'we are witnesses of this'.[56] This is of course similar to what Paul says he preached in 1 Corinthians 15. The historical reality of Jesus' death and resurrection are central to the uniqueness of the Christian faith. (2) These historically grounded accounts are, however, also theologically oriented accounts of the historical events. The sermons are not just an accounting of historical events: they are *more* than historical accounts. God's saving action in history is climaxed in Christ's death and resurrection. Thus, as we have observed, even Christ's death, though brought about through the actions of evil men, is ultimately attributed to the accomplishment of God's purposes: God's 'set purpose and foreknowledge' (Acts 2:23; cf. also 4:28); or 'this is how God fulfilled what he had foretold' (3:18); or 'in condemning him they fulfilled the words of the prophets' (13:27). Likewise, with Christ's resurrection, it is always God who 'raised him from the dead'.[57] This emphasis is the same whether the audience is Jew or Gentile. All of this is, of course, in keeping with the emphasis on God's action, the fulfilment of his purposes, and *the climax* of his saving purposes in Christ throughout Acts. (3) The focus of this Christologically oriented preaching in Acts is on the resurrection. 'Preaching the resurrection' is the way Luke summarizes their preaching at times (Acts 4:2, 33; 17:18; though there are also other formulations; cf. 17:2–3), and the resurrection of Jesus is the focus and climax of the sermons (see esp. Acts 2, 13). As noted above, even the sermon in Acts 17 is prompted by questions about the resurrection and climaxes with reference to Jesus' resurrection, which indicates that this was the goal of the sermon from the start (17:18–31; i.e. after establishing the nature of the God of the Bible). We have seen already in this chapter, however, that this focus on the resurrection does not mean that Luke downplays the death of Jesus: (a) Luke has already emphasized the importance of Jesus' death in his first volume; (b) Jesus' death is still proclaimed along with his

---

[56] Acts 2:32; 3:15; 4:33; 5:32; 10:39, 41; 13:31; 22:15, 18; 23:11; 26:16, 22.
[57] Acts 2:24; 3:15; 4:10; 5:30; 10:40; 13:32–37; 17:31.

resurrection in Acts, for the two are inseparable; (c) now that the resurrection has occurred, this is the new element in his historical account of God's saving purposes that needs to be highlighted; (d) the resurrection also demonstrates the lordship of Jesus (cf. Acts 2:35–36; 10:42; 17:31), his current reign (2:32–33) and the inauguration of God's end-time saving blessings.[58] As noted in the discussion of Jesus' death in Acts, when the apostles preached the good news of Christ's death and resurrection, they were proclaiming God's saving purposes in these events. The (wrath-bearing) death and (death-defeating) resurrection of Jesus and the resulting offer of the forgiveness of sins are inseparable.

## Response-oriented

Although apostolic preaching focuses on God's plans and purposes and culminates in the accomplishment of his saving purposes in the death and resurrection of Christ, the implications and significance of God's saving action in Christ are always highlighted. In this sense, the proclamation of the good news of God's saving action in Christ is always accompanied with warnings and promises and an appeal to respond in repentance and faith. Warnings are given because estrangement from God, opposition to God, and idolatry against God bring judgment.[59] Thus in Acts 2 the name of the Lord must be called upon in order for a person to be saved from judgment on the day of the Lord (2:21, 40, 47), and those opposed to the Lord Jesus are his enemies and members of a 'corrupt generation' who will one day be judged (2:35, 40). In Acts 3 the audience must repent so that sins might be wiped out (3:19), Christ will return (3:20–21), but all who do not listen to him will be completely cut off (3:23). In Acts 10 and 17 Christ is declared to be the judge who will one day judge 'the living and the dead' (10:42) and 'the world with justice' (17:31). In Acts 13:40 warning is given in the light of the judgment spoken of by the prophets.

Along with warnings, however, there are promises. Apostolic preaching proclaimed 'the way to be saved' (16:17, 30). The 'good news' or gospel was about what God had done in the historical events of Jesus' life, death and resurrection. Because of his

---

[58] Cf. the references earlier in this chapter to Acts 2:33, 4:10–12, 5:30–31, 13:37–38 and Paul's references to 'the hope of the resurrection' (23:6; 24:14–15, 21; 26:6–8, 22–23; 28:20) and Jesus as 'the first to rise from the dead' (26:23).

[59] Stenschke 1998: 125–144.

wrath-bearing death (Luke 22:19–20, 37, 42; 23:44–45; Acts 5:30; 10:39; 13:29) and the overcoming of death in resurrection (Luke 24:46–47; Acts 2:38; 5:31; 13:38–39) the blessings of the age to come may now be offered to those who will respond to this good news with repentance and faith in Jesus. Thus apostolic preaching involved pleading with sinners to be saved (2:40). The message was 'a message through which you and your household will be saved' (11:14) or 'a message of salvation' (13:26). In Acts 13 this 'message of salvation' is further defined in terms of 'forgiveness of sins' (13:38), 'justification' (13:39), 'eternal life' (13:46, 48) and again 'salvation' (13:47).[60] In obedience to the command of the Lord Jesus, therefore, the apostles preached 'repentance and forgiveness of sins' in Jesus' name to all nations (Luke 24:47). The preaching was direct and personal where applicable ('you killed', 'you know', 'it is to us', 'he has fulfilled for us', 'I want you to know', 'your objects of worship . . . what you worship') and repentance and faith were called for consistently. Apostolic preaching was not character-ized by merely abstract announcements of Jesus' lordship, nor was personal application left out. The good news of God's saving action in Christ demands a response, so apostolic preaching consistently called people to repentance and faith.[61]

It should be noted in this regard that although the preaching was response-oriented, the messages were not response-driven. That is, the messages were not compromised just to get a favourable response or just to make people happy. There were often *mixed* and even *hostile* responses. This does not mean, of course, that there was a lack of concern for the audience or that there was no desire to see a favourable response. The hope was that there would be a response of repentance and faith for the forgiveness of sins.[62]

### Boldness: the manner of apostolic preaching

Luke is especially fond of describing the preaching in the book of Acts as preaching with 'boldness'.[63] The noun *parrēsia* is used five times, especially in the early chapters of Acts, and the verb *parrēsiazomai* is used seven times (out of a total of nine in the NT).

---

[60] In the context of 'forgiveness' (13:38), 'justification' (13:39) here is acquittal or freedom from guilt through Jesus. Cf. Bock 2007: 459.

[61] See pp. 141–143 for a brief discussion of the relationship between the responses of faith, repentance and baptism, and the reception of the Holy Spirit in Acts.

[62] Cf. Paul's concern in Acts 20:19–21.

[63] For a full and helpful discussion of this see Wagner 2004: 39–86.

Thus, using the noun *parrēsia*, Peter states in 2:29, 'Brothers I can tell you *confidently* . . .' (in the context of derision); in 4:13 Luke states that when the Sanhedrin saw the *boldness* of Peter and John, they marvelled (in the context of opposition from 'the rulers'); in 4:29 the believers pray that the Lord would 'enable your servants to speak your word with great *boldness*'; then in 4:31 'they were all filled with the Holy Spirit and spoke the word of God *boldly*' (in the context of threats and opposition); and finally in 28:31 Luke states that Paul '*boldly* and without hindrance' 'preached the kingdom of God and taught about the Lord Jesus Christ' (in the context of house arrest).

The verb *parrēsiazomai* is used in 9:27, where Luke reports that Barnabas told the disciples in Jerusalem how Saul preached *fearlessly* in Damascus; and the verb is used again in 9:28, where Luke reports that Saul spoke *boldly* in the name of the Lord in Jerusalem (in the context of Jews plotting to kill Paul). In 13:46 we are told that Paul and Barnabas 'answered them *boldly*' (in the context of Jews being filled with jealousy and 'blaspheming' or 'speaking abusively' against Paul); again in 14:3 Paul and Barnabas spend considerable time in Iconium speaking *boldly* for the Lord (in the context 'Jews stirred up the Gentiles and poisoned their minds' and there was a plot among the Gentiles and Jews 'to mistreat them and stone them'); in 18:26 Apollos began to speak *boldly* in the synagogue (in the context of vigorous refutation and public debate); similarly, in 19:8 Paul entered the synagogue in Ephesus and 'spoke *boldly* there' (in the context of some being 'obstinate', who 'refused to believe' and 'publically maligned the way'); and in 26:26 Paul states that he speaks 'freely' to Festus (in the context of a trial and Festus' shouting that Paul is insane!).

As noted in the parentheses above, each reference to 'boldness' here is located in a context of hostility or opposition. In these contexts then 'boldness' is a freedom to proclaim the truth of God's saving purposes in the Lord Jesus along with the accompanying warnings and promises even in contexts of opposition, threats of personal harm, persecution or derision. It is the willingness 'to be clear in the face of fear'.[64]

How then did this boldness arise? First, especially in Acts 4, Luke highlights the fact that this boldness comes supernaturally as a result of the Spirit's work. Thus Peter is 'filled with the Holy Spirit' when

[64] Ibid. 42.

he speaks to the Sanhedrin (4:8) and they notice his boldness (4:13). The believers pray that they will be enabled 'to speak your word with great boldness' (4:29) and again they were 'filled with the Holy Spirit and spoke the word of God boldly' (4:31).[65] A similar point may be made from Peter's speech in Acts 2, where the same term used for the enabling from the Spirit to speak in languages in 2:4 is used of Peter being enabled to speak in 2:14.[66]

Secondly, it seems likely that the manner of preaching is linked to a conviction about the message preached.[67] Boldness comes from knowing that the kind of message one brings is God's message about what he has done in Christ, which fulfils his word of promise in the law and prophets, and which is the only means to receive forgiveness of sins and avert judgment. In this sense, in addition to what was said above about the consistent inclusion of warnings and promises in apostolic preaching, it is also helpful to observe the descriptions of this message in Acts. In table 3 below, summaries of the message preached in Acts indicate that although there are a variety of expressions used concerning the message, it is consistently described as, on the one hand, God's message (it is the message of 'God', 'the Lord', 'the kingdom of God' or 'the will of God'), and, on the other hand, as 'good news' (it is the word of 'salvation', 'grace', 'life', 'peace'). Thus it is likely that the manner of preaching is derived from the nature of the message as God's word of grace. Knowing the source of the message (God), the content of the message (God's saving action in Christ) and the eternal significance of the message (life) brings confidence in proclaiming the message. Their message after all promised not health and wealth in this life but 'new life' or 'eternal life' (5:20; 11:18; 13:46, 48).

Thirdly, returning to the theme of this chapter (and the book as a whole), it is also likely that the truth of Jesus' resurrection brought boldness in the face of opposition. The disciples knew that Jesus had conquered death (1:3) and continues to reign (2:32–36); they proclaimed a risen Saviour (2:31; 3:15; 4:2, 33; etc.); they were commissioned by the risen Lord himself (Luke 24:47–49; Acts 1:8; 9:15; 13:47; 20:24; 22:21); the Lord Jesus enables those who hear the message to respond (2:47; 5:31; 11:21; 16:14); the risen Lord Jesus continues to encourage them in the midst of hardship (18:9; 23:11);

---

[65] Cf. Eph. 6:19; Col. 4:4 (cf. also 2 Cor. 3:1–18).
[66] *Apophthengomai* (see further on pp. 131–134).
[67] Wagner 2004: 39, 64.

and Jesus himself will receive them when they 'sleep' at their death (7:59–60).

## Conclusion

The resurrection of Jesus in Acts especially highlights the arrival of the age to come as anticipated in the OT Scriptures. The resurrection is therefore integral to the outworking of God's saving promises and the inauguration of the kingdom of God. As Luke 24 and Acts 23 – 28 especially highlight, the resurrection of Jesus is the fulfilment of Israel's hope. Luke had already highlighted the saving significance of the wrath-bearing and sacrificial death of Jesus in his Gospel. In Acts, therefore, he summarizes this aspect of apostolic preaching more succinctly in order to highlight the new event in God's saving purposes – the resurrection as supreme evidence of the achievement of God's saving purposes and the arrival of the age to come. It is therefore, on the basis of the death and resurrection of Jesus, that the blessings of the age to come may be offered to all who come to the risen Lord Jesus in repentance and faith. The next chapter will examine further some of the promises of blessing for the age to come that are fulfilled in Acts.

The following tables relate to the discussions above regarding the variety of verbs used as an indication of the variety of ways in which the gospel was announced to the audiences (table 2) and the variety of ways in which the content of the message is summarized as God's message of grace (table 3). The references are not grouped in any particular order except that an attempt has been made to group similar phrases together (though variations are listed separately). The translations of the Greek text are my own.

Table 2: Verbs used in Acts to describe the action of apostolic preaching

preach/proclaim (*katangellō*, 13:5, 38; 15:36; 16:17; 17:13, 23; 26:23)
preach/proclaim (*kēryssō*, 8:5; 9:20; 10:37; 19:13; 20:25)
preaching and teaching (*kēryssō . . . didaskō*, 28:31)
proclaim and teach (*anangellō . . . didaskō*, 20:20)
proclaim (*anangellō*, 20:27)
teaching and proclaiming the good news (*didaskō . . . euangelizō*, 5:42; 15:35)
teaching and proclaiming (*didaskō . . . katangellō*, 4:2)
teaching (*didaskō*, 5:21, 25, 28; 11:26; 18:11; 21:21, 28)
to speak or teach (*phthengomai . . . didaskō*, 4:18, 20)
speak (*laleō*, 2:4, 6–7, 11; 4:1, 17, 20, 29, 31; 5:20, 40; 6:10–11, 13; 10:44; 11:14–15,
    19; 13:42, 46; 14:1, 9, 25; 16:6, 13–14, 32; 17:19; 18:9; 21:39; cf. also the use of *legō*)

Table 2: (cont.)

| |
|---|
| spoke and debated (*laleō . . . syzēteō*, 9:29) |
| speak and preach the good news (*laleō . . . euangelizō*, 11:20) |
| preach the good news (*euangelizō*, 8:4, 12, 35, 40; 10:36; 13:32; 14:7, 15, 21; 16:10; 17:18) |
| testify and proclaim and preach the good news (*diamartyromai kai laleō . . . euangelizō*, 8:25) |
| to preach and to testify (*kēryssō . . . diamartyromai*, 10:42) |
| testify . . . bear witness (*diamartyromai . . . martyreō*, 23:11) |
| warned and pleaded (*diamartyromai . . . parakaleō*, 2:40) |
| testify solemnly/declare (*diamartyromai*, 18:5; 20:21, 24) |
| explained, declared, tried to convince (*ektithēmi, diamartyromai, peithō*, 28:23) |
| testify (*martyromai*, 20:26; 26:22) |
| preached fearlessly/speaking boldly (*parrēsiazomai*, 9:27–28; 13:46; 14:3; 18:26; 26:26) |
| spoke, taught, preach boldly (*laleō . . . didaskō . . . parrēsiazomai*, 18:25–26) |
| speaking boldly, reasoning, persuading (*parrēsiazomai . . . dialegomai . . . peithō*, 19:8) |
| reasoning (*dialegomai*, 17:17; 18:19; 19:9; 20:7, 9; 24:25) |
| reasoned, persuading (*dialegomai . . . peithō*, 18:4) |
| persuade (*peithō*, 13:43; 17:4; 19:26; 26:28; 28:24) |
| reasoned, explaining, proving, proclaiming (*dialegomai, dianoigō, paratithēmi, katangellō*, 17:3) |
| proving (*symbibazō*, 9:22) |
| refuted (*diakatelenchomai*, 18:28) |

Table 3: Summary descriptions of the message preached in Acts

| |
|---|
| the word of God (*ho logos tou theou*, 4:31; 6:7; 8:14; 11:1; 13:5, 7, 46; 17:13; 18:11) |
| the word of the Lord (*ho logos tou kyriou*, 8:25; 13:44, 48–49; 15:35–36; 16:32; 19:10, 20) |
| the word/message (*logos*, 4:4; 6:4; 8:4; 11:19; 14:25; 17:11) |
| your word (*ton logon sou*, 4:29) |
| the word of this salvation (*ho logos tēs sōtērias tautēs*, 13:26) |
| the word of his grace (*ho logos tēs charitos autou*, 14:3; 20:32) |
| the word of the gospel (*ho logos tou euangeliou*, 15:7) |
| in Jesus the resurrection from the dead (*en tō Iēsou tēn anastasin tēn ek nekrōn*, 4:2) |
| what we have seen and heard (*ha eidamen kai ēkousamen*, 4:20) |
| the resurrection of the Lord Jesus (*tēs anastaseōs tou kyriou Iēsou*, 4:33) |
| the teaching about the Lord (*hē didachē tou kyriou*, 13:12) |
| the full message of this new life (*panta ta rhēmata tēs zōēs tautēs*, 5:20) |
| a message (*rhēma*) through which you will be saved (*sōthēsē*) you and all your household (11:14) |
| the way to be saved (*katangellousin hymin hodon sōtērias*, 16:17) |
| preach the good news/gospel (*euangelizō*, 8:25, 40; 13:32; 14:7, 15, 21; 15:35; 16:10) |
| what God promised our fathers he has fulfilled for us, their children, by raising up Jesus (13:32–33) |

Table 3: (cont.)

---

the good news that the Christ is Jesus (*euangelizomenoi ton Christon Iēsoun*, 5:42; 18:5, 28)

the Christ (*ton Christon*, 8:5)

that he (Jesus) is the Christ (*hoti houtos estin ho Christos*, 9:22)

the good news about Jesus (*euēngelisato autō ton Iēsoun*, 8:35)

that Jesus is the Son of God (*ton Iēsoun hoti houtos estin ho huios tou theou*, 9:20)

the good news about the Lord Jesus (*euangelizomenoi ton kyrion Iēsoun*, 11:20)

to believe in . . . Jesus (*hina pisteusōsin . . . eis ton Iēsoun*, 19:4)

the kingdom of God (*peri tēs basileias tou theou*, 19:8)

that it was necessary for the Christ to suffer and to rise from the dead . . . this Jesus is the Christ (*hoti ton Christen edei pathein kai anastēnai ek nekrōn . . . houtos estin ho Christos [ho] Iēsous*, 17:3)

the good news about Jesus and the resurrection (*ton Iēsoun kai tēn anastasin euēngelizeto*, 17:18)

the good news of the kingdom of God and the name of Jesus Christ (*euangelizomenō peri tēs basileias tou theou kai tou onomatos Iēsou Christou*, 8:12)

the good news of peace through Jesus Christ (*euangelizomenos eirēnēn dia Iēsou Christou*, 10:36)

repentance to God and faith in our Lord Jesus (*tēn eis theon metanoian kai pistin eis ton kyrion hēmōn Iēsoun*, 20:21)

repent and turn to God (*metanoein kai epistrephein epi ton theon*, 26:20)

the gospel of God's grace (*to euangelion tēs charitos tou theou*, 20:24)

the whole will of God (*pasan tēn boulēn tou theou*, 20:27)

preaching the kingdom (*kēryssōn tēn basileian*, 20:25)

faith in Christ Jesus . . . righteousness, self-control and the judgment to come (*peri tēs eis Christon Iēsoun pisteōs . . . dikaiosynēs kai enkrateias kai tou krimatos tou mellontos*, 24:24–25)

the Christ must suffer, and by being first to rise from the dead, he would proclaim light . . . (*ei pathētos ho Christos, ei prōtos ex anastaseōs nekrōn phōs mellei katangellein*, 26:23)

declaring the kingdom of God and . . . about Jesus (*diamartyromenos tēn basileian tou theou . . . peri tou Iēsou*, 28:23)

preaching the kingdom of God and teaching about the Lord Jesus Christ (*kēryssōn tēn basileian tou theou kai didaskōn ta peri tou kyriou Iēsou Christou*, 28:31)

---

# Chapter Three

# Israel and the Gentiles: the kingdom and God's promises of restoration

So far we have observed that the emphasis on the outworking of God's saving promises in Acts is specifically describing the continued outworking of the inaugurated kingdom of God. In Acts the inaugurated kingdom of God is continued through the reign of the risen Christ, whose resurrection and exaltation demonstrate that the age to come and the hoped-for blessings of that age have already arrived. This chapter will now further develop this emphasis on the arrival of the blessings of the age to come by focusing on the fulfilment of God's promises for the restoration of his people in Acts. We will examine those programmatic verses in the opening section of Acts where Jesus' answer to the disciples' question says so much about how the narrative of Acts will proceed (1:6–8). We will then note the significance of Acts 2, 8, 13 and 15 as evidence that Luke is demonstrating in the narrative of Acts the outworking of God's promises of restoration for his people.

## Kingdom restoration and Israel? (Acts 1:6–8)

The promise of the Lord Jesus in Acts 1:8 that the disciples will receive power when the Holy Spirit comes upon them and that they will be witnesses in Jerusalem, all Judea and Samaria, and to the ends of the earth is widely recognized as a programmatic introduction to the way the narrative of Acts unfolds. What is not so widely agreed upon, however, is the way this promise of Jesus relates to the question the disciples raise in 1:6 concerning Israel and the restoration of the kingdom. We will see that, in its context, this promise of the Lord Jesus provides more than a geographical outline for the narrative of Acts; it provides further evidence that Acts is about the inaugurated kingdom of God in this age. We will begin by placing the disciples' question and Jesus' answer in its immediate context before clarifying the relationship between the disciples' question and Jesus' answer to that question.

First, in terms of the immediate context, it should be noted that verse 6 is directly linked to the setting described in the previous verses with the conjunction *oun*, 'therefore' ('so' NIV). As we have already seen, in these verses the topic of discussion during the forty days between Jesus' resurrection and ascension consisted of 'many convincing proofs that he was alive' and discussion about the kingdom of God. It was during this time in which the kingdom of God was the topic of discussion that Jesus told the disciples to wait in Jerusalem for 'the gift my Father promised'.[1] This is the promise (as he reminded them of his own words) that they would be baptized with the Holy Spirit. Thus we have in these few verses an emphasis on Jesus' resurrection and his teaching to the disciples concerning the kingdom of God. More specifically, the focus narrows down to Jesus' teaching his disciples concerning the 'promise' of the Father (a term that invites readers to understand the Spirit in terms of OT promises), the coming of the Holy Spirit in keeping with Jesus' own words, and the location of this baptism as Jerusalem. It is because of this teaching concerning the nature of the kingdom of God ('therefore') that the disciples ask their question in verse 6.

Secondly then, sometimes Jesus' answer in verses 7–8 is understood to be a discussion of something unrelated to the question raised by the disciples in verse 6. This is sometimes expressed in two opposing interpretations of this relationship between the disciples' question and Jesus' answer. (1) Jesus' answer is sometimes understood as an implicit postponement of (though not disagreement with) what the disciples were supposedly looking for in verse 6.[2] In this view the disciples are still looking for a kingdom dominated by blessing to national Israel. Jesus' reply, however, speaks of events associated with the church age (i.e. the pouring out of the Holy Spirit and proclamation to the ends of the earth). Therefore, according to this view, Jesus redirects their attention to the immediate

---

[1] The *kai* (and) at the beginning of v. 4, although capable of a variety of translations, seems to imply a continuation from v. 3 ('on one occasion', NIV) rather than the beginning of something disconnected from this context.

[2] Cf. the recent popular-level articulation of this in Pentecost 2010: 31–34. Though see Bock 1992: 37–67, esp. pp. 45–46, for a discussion of these verses in the context of a more nuanced 'progressive dispensational' position.

future, implying in his reference to times or dates that their Israelite concerns will be taken care of in the future.

(2) In contrast to the previous view, Jesus' answer is sometimes understood as a *rebuke* to the disciples and therefore his answer is thought to be a change of topic to what the disciples were looking for.[3] In this second view the disciples are entirely wrongheaded in still focusing on national Israel. They have misunderstood the universal emphasis of Jesus' mission entirely and are still stuck with purely nationalistic and political views of the kingdom. Jesus' reply, therefore, redirects their attention away from a national and political kingdom to a universal mission empowered by the Holy Spirit.

In both of these approaches Jesus' answer changes the topic and does not directly answer the disciples' question about the restoration of the kingdom and Israel. Either he talks of the church age while implicitly postponing a restoration of Israel to the future, or he talks of a universal mission empowered by the Holy Spirit in contrast to the disciples' focus on purely national and political concerns for ethnic Israel. There are a number of indicators, however, that Jesus is in fact answering the disciples' question and that the details of his answer in 1:8 relate to their question.

We will see below that Jesus rejects only the attempt to calculate the timing of the restoration rather than their interest in Israel and the kingdom. Jesus' answer neither postpones that fulfilment to the distant future nor rejects such a prospect for the present. Although there are complex issues related to the timing of these plans and their full consummation, the inauguration of God's kingdom, or the fulfilment of God's saving promises for his people, are about to be worked out in the pouring out of the Holy Spirit and the declaration of Jesus' reign in Jerusalem, Israel and beyond![4]

Evidence that Jesus is providing an answer to the disciples' question regarding the restoration of the kingdom and Israel's inclusion

---

[3] D. Hill 1984: 16–26; Stott 1990: 41.

[4] It should also be noted that emphasis on the fulfilment of God's promises for Israel in the early chapters of Acts does not necessarily entail a rejection of the Jewish people altogether in the final verses of Acts (nor does it contradict Paul's hope for Israel in Rom. 9 – 11). The pattern is repeatedly shown throughout Acts that even though some Jews in a particular location reject the gospel, leading to a greater focus on Gentiles, other Jews regularly respond and Paul continues to approach Jews in the next location (cf. Acts 13:46 and 14:1–7; 18:7 and 18:7–11; cf. also 18:19; 19:8–10; 26:20). There is every indication, therefore, that hope for Jewish responses to the gospel continues beyond Acts 28 (hence Paul welcomes 'all' who come to him in 28:30, contra J. T. Sanders 1987).

in that kingdom includes the following. First, in the immediate context it is Jesus' forty-day instruction concerning the kingdom that leads to their question concerning the kingdom. It is unlikely, therefore, that Luke intends us to view the disciples as completely ignorant here. Secondly, Luke has already demonstrated the close tie between Jesus' teaching on the kingdom of God in verse 3 and Jesus' teaching about the pouring out of the Holy Spirit in verses 4–5. It is likely, therefore, that Jesus is relating the two again when he refers to the pouring out of the Holy Spirit in verse 8 in response to the disciples' question about the kingdom in verse 6.[5] Thirdly, Israel *is* in fact mentioned in Jesus' reply. When Jesus refers to Jerusalem as well as to 'all Judea and Samaria', he is of course referring to Israel. Jerusalem was the religious capital of Israel, and the phrase 'all Judea and Samaria' was representative of the southern and northern kingdoms of Israel respectively. In the light of the division of Israel almost from the outset of its history under kings (Solomon being the last king to rule over a united Israel) and the prophetic hopes found in passages such as Ezekiel 37 for a united Israel, any talk of restoration would have to include some reference to the division between north and south known throughout much of Israel's history.[6] Fourthly, the language of 'restoration' in the disciples' question recalls the promises and hopes of the OT for God's people.[7] It is the fulfilment of God's OT promises for his people that Luke repeatedly highlights throughout Acts. We will now examine Jesus' promise in verse 8, where OT promises of restoration are alluded to and which are programmatic for the narrative of Acts.

OT hopes for the blessing and transformation of God's people are reflected in Jesus' words 'when the Holy Spirit comes on you', 'you will be my witnesses' and 'to the ends of the earth'. The language of Jesus in these three phrases reflects the wording of phrases in Isaiah that look forward to a coming salvation brought about by God and his (suffering) Servant.[8] Though any one phrase on its own may not make a strong case for seeing the hopes of Isaiah here, the pervasive influence of Isaiah throughout Acts together with the combination of these three allusions to Isaiah indicate that the hopes

---

[5] Ziccardi 2008: 102–104. Ch. 4 will discuss the role of the Holy Spirit.

[6] Further discussion of this will follow when we examine Acts 8 below (pp. 112–116) in this chapter.

[7] Cf. Isa. 1:26; 9:7; Jer. 16:14–15; 23:5–8; 33:15–17; Hos. 3:5; Amos 9:11–12; Zech. 9:9–10.

[8] This has been developed by Pao (2000: 91–93); cf. also Marshall 2007: 528.

of Isaiah are found here in Jesus' words.[9] The phrase 'when the Holy Spirit comes on you' reflects the wording of Isaiah 32:15. The context of Isaiah 32 refers to the end of the desolation of Judah and the coming of the new age with the pouring out of the Holy Spirit (cf. also Isa. 44:3–5).[10] The phrase 'you will be my witnesses' reflects the wording of Isaiah 43:12. In the context of Isaiah 43 the people of God will be transformed and become witnesses to the salvation of God when the new age arrives (cf. also Isa. 44:8); they will know and believe that the Lord is the only Saviour. This transformation, of course, is in contrast to the way Israel is described in Isaiah 42:18–25 as deaf and blind. The phrase 'to the ends of the earth' reflects the wording of Isaiah 49:6. In Isaiah 49 a Servant who represents Israel ('you are my servant, Israel', 49:3), who is yet distinct from Israel in that he will restore Israel (49:5–6), will also include Gentiles in this restoration. Given the clear parallel in Isaiah 49:6 between 'a light for the Gentiles' and 'salvation to the ends of the earth', and the use of Isaiah 49:6 in Acts 13:47 to refer to ministry among Gentiles (cf. 13:46, 48), the phrase 'to the ends of the earth' in 1:8 refers also to the inclusion of Gentiles in this restoration program.[11] What Jesus does then in his reply to the disciples is affirm that God's promises of restoration are about to be fulfilled. As Pao correctly observes, Jesus' reply includes 'one city, two regions, and a reference to the Gentiles' and therefore should be taken in 'theopolitical terms' and not merely as geographical markers.[12] This sequence of restoration

---

[9] Allusions to Isaiah in Acts 1:8 have been noted by many. Cf. Pao 2000: 91–96; Turner 1996: 299–303; Tiede 1986: 278–286. On the influence of Isaiah in the book of Acts as a whole see Pao 2000, who highlights the 'Isaianic New Exodus', and Mallen 2008, who emphasizes the mission of the Servant in bringing salvation. For earlier succinct studies on the extensive use of Isaiah in Acts see J. A. Sanders 1982: 144–155 and Seccombe 1981: 252–259.

[10] Pao (2000: 92) notes that Luke 24:49 contains the phrase 'from on high', which is found in Isa. 32:15.

[11] Some suggest that although Jesus (and Luke) may intend a reference to Gentiles, the disciples themselves would not have recognized this but would only have thought in terms of Jews dispersed throughout the world (Bock 2007: 66). In support of this, it is claimed that otherwise there would be no difficulty in including Gentiles in Acts 10 – 11. However, in the light of the commission to 'all nations' in Luke 24:47 and the association of the phrase 'ends of the earth' with Gentiles in Isa. 49:6, it is just as likely that the disciples did in fact understand a reference to the inclusion of Gentiles here. Note also that in Acts 11:20 (which takes us back to the scattering that took place at the death of Stephen in Acts 8:1) the good news about Jesus is told to Greeks. The difficulties in Acts 10 – 11 and 15 have more to do with understanding *how* the Gentiles may be included in the people of God and their status in the people of God than *whether* they should be included. Cf. Schnabel 2004, 1: 709.

[12] Pao 2000: 127.

to Israel followed by the inclusion of Gentiles may also be found in Peter's speech in Acts 3:26. Peter states that not only have all the prophets foretold these days, but God has also raised up his servant, the Lord Jesus, and has sent him to Israel 'first' to bless them in turning them from their wickedness.[13]

Thus, in his reply to the disciples, Jesus does not reject their enquiry into God's promises of restoration, whether in redirecting this hope to a distant future or in rebuking a nationalistic focus. He is, rather, affirming and clarifying their role in this restoration. As God has promised, this restoration will involve the enabling of God's Holy Spirit, the transformation of God's people who bear witness to the Saviour, and the inclusion of the nations. There are, of course, developments in this programme. Jesus is the one who will bring about this restoration ('Lord, are *you* . . . going to restore the kingdom . . . ?') and Jesus himself is the one who will be the object of the disciples' witness ('you will be *my* witnesses', which places him in the position of the Lord God in Isaiah). Furthermore, the way that Gentiles will be included among God's people has yet to be seen in the narrative of Acts. Nevertheless, the emphasis of Jesus' words is on the fulfilment of God's saving promises for his people. In the context of Jesus' forty-day instruction and the disciples' question concerning the kingdom, the fulfilment of these saving promises will characterize the outworking of the inaugurated kingdom of God. Acts 1:8 then is the programmatic verse for how the narrative of Acts will unfold.[14]

---

[13] Peterson 2009: 185.

[14] It might be objected that the language of 'restoration' is used in Acts 3:21 for something that will occur only *after* Jesus returns. Thus Bock (2007: 176–177) notes parallel terms in 1:7 and 3:19–21. This view is especially based on the preposition *achri* (until) in 3:21 ('he must remain in heaven *until* the time comes for God to restore everything as he promised long ago through his holy prophets'). It should be noted that this would not contradict the view presented here that the restoration of what God has promised is taking place 'already'. The emphasis on fulfilment in Acts already indicates this. Acts 3:21 would then refer to the 'not yet' aspects of that fulfilment (the 'consummation' of the kingdom). However, Pao (2000: 133–135) notes that the same preposition is used in Acts 20:6 to mean 'after' (these two passages are Luke's only uses of the preposition with a plural object). Translating the preposition as 'after' (as it should be in 20:6) then results in the translation 'whom heaven must receive until after the times of restoration of all that God spoke by the mouth of his holy prophets from of old'. This, coupled with the use of the phrase 'time of universal restoration' in the LXX for Israel's restoration, indicates that Peter is referring to a process that will reach its completion at the end of times. It should also be noted that in this same context (of 3:21) Peter declares that 'all the prophets . . . have foretold these days' (3:24), which is clearly a reference to the time of fulfilment contemporaneous with Peter's audience.

# Pentecost and 'all Israel' (Acts 2)

In Acts 1 the kingdom of God has been related to the ongoing reign of Christ, the pouring out of the Holy Spirit, the people of Israel and the disciples' role in the outworking of the promises of God. In Acts 2 these themes continue and are related together in further clarity. The question raised after the events of Pentecost 'What does this mean?' (2:12–13) becomes the launching pad for Peter's lengthy explanation concerning the significance of these events. As we have observed already, the enthronement and reign of Jesus is the primary focus of Acts 2. The pouring out of the Holy Spirit is evidence of his resurrection and reign on the Davidic throne (2:30–33) and his authority as Lord at the right hand of God (2:33–36). Although we will focus more specifically on the role of the Holy Spirit in the next chapter, we will note here that these themes of Jesus' lordship and his pouring out of the Holy Spirit are also placed within the framework, introduced in Acts 1, of Israel's restoration in fulfilment of God's saving promises.[15]

In his description of what takes place in the pouring out of the Spirit and the speaking of various languages in 2:1–13, Luke repeatedly highlights a comprehensive picture of Israel gathered together at Pentecost. In verse 5 he states that there were Jews from 'every nation under heaven'! Then Luke proceeds in verses 9–11 to give a comprehensive list of all those who heard these Galileans declaring the wonders of God in their own native languages. When we note not only the comprehensiveness of the list but also the geographical locations of those listed, we see that Luke is highlighting the arrival of Jews from far and wide. Visually, the map on p. 111 from *The NIV Study Bible* of 'Countries of People Mentioned at Pentecost' highlights nicely the arrival of Jews from the east, west, north, south and even those from the islands in the sea (Crete) and the distant peoples on the outskirts (Arabia), all to Jerusalem – the centre of this world. He even makes sure to note that those from Rome were both

---

[15] The reference in Acts 2:1 to 'when the day of Pentecost was being fulfilled' (*en tō symplērousthai*) is already an indication that the day of Pentecost is meant to be understood within the general framework of the fulfilment of God's promises. Tannehill (1990: 26–27) refers to the use of the term in Luke 9:51. The prophecies in view here then would be Luke 24:49; Acts 1:4–5, 8; Isa. 32:15; 44:3–5; Joel 2; though, in view of Jesus' description of the Holy Spirit as 'promised' (Acts 1:4; cf. also 2:33), the language of 'fulfilment' here may also refer to the Father's promises concerning the Holy Spirit elsewhere in the OT (i.e. Ezek. 36 – 37).

Jews and converts to Judaism (2:11). It is as if everyone associated with Israel from the four corners of the earth is here.[16] The comprehensiveness of this description and the emphasis on the return of Jews from all directions highlights one of the expectations for the last days, that the exiles would return and Israel would be restored.

Further evidence that a 'last days' restoration of Israel is taking place here comes in Peter's explanation in 2:14–36 answering the question 'What does this mean?' (2:12).[17] Throughout his explanation Peter continues this emphasis on the comprehensiveness of Israel in the way he addresses the audience. Note the following:

2:14 'People of Judea and *all* of you who live in Jerusalem . . .'[18]
2:22 'People of *Israel* . . .'
2:36 'Therefore let *all the house of Israel* know . . .'

Peter's opening reference to 'Judea and Jerusalem' recalls the words of the Lord Jesus in 1:8 concerning the first stage of the restoration programme. The comprehensive references to the 'people of Israel', and especially the climactic and emphatic reference to 'all the house of Israel' in Peter's concluding words, recall the disciples' question in 1:6 concerning Israel as well as the comprehensive picture of the gathering of all Israel already provided by Luke in the immediately preceding verses (2:5–11). Richard Bauckham's study on the restoration of Israel in Luke-Acts also draws attention to the references to Jews 'from every nation under heaven' (Acts 2:5) and the concluding reference in Peter's sermon to 'the whole house of Israel' (Acts 2:36) as evidence for the restoration of Israel. He particularly notes the concentrated use of the term 'the whole house of Israel' in Ezekiel 37, where it is associated with

> the reunification of the southern and northern tribes and their restoration to the land (37:15–22), the giving of God's Spirit to revive and restore his people (37:14; 39:29), and the rule of the new David (37:24–25). Accordingly, in Acts 2 Israelites from the whole diaspora return to God ('repent': Acts 2:38)

---

[16] Spencer (2004: 44) uses the phrase 'four corners of the earth' in this context.

[17] Though it should be noted that throughout this account Peter is associated with the other apostles (cf. 2:14, 37, 42).

[18] The term for 'people' in 2:14 and 22 is *andres* (men). However, as 17:34 indicates, the term may include women. Thus the translations 'People of Judea' or 'People of Israel' are used here. In 2:36 the NIV has 'all Israel'.

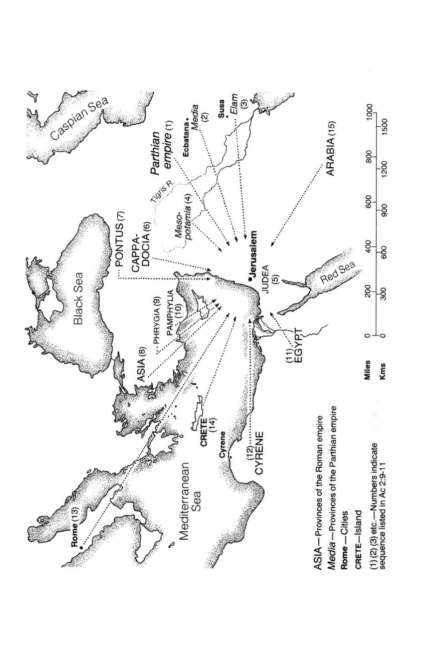

Caspian Sea

Black Sea

Mediterranean Sea

Red Sea

**Parthian empire (1)**

Ecbatana • *Media* (2)

Susa • *Elam* (3)

Tigris R.

*Meso-potamia* (4)

•Jerusalem JUDEA (5)

CAPPA-DOCIA (6)

PONTUS (7)

ASIA (8)

PHRYGIA (9)

PAMPHYLIA (10)

(11) EGYPT

ARABIA (15)

CRETE (14)

Cyrene

(12) CYRENE

Rome (13)

ASIA — Provinces of the Roman empire
*Media* — Provinces of the Parthian empire
**Rome** — Cities
**CRETE** — Island

(1) (2) (3) etc. — Numbers indicate
sequence listed in Ac 2:9-11

Miles   0      200      400      600      800      1000

Kms    0      300      600      900      1200     1500

and receive from the Davidic Messiah, enthroned in heaven, the promised gift of the Spirit (Acts 2:33, 38–39).

Bauckham concludes that the phrase 'the whole house of Israel' is 'a term which naturally encompasses all twelve tribes, in the diaspora as well as in Jerusalem, and which readily suggests restoration (Ezek. 20:40; 36:10; 37:11, 16; 39:25; 45:6)'.[19]

Final confirmation that the events of Pentecost are meant to be understood within the framework of the fulfilment of God's promises for the end-time restoration of his people comes at the very beginning of Peter's explanation. After stating that 'this is what was spoken by the prophet Joel', Peter notably adjusts the opening words of his quotation from Joel. In place of the general introductory wording found in Joel 2:28, '*and afterwards* I will pour out my Spirit', Peter states, '*In the last days*, God says, I will pour out my Spirit.'[20] Thus in Acts the quotation from Joel is specifically related to God's end-time promises of blessing for his people (the implications of the universal note in Joel and in Peter's sermon are, of course, developed later in the narrative of Acts). The answer then to the question 'What does this mean?' is that Jesus is Lord and his enthronement as the Davidic King has ushered in the last days, the new age of the Spirit, in fulfilment of God's ancient promises for his people. Israel is being restored, the exiles are returning to God and the promised age of the Spirit is here because Jesus is Lord and is reigning even now from the right hand of the Father!

## Samaria and the restoration of Israel (Acts 8:1–25)

Having focused on the restoration plan of God in Jerusalem and Judea in Acts 1 – 7, Luke then focuses attention on Samaria in Acts 8. That Luke has a particular interest in Samaria may be seen in the number of references to Samaritans throughout Luke-Acts.[21] Here

---

[19] Bauckham 2001: 473 (essay repr. in Bauckham 2008: 325–370). As further evidence for this, Bauckham notes the spread of the northern tribes in the diaspora and the list of diaspora Jews in Acts 2 (particularly Media in 2:9).

[20] The allusion to Isa. 2:3 in the opening words ('in the last days') of Peter's quote from Joel will be mentioned further in chs. 4 and 5.

[21] Cf. Luke 9:51–56; 10:30–37; 17:11–19; Acts 1:8; 8:1–25; 9:31; 15:3. Cf. Ravens 1995: 72–106.

in 8:1–25 references to Samaria or Samaritans occur in 8:1, 5, 9, 14 and 25.

The background to the relationship between Jews and Samaritans goes back to 1 Kings 12 (see esp. vv. 16–20) and the rebellion of the northern kingdom against the house of David, Jerusalem and Judea. Omri built the city of Samaria (1 Kgs 16:24) and it became the capital of the northern kingdom. The end of the northern kingdom eventually came (2 Kgs 17) when, following the capture of Samaria and the exile of the northern kingdom of Israel to Assyria (2 Kgs 17:5–23), the king of Assyria 'brought people from Babylon, Cuthah, Avva, Hamath and Sepharvaim and settled them in the towns of Samaria to replace the Israelites' (2 Kgs 17:24). Later, in order to keep them from being judged by the Lord, the king of Assyria sent a priest back to Samaria to teach them how to worship the Lord (17:25–28). Although they 'worshipped the Lord', they also 'served their own gods in accordance with the customs of the nations from which they had been brought' (17:33; cf. 17:29–41).[22]

Moving closer to the time of the NT, in intertestamental times the Samaritans sought permission from Alexander the Great to build a temple on Mount Gerazim, denounced the Jews when Antiochus Epiphanes persecuted them, and dedicated their temple to Zeus – not exactly a high point in the biblical faithfulness of the northern kingdom! The Jewish Maccabean ruler John Hyrcanus destroyed the temple in approximately 128 BC and later destroyed the city of Samaria in approximately 108 BC. Herod the Great rebuilt the city of Samaria but renamed it Sebaste in honour of Caesar Augustus in 27 BC.[23] So, leading up to this time, relationships were not exactly friendly between Jews and Samaritans. Samaritans were viewed as the descendants of Jeroboam's rebellion against the house of David in Judah and Jerusalem (1 Kgs 12:16–20) who set up a second monarchy, and continued this trend as religious compromisers characterized by the syncretistic worship of the Lord and the gods of the nations (2 Kgs 17). There is little surprise then in Luke 17:18 that the Samaritan, as the only one who returns to give thanks to Jesus for being healed of leprosy, is called a 'foreigner'. Although they are not called Gentiles in the NT, they are nevertheless grouped with

---

[22] Cf. Younger 2004: 254–280.

[23] The Greek *Sebastos* being used for the Latin *Augustus*. Cf. the succinct summary of Samaria's history in Ferguson 1993: 386, 500.

Gentiles and viewed as outside God's covenant people.[24] The ultimate insult from the Jews to Jesus in John 8:48 appears to be that
'you are a Samaritan and demon-possessed'.

Nevertheless, there remained the prophetic hope expressed in
Ezekiel 37 that the restoration of Israel, described in terms of a resurrection with the presence of God's Spirit in verses 1–14, would involve
a restoration of the northern and southern kingdoms of Israel in
verses 15–27. This restoration would be characterized by a gathering
of Israelites from the nations where they had gone (v. 21) and a reunit-
ing of the northern and southern kingdoms under one king (v. 22).
In keeping with God's covenant promises that they will be his people
and he will be their God (vv. 23, 26–27), they will be united under a
Davidic King (vv. 24–25) and God will dwell among them (vv. 26–28).
Thus, although they had not been under one king since Solomon,
there was hope that one day great David would have a greater son
who would reign over a restored people of God united under his rule.

Luke-Acts has particularly emphasized the Davidic descent of
Jesus and his rule in fulfilment of the hope for a descendant of David
to rule for ever (Luke 1:32–33; 2:1–12). This is especially highlighted
in Acts 2, where the pouring out of the Spirit is evidence that this
hope has been fulfilled in the resurrection and ascension of Jesus
to rule at the right hand of the Father (cf. Acts 2:30–36). Given the
emphasis on the resurrection of Jesus, the pouring out of the Spirit
in Jerusalem and the response of 'all the house of Israel' in Acts 2,
expectations ought to arise regarding the promises for the northern
kingdom (i.e. as found in Ezekiel). These expectations have stead-
ily built throughout Luke's Gospel with references to Samaritan
responses to Jesus, and continue with Jesus' reference to 'all Judea
and Samaria' in the programmatic statement in Acts 1:8.[25] When
read in the light of these eschatological hopes, it becomes clearer
that the reference to Samaria in 1:8 is more than a geographical
reference regarding the next stage of the spread of the gospel. It
undoubtedly includes that geographical element, but it is more than
that: it is the continued outworking of the fulfilment of God's saving
promises for his people.[26]

---

[24] Note Matt. 10:5–6, where they are distinguished from Gentiles and 'the house of
Israel', and John 4:7–10, where John remarks in an aside that 'Jews do not associate
with Samaritans'.

[25] As noted above, see Luke 9:51–56; 10:30–37; 17:11–19.

[26] The following discussion summarizes Pao 2000: 127–129. Cf. also Ravens 1995:
92–93.

When we come to the events that take place in Acts 8, it is likely that the introduction to this section concerning the persecution that led to the scattering of the disciples 'throughout Judea and Samaria' deliberately recalls Jesus' words in 1:8 concerning 'all Judea and Samaria'.[27] At the outset of the events in Acts 8 there is an interesting textual variant in Acts 8:5. Although some versions read that Philip went down to 'a city in Samaria' (NIV, TNIV, HCSB, RSV), most commentators recognize that there is stronger textual evidence for translating this as 'the city of Samaria' with a definite article rather than an indefinite article.[28] The perceived difficulty with this textual evidence, however, is that there was no city called 'Samaria' at that time (as noted above, Herod had renamed it Sebaste in 27 BC). Thus it is thought that the sense of the verse should be 'a city in Samaria'. Given the weight of the textual evidence as the correct reading, however, the translation 'the city of Samaria' should stand. Pao is probably correct, therefore, to suggest that Luke is referring to the capital city as it was known in OT times and thus recalling the city of Samaria as symbolic of the northern kingdom.[29]

The emphasis on Samaria as a collective term, however, is maintained throughout this account. Thus, following an emphasis on the widespread influence of Simon and his sorcery upon the people of Samaria as a whole in 8:9–11,[30] Luke notes in a blanket statement that 'Samaria had accepted the word of God' (8:14). On the one hand, this highlights the power of the gospel to transform lives and confirms the validity of the message Philip preached (cf. 8:12). Nevertheless, as Pao also correctly observes, 'This blanket statement concerning the conversion of an entire city or region appears only here in the narrative of Acts; and this peculiar fact can only be understood when the symbolic value of the name "Samaria" is recognised.'[31] Thus (1) prophetic hopes for the inclusion of the

---

[27] Pao (2000: 128) notes that 'the occurrence together of both "Judea" and "Samaria" is a unique Lukan feature that appears in the New Testament only in Acts' (referring to 1:8; 8:1; 9:31).

[28] Cf. Peterson 2009: 280; Bock 2007: 337; Metzger 1994: 311. The translation 'the city of Samaria' is found in the ESV, AV, NKJV, NASB and NLT. Manuscripts which omit the article are C D E Ψ 33 1739 𝔐. Manuscripts which retain the article include 𝔭[74] ℵ A B 69 181 460* 1175 1898.

[29] Pao 2000: 128. Pao notes that Barrett (1994: 402) and Hengel (1983: 123–126) are also favourable to this suggestion. Cf. also Bock 2007: 337.

[30] In Acts 8:9–11 the emphasis on the people as a whole is seen in the descriptions of them as 'the nation/people of Samaria' (*to ethnos tēs Samareias*, 8:9) and 'all from the least to the greatest' (*pantes apo mikrou heōs megalou*, 8:10).

[31] Pao 2000: 128.

northern kingdom under the reign of the coming Davidic King, (2) the focus in Luke-Acts on the Davidic reign of the Lord Jesus and the fulfilment of God's end-time promises, and (3) the emphasis on the acceptance of the word in Samaria as a whole in Acts 8:4–25 all indicate that God's saving promises for his people are continuing to be fulfilled in the inclusion of Samaria under the reign of the Davidic King Jesus in Acts 8.

## Outcasts and the restoration of Israel (Acts 8:26–40)

In the narrative of Acts to this point there has been an emphasis on the fulfilment of God's saving promises in the rebuilding of the Davidic kingdom through the ascension of the Lord Jesus to the throne of David (2:30–33), the pouring out of the promised Holy Spirit of the last days (2:16–17), the ingathering of the exiles of Israel (2:5, 9–11) and the repentance and turning to the Lord of Israel in Jerusalem, Judea and Samaria, which unite under the one Davidic King (2:38–47; 4:4; 8:4–25). The remainder of Acts 8 continues this emphasis on the fulfilment of God's saving promises. In view now are the promises to include outcasts among the people of God.[32] This is particularly seen in the overwhelming emphasis in the passage on the identity of the man Philip speaks to as simply 'the eunuch'. Although in 8:27 the man is said to be an 'Ethiopian', an 'important official' and a 'eunuch', it is only this designation as a 'eunuch' that is continued for him throughout the rest of the account. There are four more references to the actions of the man who is simply designated as 'the eunuch': 'the eunuch' asks Philip about a passage of Scripture (v. 34), 'the eunuch' asks about baptism (v. 36), 'the eunuch' goes down into the water with Philip for baptism (v. 38), and after Philip is taken away we read that 'the eunuch' did not see him again but went on his way rejoicing (v. 39). An attentive reader wondering what Luke is trying to highlight about the identity of this man should be wondering why he is so often called 'the eunuch'.[33]

Given the emphasis on the fulfilment of Isaiah throughout Acts

---

[32] Again, for Acts 8:26–40, see Pao 2000: 140–142. Marshall (2007: 573) summarizes various approaches to this section and the reasons for including it here in Acts.

[33] Pao (2000: 141) notes that the ethnic identity of the man is not settled with the description of him as Ethiopian. He may still simply be an 'Ethiopian Jew', as the list of people groups in Acts 2:9–11 were 'Jews from every nation under heaven'.

(and in the key statement of Acts 1:8), together with the fact that a quotation from Isaiah 53 forms the focal point of this episode in Acts 8, it is most likely that the emphasis on the man as 'the eunuch' is meant to recall the promises for eunuchs in Isaiah 56. Isaiah 56 looks forward to the time of God's salvation when the exclusion of those with defects from the assembly of God's people in Deuteronomy 23:1–7 will be overturned.[34] This salvation will be a time when the Lord says:

> Let no foreigner who has bound himself to the LORD say,
> 'The LORD will surely exclude me from his people.'
> And let not any eunuch complain,
> 'I am only a dry tree.'
>
> (Isa. 56:3)

The Lord says to the eunuchs that

> to them I will give within my temple and its walls
> a memorial and a name
> better than sons and daughters;
> I will give them an everlasting name
> that will not be cut off.
>
> (56:5)

To these foreigners and eunuchs who love the name of the Lord and worship him the Lord will give joy in his house of prayer (56:6–7). The concluding verse of this section ties this inclusion of eunuchs to the restoration of Israel and the return from exile (56:8).[35]

Thus this 'eunuch' who is reading Isaiah has a special interest in the ministry of the Suffering Servant of Isaiah. How might the humiliation and ministry of this despised and rejected Servant (in Isa. 53) relate to him, a despised and rejected eunuch (referred to just a little further on in that same section of Scripture)? Is the prophet talking about himself,[36] or is there another who will come and bring about the restoration this Servant will bring by bearing the punishment that brings peace? In this episode Luke highlights the continuing fulfilment of God's promises to restore his people. The Davidic

---

[34] Cf. also A. J. Thompson 2008a: 96–98.
[35] Pao 2000: 142.
[36] Cf. Isa. 20:3.

King reigns over his people and, as Isaiah anticipated, the scattered people of Israel and those excluded from the assembly of Israel are united through the message of the good news of forgiveness brought about through the death and resurrection of the Lord Jesus.

## The Servant who restores Israel and brings salvation to the Gentiles (Acts 13:47)

A further indication that the fulfilment of God's saving promises is the framework for understanding Acts is found in Acts 13:47. In this passage Paul and Barnabas quote the words from the second 'Servant Song' in Isaiah 49:6, 'I have made you a light for the Gentiles, / that you may bring salvation to the ends of the earth', as being directed to them and justifying their turn to the Gentiles.

In the wider context of Isaiah 49, Cyrus has been named as the 'anointed' one who will enable the captives to return to Judah (44:24 – 45:8; 47:1 – 48:22), and Israel is then supposed to bear witness to God's salvation (43:10–13). However, Israel is described in this section of Isaiah as a complaining (40:27), fearful and dismayed (41:10), deaf and blind (42:18–19), and disobedient (42:23–24) 'Servant' (41:8–20). The question that arises in this context then is 'how will the blind, deaf, rebellious Servant Israel be any different just because Cyrus has sent them home?'[37] The answer that the 'Servant Songs' progressively unfold is that a perfect Servant will embody all that Israel should have been and will give himself to remove sin and restore the relationship between God and sinful people. As noted above (regarding Acts 1:8), the Servant in Isaiah 49 both represents Israel ('you are my servant, Israel', 49:3), embodying all that Israel should have been, and yet is also distinct from Israel since the task of the Servant is to restore Israel (49:5–6). Thus the focus in this Servant Song shifts from physical captivity to moral and spiritual captivity. This Servant will be an infinitely greater deliverer than Cyrus: he will restore Israel *to God* (49:5–6) and bring *light* in the face of darkness (v. 6).[38]

[37] Oswalt 1998: 287.
[38] Ibid. Note also that in 49:9b–12 those 'returning' are not just the ones taken to Babylon. There is a great crowd from the north, west and the south (the region of Aswan). The emphasis in this context is on the mission to the Gentiles that will follow the restoration to the Lord of the Lord's people by the Servant. Furthermore, in 50:10–11 the people are described as those who obey the word of the Servant. Cf. Webb 1996: 200.

In the light of passages such as Isaiah 43:10 and 44:1–2, however, it should also be noted that just because there will be a greater Servant who will embody all that Israel should be and who will restore Israel, this does not mean that the servant role of restored Israel has been abrogated. In the immediate context of this Servant Song in Isaiah 49 the 'returning' people are told that the Lord will make them a 'covenant for the people' (49:8). In Isaiah 42:6 this phrase was applied to the Servant along with the phrase 'light for the Gentiles'. As Motyer observes, the phrase 'covenant for the people' in 42:6 suggests that the Servant will be 'the means through whom people will come into a covenant relation with the Lord'.[39] The use of the same phrase in Isaiah 49:8 with reference to the returning people of God indicates that God will achieve the extension of his salvation to all peoples through the Servant (who restores the people to God) and through his restored people (who announce this restoration to the nations, 49:9). Thus, 'As they are brought back into a right relationship with God, God's people become one with God's Servant in his worldwide mission.'[40]

It is this understanding of the inclusion of the restored people of God in the mission of the Servant that enables us to understand how Paul and Barnabas are able to apply to themselves a commission that is given to the Servant.[41] Allusions to this terminology from Isaiah 49:6 in Luke-Acts are applied therefore to Jesus by Simeon in Luke 2:32 and to Jesus' followers in Acts 1:8 and 13:47. In Luke 2 Simeon is described as 'waiting for the consolation of Israel' (Luke 2:25). Then when Simeon sees the baby Jesus, he takes the Lord Jesus in his arms and praises God, saying that now he has 'seen your salvation, which you have prepared in the sight of all people, a light for revelation to the Gentiles and for glory to your people Israel' (2:30–32). Allusions to Isaiah 49:6 (and 42:6) are clearly in view here. Simeon applies this role of being God's salvation and a light to the Gentiles to Jesus.[42] In keeping with the context of the Servant Songs

---

[39] Motyer 1993: 322.

[40] Webb 1996: 195.

[41] Note the shift from the plural 'the Lord has commanded us' to the singular 'I have made you (sing.) a light for the Gentiles' (Acts 13:47). Contra Koet (1989: 113–118) the plural is not to be understood as an invitation to collective Israel here. Paul and Barnabas are describing their mission here (note the first person plurals in vv. 46 and 47, 'we had to speak . . . we now turn . . . for the Lord commanded us . . .').

[42] Note also that, as we have seen, in Acts 8:35 Philip tells the eunuch about Jesus from the Servant Song of Isa. 53. Cf. Bock (1987: 262–270) and Mallen (2008: 102–105) for further discussion of the 'Servant-Christology' in Luke-Acts. D. E. Johnson

in Isaiah then, Paul and Barnabas are able to fulfil this mission of being a 'light for the Gentiles' and bringing 'salvation to the ends of the earth' because of their identification with the perfect Servant who enables his followers to carry out his mission.[43] As Barrett correctly concludes, Paul is a light to the Gentiles 'only in virtue of the Christ he preaches; Christ is a light to the Gentiles as he is preached to them by his servants'.[44] The implication of this citation from Isaiah 49, therefore, is that God is accomplishing the fulfilment of his saving promises. Israel is being gathered to God, as the early chapters of Acts have indicated. Therefore, the rest of the servant's commission to bring salvation to the Gentiles is now underway. This sequence of restoration for Israel and inclusion of Gentiles is also found in Acts 15.

## The rebuilding and restoring of David's fallen tent (Acts 15:13–18)

How may Gentiles participate in the saving promises of God, and what will be required of them? In the narrative of Luke-Acts the fact that Gentiles would be included in God's kingdom has been clear since Luke 2:32, though Luke 24:47 and Acts 1:8 showed that this was still to take place after Jesus' earthly ministry. God's acceptance of Gentiles was especially highlighted in Acts 10 – 11.[45] Acts 15, however, clarifies how they will participate in this saving plan and how their participation relates to God's promises to restore his people.

---

1990: 343–345 also notes Servant texts in Luke 1:79 (allusion to Isa. 42:7); 3:22 and 9:35 (allusion to Isa. 42:1); 4:18–19 (citation of Isa. 61:1–2); 7:22 (allusions to Isa. 35:5; 42:7; 61:1–2); 9:51–53 (allusion to 50:6–9); 22:20 (allusion to Isa. 53:12); 22:37 (citation of Isa. 53:12); Acts 3:13–14, 26 (allusion to Isa. 53:13); 4:27, 30 (allusion to Isa. 61:1); and 8:32–35 (citation of Isa. 53:7–8). Furthermore, the use of *pais* (*theou*), 'servant (of God)', the typical LXX translation of '*ebed yâweh* in the Servant Songs of Isaiah, is applied to Jesus only in Acts 3:13, 26, 4:27, 30 in the NT.

[43] Thus, although God obviously gives this instruction in Isaiah, the context of Acts 1:8 (note the use of *entellomai*, which is found in Acts only in 1:2 and 13:47), together with the commission from the Lord Jesus in Paul's conversion (cf. Acts 9:15; 22:21; 26:17–18) indicate that 'the Lord' who commands here is the Lord Jesus (which further identifies the Lord Jesus with the God of Isaiah; he is the Lord as well as the Servant of the Lord).

[44] Barrett 1994: 658. Note also the association between Jesus and his disciples in Luke 10:16. In the light of Acts 26:23 there is also a sense in which the Lord Jesus himself enables the preaching and is himself 'proclaiming light to his own people and to the Gentiles' through Paul and the apostles (cf. Luke 21:15).

[45] Cf. also Acts 13:47–48. The role of the Holy Spirit in this restoration will be discussed in ch. 4.

The narrative context of Acts 13 – 14 particularly helps to high-light the significance of the claim made by some from Judea in Acts 15:1 that circumcision is required of Gentiles in order for them to be 'saved' (15:1, 5).[46] Acts 13 – 14 has just recounted a mission in which the 'message of salvation' is addressed to Jews and Gentiles together (13:26) concerning the promised Saviour, Jesus (13:23). Jews and Gentiles are both urged to respond in the same way: they are urged to 'believe' (13:39, 46, 48; 14:1). Although a variety of terms are used, both groups are offered 'salvation': forgiveness of sins, justification and eternal life are offered to 'everyone who believes' (13:26, 38–39, 46–48). Thus those who respond positively (both Jews and Gentiles) to Paul and Barnabas are those who have 'believed' (14:1), and those who respond antagonistically are those who 'refused to believe' (14:2). The concluding summary to this 'work' of God's grace is that God had 'opened the door of faith to the Gentiles' (14:27). In this narrative context the claim that something else, namely circumcision, is 'required' for salvation is a departure from what has been proclaimed in Acts 13 – 14.

The account of the Jerusalem Council summarizes a report from Peter, then from Paul and Barnabas, and finally James's conclusion. Peter perceives that the central issue in this debate is the nature of the gospel, and so he reminds the Council about the core features of his meeting with Cornelius: (1) God took the initiative in ensuring that the Gentiles heard the gospel and that their response would be one of belief (15:7); (2) both Jew and Gentile have received the same Holy Spirit by faith, indicating God's acceptance of them (15:8–9); (3) both Jew and Gentile are saved by grace (15:11).[47] Thus God himself has accepted Gentiles as his people not on the basis of circumcision but by grace, and the only requirement is faith. The account of Paul and Barnabas is summarized briefly as a supporting argument that God has worked through them among the Gentiles.

James's opening words refer to Peter's argument and highlight again God's initiative in including Gentiles. James's summary of God's action in including the Gentiles, however, uses language from the OT that reflects God's action for his people, Israel. Thus James begins by stating that God had 'visited' the Gentiles.[48] This termi-

---

[46] C. Green 2005: 87–92. The role of the law will be discussed in ch. 6.

[47] Thus the issue raised at the Council is theological rather than an issue of contextualization. Cf. Wiarda 2003: 233–248 (esp. 233–236).

[48] *Episkeptomai* (15:14, 'showed his concern' NIV).

nology reflects a way of speaking about God coming to save his people Israel.[49] The following phrase also reflects language from the OT but adds a twist. The statement that God visited to take 'from the Gentiles a people for himself' indicates in this context that God is taking Gentile people for himself out of the Gentiles/nations. In the OT, however, the phrase normally indicates that God has chosen his people Israel out from among the nations (i.e. Gentiles).[50] Now this same terminology is being used of God's action in choosing Gentiles. The language that James uses here therefore indicates that he views the Gentiles who have placed their faith in the Lord Jesus as being just as much a part of God's people as Jews who have also placed their faith in the Lord Jesus.

James then declares that the words of the prophets are in harmony with this action of God in accepting the Gentiles (15:15). James's reference to 'the prophets' (in the plural), together with allusions to other texts in his quotation, indicates that this acceptance of Gentiles is part of wider prophetic expectations concerning God's saving promises for Gentiles and is not limited to the section from the prophet Amos that will form the substance of his quotation.[51] The quotation from Amos, however, indicates that there will be a sequence. First there will be a restoration of the Davidic kingdom. This is described with three parallel phrases:

> I will return and rebuild David's fallen tent.
> Its ruins I will rebuild,
> and I will restore it.

> (Acts 15:16)

The reference to 'the dwelling of David' is a reference to the restoration of the Davidic kingdom under Davidic rule and therefore anticipates the restoration of Davidic kingship *as well as* the restoration of the eschatological people of God under the rule of the Davidic

---

[49] Cf. Exod. 3:16; 4:31; 13:19; Ruth 1:6.

[50] Cf. Exod. 23:22 (LXX); Deut. 7:6; 14:2. Note that up to this point in Luke-Acts (cf. Acts 2:47; 3:23; 4:10; 5:12; 7:17, 34; 13:17) the term *laos* (people) is usually reserved for Israel. A shift appears to occur here and in 18:10 where Gentiles are included in this term for God's people (contra Jervell 1996: 23, 34).

[51] Given the allusions to other texts in this section, this is a better option than the suggestion that he is referring to the book of the twelve 'Minor Prophets' (contra Peterson 2009: 430, n. 41). Marshall (2007: 589–593) notes allusions to Zech. 2:11, Jer. 12:15 and Isa. 45:21 in Acts 15:16–18.

King.[52] Luke 1:32–33 also highlights the restored Davidic throne and reign together with the restored Davidic kingdom. Likewise, Zechariah's praise to God in Luke 1:68–69 combines praise for a restored Davidic house with the restoration of God's people. The restoration of the Davidic kingdom was especially emphasized in Acts 2: the resurrection and exaltation of the Davidic King to reign on the Davidic throne in Acts 2:30–36 led to the pouring out of the Holy Spirit (the end-times promise) and the inclusion of the exiles of 'the whole house of Israel'. We observed above that prophetic hopes (i.e. Ezek. 37) for the restoration of the northern kingdom of Samaria into the Davidic kingdom under the reign of the Davidic King are also likely to be the reason why Luke highlights Samaria's acceptance of the good news of the kingdom of God in Acts 8 (cf. 8:12). The fulfilment of the promises to David is especially the focus in Acts 13.[53] The restoration of the Davidic kingdom in Acts 15 is therefore once again a significant feature of the fulfilment of God's saving promises in Luke-Acts.

Amos indicates that the purpose of this restoration is that there will then be a large number of Gentiles who will seek the Lord.[54] The sequence, therefore, will be a restoration of the Davidic kingdom, followed by an inclusion of Gentiles in this eschatological people of God who have been claimed ('named') by the Lord.[55] James perceives that this pattern, anticipated by the prophets and succinctly stated by Amos, has taken place, by God's grace, in their midst: the promises of salvation for God's people are accomplished through the crucified and resurrected Christ, and men and women from 'all the house of Israel' (exiles, Judea and Samaria, outcasts) have responded with faith in Jesus; now Gentiles too are placing their faith in Jesus. Thus James recognizes that God is fulfilling his

[52] Strauss 1995: 180–192; Turner 1996: 312–315; Peterson 2009: 431. Contra Haenchen 1971: 99, who views this as a reference solely to the resurrection, and Bauckham 1995: 452–458, who views this as a reference to the eschatological temple.

[53] Cf. Acts 13:23 and esp. 13:34, which cites the fulfilment of the promises to David anticipated in Isa. 55:3.

[54] A purpose clause is indicated in 15:17 where *hopōs* is followed by the subjunctive *ekzētēsōsin* ('*that* the rest of men *may seek* the Lord', RSV). Marshall (2007: 589–593) succinctly summarizes the range of issues related to the textual variations in Acts 15:17 from the Hebrew text of Amos 9:11–12.

[55] Peterson (2009: 432) notes that the passive tense of *epikeklētai* ('have been called', indicating divine agency) and the reference to God's 'name' in v. 17 provide the basis for James's observation concerning God's action in taking a people for his 'name' in v. 14.

saving promises to accept Gentiles in this Davidic kingdom through their faith in the Davidic King Jesus.[56]

# Conclusion

In Acts, Luke emphasizes that God is keeping and fulfilling his saving promises and his kingdom has been inaugurated. The close relationship between the nature of God's kingdom in this era (following Jesus' death, resurrection and ascension) together with God's promises of salvation (for Israel as well as for the Gentiles) is established in the first chapter of Acts. In response to the disciples' question concerning the kingdom, Jesus clarifies that God's promises will be fulfilled: Israel will be restored and salvation will come to the Gentiles. The narrative of Acts then shows the unfolding of those saving promises as thousands of Jews respond to the message of the saving reign of the Davidic King, Samaria hears and responds to the good news of the kingdom of God and the name of Jesus Christ, outsiders (as illustrated in the previously excluded eunuch) joyfully respond to the good news about Jesus (as Isa. 56 anticipated) and Gentiles also receive salvation through faith in the Lord Jesus according to God's promises in the prophets (Acts 13, 15). Readers such as Theophilus may be assured, therefore, that God's plan of salvation is being carried out according to his purpose and promises. Gentiles are receiving God's salvation not because God has failed to keep his word to Israel, nor because they must accept circumcision. Rather, Gentiles belong because God himself has included them by grace among his restored people by enabling them to hear the same good news of forgiveness of sins through faith in the crucified and risen Davidic King. Furthermore, this is what God promised he would do and this is what Jesus said would happen. God's saving kingdom through the reign of the Lord Jesus is continuing according to plan. Throughout Acts, a sign that Jew and Gentile belong together as one people of God is the fact that Jew and Gentile together have received the same promised Holy Spirit. It is to this aspect of the fulfilment of God's promises that we now turn.

---

[56] Cf. pp. 182–187 for a discussion of the role of the 'Jerusalem decree' in 15:19.

## Chapter Four

# The promise of the Father: the gift of the Holy Spirit

The overall argument of this book has been that the book of Acts is best understood within the framework of inaugurated eschatology. Luke aims to teach about the nature of the kingdom of God in this era between the inauguration of the kingdom in Jesus' life, death, resurrection and ascension, and the consummation of the kingdom at Jesus' return. This focus on the inaugurated kingdom, therefore, is why Luke draws attention to the continuing reign of the Lord Jesus (he is enabling the spread of the word and the establishment of local churches even in the midst of opposition), the significance of the resurrection (this especially highlights the arrival of the blessings of the age to come that may be offered on the basis of Christ's death and resurrection) and the restoration of God's people (God's saving promises for Israel and the Gentiles are being fulfilled). This framework of inaugurated eschatology also helps us to understand Luke's focus on the role of the Holy Spirit in Acts. The Holy Spirit has been poured out in fulfilment of God's promises for the last days because God's kingdom has been inaugurated through Jesus' life, death, resurrection and reign on the throne of David. Thus, following a brief reminder of the prophetic hope for the Spirit, this chapter will highlight the following key features of Luke's teaching about the Spirit in Acts: the Spirit and the kingdom, the Spirit and the reign of the Lord Jesus, the enabling power of the Spirit, the transforming work of the Spirit, the Spirit and the unity of God's people, and the reception of the Spirit.

## The prophetic hope of the Spirit

Although the Holy Spirit was at work among God's people in the OT, enabling the hearts of the remnant among the people of Israel to respond to God and empowering individuals to accomplish particular tasks, the prophets hoped for more.[1] Isaiah (32:15; 44:3), Ezekiel

---

[1] Cf. Hamilton 2006: 25–55 for a discussion of the teaching in the OT on the Holy Spirit.

(36:27; 37:14; 39:29) and Joel (2:28–29) in particular look forward to a time when God will pour out his Spirit in fullness upon all his people.[2] In these texts the prophets look forward to a time beyond the experience of Israel as disobedient and under God's judgment in exile to a time when God will again restore his people. In that time God will establish a new covenant relationship with his people, cleanse their hearts, forgive their sin, dwell among and enable them to obey him and declare his name to the nations. Thus the pouring out of the Spirit was essential to the hope of the 'last days' when God's people would be restored. It is for this reason that any explanation of the 'inauguration of God's kingdom' must include teaching about this aspect of Israel's hope.

## The kingdom of God and the promised eschatological gift of the Spirit

This rather long subheading is an attempt to capture in one phrase the 'eschatological' framework Luke provides for understanding the importance of the day of Pentecost. In Acts 1:1–8, Luke, in preparation for the major event of Pentecost in Acts 2, relates the coming of the Spirit directly to Jesus' teaching on the kingdom as well as to the prophetic hope for the coming age.[3] First, to recap the findings in chapter 3 briefly, Luke closely associates Jesus' forty-day teaching on the kingdom of God to his disciples in Acts 1:1–3 with Jesus' instruction concerning the pouring out of the Holy Spirit in 1:4–5. The close relationship between these two topics of Jesus' teaching is indicated by Luke's placement of the scene in 1:4–5 within the period of instruction on the kingdom he has just described. The use of *kai* (and) at the beginning of verse 4 in the context of this forty-day period indicates that Luke is not beginning a new section here but rather is providing a particular example, as he often does, of the general summary he has just given.[4] Thus the imminent arrival of the Father's promised gift is a crucial aspect of the inaugurated kingdom of God.[5]

Jesus' reference to the Holy Spirit as (lit.) 'the promise of the

---

[2] Because Jeremiah's prophecy of a new covenant that transforms hearts is similar to Ezekiel, Jer. 31 may also be added to this list.

[3] Ziccardi 2008: 102–106.

[4] See e.g. 2:42–47 and 3:1–2 (see the discussion on p. 150). See also 4:34–35 followed by a positive example in 4:36–37 and a negative example in 5:1–2.

[5] Cf. O'Toole 1987: 149; Turner 1996: 294–297.

Father' in 1:4 not only looks back to the same phrase used by Jesus in Luke 24:49, but also looks further back to the prophetic hope where this promise is found.[6] Jesus does not indicate in Acts 1:4 where in the OT this promise of the Father may be found. However, the terminology of being clothed with power 'from on high' in Luke 24:49 (which the wording of Acts 1:4 recalls) and the terminology of the Holy Spirit 'coming upon you' in Acts 1:8 (which Acts 1:4 anticipates) both recall the same passage in Isaiah (32:15).[7] The pouring out of the Spirit from on high in Isaiah 32 brings Judah's desolation to an end and also brings the arrival of the new age of righteousness and peace.

Secondly, the disciples' question in Acts 1:6 concerning the timing of the restoration of the *kingdom* to Israel is also closely related to these opening verses in Acts where Jesus' instruction regarding the kingdom and the coming of the Holy Spirit have been related. This close connection is seen in the conjunction *oun* (therefore) at the beginning of 1:6 and the reoccurrence of the term *basileia* (kingdom) in 1:3 and 1:6. In the previous chapter we observed that Jesus' response in 1:7–8 does in fact answer the disciples' question: he explains how the restoration of the kingdom relates to the people of Israel (though he refuses to outline the time frame) in language that recalls the hopes of Isaiah. In this sense then, in 1:6–8 Jesus again relates the two topics of the inauguration of the kingdom and the pouring out of the Spirit.[8]

Luke's concern to highlight the significance of the pouring out of the Holy Spirit as an eschatological fulfilment of God's promise is further seen in Acts 2. Given the lengthy account of Peter's sermon explaining 'what this means' (2:12), and the lengthy quotation of Joel within Peter's explanation, this chapter is obviously essential for understanding the role of the Holy Spirit in the book of Acts. The most obvious point of Peter's explanation of what is taking place on the day of Pentecost is that this is the fulfilment of God's promise to pour out the Holy Spirit upon his people. Peter could not be clearer when he states that 'this is what was spoken by the prophet Joel'

---

[6] Cf. also the references to the Spirit as 'the promise' in 2:33 and 2:39 (2:39, in this context, probably refers to 'the promise of the Holy Spirit' in 2:33).

[7] Pao 2000: 92; Turner 1996: 300–303.

[8] As mentioned in the last chapter, the cluster of phrases in Acts 1:8 that refer to the Holy Spirit 'coming upon you' (Isa. 32:15; 44:3), the disciples being 'my witnesses' (43:10–12; 44:8) and the extension of the witness to 'the ends of the earth' (49:6) all recall passages from the prophet Isaiah.

(2:16). Thus what Jesus referred to as the 'promise of the Father', in language that alluded to the promises found in Isaiah, is now specified in terms of the promise found in Joel. Specifically, the promise is stated as, 'God says "I will pour out my Spirit."' That Peter understands this promise as related to the wider eschatological hope of the OT is indicated by his change of wording from 'afterwards' (as found in Joel 2:28) to 'in the last days' (Acts 2:17) at the beginning of his quotation of Joel. This additional phrase seems to come from Isaiah 2:2, a passage that looks forward to the day when the nations will come to the Lord's house and 'the word of the LORD' will go out from Jerusalem.[9]

As indicated in chapter 3, it is also possible that Luke is alluding to Ezekiel in Acts 2.[10] As Bauckham has noted, the phrase 'the whole house of Israel' (*pas oikos Israēl*) used by Peter in Acts 2:36 is particularly reminiscent of the context of Ezekiel 37.[11] In Ezekiel 37 'the whole house of Israel' is associated with the regathering of Israel's exiles (37:21), the reunification of the southern and northern kingdoms (37:15–22), the 'resurrection' of Israel and the giving of God's Spirit (37:14; 39:29), the reign of a Davidic King as one king over one united kingdom (37:24–25), and the dwelling of God with his people in the fulfilment of the covenantal promises and for the instruction of the nations (37:26–28). In Acts 2 Israelites from 'every nation under heaven' are present and in one day about three thousand return to God ('repent', 2:38) and receive from the resurrected and enthroned Davidic Messiah the 'promise of the Spirit' (2:33, 38–39).[12] This cluster of themes associated with the prophetic hope of Ezekiel indicates that the pouring out of the Spirit in Acts 2 on

---

[9] Isa. 2:3; Mic. 4:2. Bruce 1990: 89; Bock 2007: 112; Peterson 2009: 141. Pao 2000: 156–159 discusses the relationship between Isa. 2 and Mic. 4, and the relationship between Isa. 2:2–4 and 40 – 55 (and the significance of the spread of the word in the context of Acts). Pao also notes that this exact phrase (*en tais eschatais hēmerais*) is found only in Isa. 2:2 and Acts 2:17 in the LXX and NT (though a similar phrase is found in 2 Tim. 3:1 and Jas 5:3; cf. also Heb. 1:2; 2 Pet. 3:3).

[10] This is less direct, however, than the more obvious citation from Joel in Acts 2 and the allusions to Isaiah in Acts 1.

[11] Bauckham 2001: 473. Cf. Ezek. 37:11, 21 (though the phrase 'house of Israel' is a more common designation in the OT, it is also found much more often in Ezekiel than anywhere else in the OT). Cf. also Ezek. 39:29, where the Lord describes the regathering of Israel as a time when 'I will no longer hide my face from them, for I will pour out my Spirit on the house of Israel'. In Ezek. 36:21–32 the placement of God's Spirit in his people and the restoration of the 'house of Israel' are for the sake of the Lord's holy name.

[12] Observations from Ezek. 37 and Acts 2 are adapted from Bauckham 2001: 473. Repr. 2008: 325–370.

'the whole house of Israel' is also meant to recall the promises of the Spirit associated with Ezekiel.[13]

In summary: in Acts 1 – 2, with descriptions of the Holy Spirit as 'the promise', allusions to the prophetic hope of the Spirit in Isaiah, a direct quotation from the prophecy in Joel introduced as spoken by God about 'the last days', together with language that recalls Ezekiel's prophecy for 'the whole house of Israel', Luke is emphasizing in a variety of ways that the pouring out of the Holy Spirit is to be understood as the fulfilment of God's promise for the last days. The fulfilment of this promise of the Spirit is therefore part of the evidence that the kingdom of God has been inaugurated. The reason for this pouring out of the promised Holy Spirit, however, is because the Lord Jesus has risen from the dead and ascended to reign at the right hand of the Father.

# The Holy Spirit is bestowed by the risen and exalted Lord Jesus

As we have already seen, Luke is particularly highlighting the accomplishment of God's promises through the Lord Jesus. Thus it is through the death, resurrection and current reign of the Lord Jesus that God's saving purposes are accomplished. In terms of the restoration of Israel it is the Lord Jesus who is accomplishing this promised restoration (1:6). In Acts the pouring out of the Holy Spirit therefore not only follows the death and resurrection of Jesus as the next stage in God's salvation-historical purposes, but Jesus himself, as the reigning Lord, is the one who pours out the Spirit. In this sense then, within this broad framework of the restoration of Israel, the Holy Spirit in Acts is the 'executive power of the exalted Christ' to bring about the Messiah's restoration of Israel.[14]

At the end of Luke's Gospel, not only does Jesus command his disciples to remain in the city until they have been 'clothed with power from on high', but he also declares that 'I am going to send you what my Father has promised' (Luke 24:49). The risen Lord

---

[13] Turner (1996: 48–53, 344) disagrees with Dunn (1970: 47–49) and argues that Luke does not intend any reference to Ezek. 36 in Acts 2. Bauckham's observations from Ezek. 37, however, strengthen this possibility.

[14] Turner 1996: 265–266, 301–303, 306. Cf. Pao 2000: 131–135. Cf. also Buckwalter 1996: 180–182, 193–205, though Buckwalter primarily shows parallels between Jesus' role and the role of Yahweh in the OT as part of a 'Christological apologetic'.

Jesus clearly states here that he himself is going to be the one who will send the 'promise of the Father'. This focus on Jesus' role in sending the Spirit is not indicated again in Acts 1:5, where Jesus simply states that they 'will be baptized with the Holy Spirit', nor does it reoccur in 1:8, where Jesus states that they 'will receive power when the Holy Spirit comes on' them. Nevertheless, as we saw in chapter 1, Luke indicates that the account of Jesus' ascension in Acts 1 is important for understanding how the events in Acts 2 come about: (1) Acts 1 refers to 'the day' Jesus was 'taken up' (1:2 and 22) and Acts 2 then refers to 'the day' of Pentecost (and later records that about three thousand were added 'that day', 2:1, 41); (2) Acts 1:10–11 emphasizes four times in two verses that Jesus was taken up 'into heaven'.[15] Thus, after reading in Acts 1 of 'the day' when Jesus went up 'into heaven', readers are prepared to understand that when Acts 2:2 then refers to 'the day' of Pentecost, when a sound like a strong wind came 'from heaven', the risen and ascended Lord Jesus of Acts 1 is behind the events of Acts 2.[16]

A more explicit statement of the relationship between Jesus' exaltation and the pouring out of the Holy Spirit is found in Peter's explanation in 2:33. The verse begins with (lit.), 'Therefore, having been exalted to the right hand of God . . . he has poured out . . .' The conjunction *oun* ('therefore', omitted in the NIV) in this context indicates that the pouring out of the Holy Spirit is the consequence of Jesus' resurrection and exaltation (and having received the 'promised Holy Spirit' from the Father). Peter concludes that the pouring out of the Spirit is evidence that Jesus is the Lord upon whom we must call in order to be saved (2:21 and 34–36) and the Messiah who reigns from the throne of David. Thus he is the Davidic King in the line of David anticipated in Psalms 16:8–11 and 132:11 as the one who would sit on David's throne, and yet he is also David's Lord who reigns from a position of power and authority at God's right hand.[17] The exalted Lord is reigning and this is seen in the pouring

---

[15] The same phrase *eis ton ouranon* is used on each occasion, though the NIV alternates between 'sky' and 'heaven'.

[16] The phrase in 2:2 is *ek tou ouranou*. The description of those present in 2:5 as Jews from 'every nation under heaven' (*hypo ton ouranon*) is perhaps another indication in this context of the universal sovereignty of the Lord Jesus (cf. also 2:34). Cf. Sleeman 2009: 94–96 for a discussion concerning the Christological significance of this phrase.

[17] Ps. 132:11 is alluded to in Acts 2:30. The use of *dexia* (right hand) in Acts 2:34 (citing Ps. 110:1) and the phrase *en tē dexia sou* (at your right hand) in Ps. 16:11 (just after the citation used in Acts 2:25–28) indicate that a locative sense is intended here.

out of the end-times promise of the Spirit.[18] Furthermore, as we noted in chapter 2, the divine authority of Jesus is also seen in the parallels between (1) Acts 2:17–18 (citing Joel 2:28–29), where it is explicitly stated that God 'will pour out' the Holy Spirit,[19] and (2) Acts 2:33, where Peter strikingly says that the exalted Jesus 'has poured out' the Holy Spirit.[20] Thus in Acts the Holy Spirit is both the eschatological promise of the Father and is also evidence (being poured out by Jesus himself) that Jesus is the hoped-for Davidic King, is reigning now and by his resurrection has inaugurated the last days and the restoration of Israel.

## God's empowering presence

The most obvious stated purpose for the coming of the Spirit in Acts is to empower God's people to speak for him, proclaiming his salvation.[21] The promised restoration of God's people is accomplished by the risen Lord Jesus, through his sending of the Holy Spirit, who enables God's people to announce the message in order that others may hear, respond and also participate in God's saving promises.

Thus Jesus promises in 1:8 that the disciples will receive power when the Holy Spirit comes upon them, and the result of this reception of power will be that the disciples will be witnesses of him. Luke 24:48–49 had already made this same connection between Jesus' disciples as witnesses and the requirement first to wait in Jerusalem until they were 'clothed with power from on high'. Similarly, in Peter's quotation from Joel the immediate consequence of the pouring out of God's Spirit on all people is that 'your sons and daughters will prophesy' (Acts 2:17). This function of the Spirit is particularly emphasized in 2:18, where, following the mention that God will pour out his Spirit, Peter's quotation adds, 'and they will prophesy' (an addition not found in Joel).[22]

---

This 'position' of the Lord Jesus, however, is one of power and authority. Strauss 1995: 140–141; Turner 1996: 295–296; Peterson 2009: 150.

[18] Hence the description of the Holy Spirit in Acts 16:7 as 'the Spirit of Jesus'; i.e. the Spirit sent by the authority of Jesus.

[19] 2:17, *legei ho theos encheō* (*I* will pour out . . .).

[20] 2:33, *tēn te epangelian tou pneumatos tou hagiou . . . execheen* (the promise of the Holy Spirit . . . *he* has poured out).

[21] The wording of the heading for this section comes from Fee's well-known book on the Holy Spirit in Paul's letters (1994).

[22] The reference to young men seeing visions and old men dreaming dreams between these two references and 'prophesying' indicates that dreams and visions

What then does it mean to 'prophesy' in this context? The passage cited by Peter particularly stresses the activity of the Spirit on 'all' of God's people. This emphasis on 'all' of God's people receiving God's Spirit was already hinted at earlier in Acts 2 in verses 3–4. What looked like tongues of fire came to rest on '*each* of them' and '*all* of them were filled with the Spirit'. Peter states that this is what Joel spoke about: a time in the last days when God will pour out his Spirit on 'all' of his people (2:17). This emphasis on the totality of God's people is then filled out in three groups which highlight the fact that there will be no distinction in age or gender among the people who receive God's Spirit: 'sons and daughters . . . young men and old men . . . servants, both men and women'. It is all of God's people then who are said to receive his Spirit, but it is also all of God's people who are said to 'prophesy' here. The difficulty, however, is that in Acts itself only a select few are said to be 'prophets' (11:27; 13:1; 15:32; 21:10) and the activity of 'prophesying' is rare (19:6; 21:9). The act of 'prophesying' in Acts 2, therefore, must be understood within the context of what Peter says in this quotation from Joel. That is, that there is a broader sense of the word in which all of God's people 'prophesy'. In contrast to the work of the Spirit in the OT when the Holy Spirit empowered only certain people, prophets, to mediate God's word to the people, now all of God's people are able to speak for God. Although not explicitly cited by Peter, it appears that Moses' hope is being fulfilled: 'I wish that all the LORD's people were prophets and that the LORD would put his Spirit on them' (Num. 11:29).[23] Now that the promised Christ has come and God's saving promises have been revealed in Christ, all of God's people are enabled by his Spirit to announce the fulfilment of God's saving plan and promises when they proclaim Christ. The 'least in the kingdom of God' is greater than John the Baptist (Luke 7:28)!

An illustration of this may be found in Peter's sermon itself. In

here are also associated with prophesying; they were a means of knowing the will of God that was to be proclaimed (cf. for visions Isa. 1:1; Jer. 14:14; Ezek. 1:1; 8:2–4; and for dreams Dan. 1:17; Zech. 10:2). Peterson (2009: 141–142) notes that visions occur occasionally in Acts (Ananias and Saul in Acts 9:10–12; Cornelius and Peter in Acts 10 – 11; Paul in 16:9; 18:9–10; 27:23), and dreams are not explicitly mentioned (though Paul's visions take place at night). It seems that this reference to dreams and visions for young men and old men situated between references to all people prophesying is meant to be understood as another, poetic, way of saying the same thing: 'all will prophesy'.

[23] Cf. also Jer. 31:34.

Acts 2:4 the word used to refer to the Spirit's enabling of 'all who were filled with the Holy Spirit' to speak in other languages is *apoph-thengomai* (as the Spirit *enabled* them).[24] The same term is used a few verses later to refer to Peter's activity as he lifted his voice and 'addressed' the crowd (2:14). The use of the same term twice in this immediate context to refer to the activity of speaking indicates that Peter's address is also enabled by the Spirit. Peter then points to the fulfilment of Scripture and God's purposes in Jesus' life, death, resurrection and ascension to reign, and urges people to embrace Jesus (who is the fulfilment of God's saving promises). It is in this sense then that Peter speaks for God and himself exemplifies the words of God 'I will pour out my Spirit in those days, *and they will prophesy.*'

This link between the enablement of the Spirit and the ability to speak for God is also highlighted throughout Acts with the verb *pimplēmi* (filled) followed by an activity of speaking.[25] As noted above, in Acts 2:4 Luke states, 'They were filled with the Holy Spirit, and began to speak ...' Similarly, in 4:8 Peter is 'filled with the Spirit' and declares to the temple leadership that salvation is found in the name of Jesus alone. In 4:31 those at the prayer meeting were 'all filled with the Holy Spirit and spoke the word of God boldly'. In 6:10, although the verb *pimplēmi* is not used, the Spirit enables Stephen to speak. Following Ananias' promise that Saul will be 'filled with the Spirit' (9:17), Saul 'at once' began to preach in the synagogues (9:20). A more traditional description of prophetic revelatory speech is found in 13:9–11, where Paul is 'filled with the Holy Spirit' and then pronounces judgment upon Elymas. The examples in Acts 4 and 6 in particular are reminiscent of Jesus' promise in Luke 12:12 that the Holy Spirit will teach his disciples what to say when brought before synagogues, rulers and authorities (Jesus later states, '*I* will give you words and wisdom', Luke 21:15). Other uses of the verb *pimplēmi* in Acts 3:10, 5:17, 13:45 and 19:29 with reference to being 'filled' with wonder, jealousy or confusion indicate that the meaning of being 'filled with the Holy Spirit' followed by the action of speaking seems to be a reference to the controlling activity of the Spirit that extends to the provision of the words to say, which are most appropriate to the occasion in which the good news about

---

[24] The speaking in other languages then, as with Peter's sermon, in this context, is a subset of the activity of 'prophesying'. Those who speak in other languages are described as 'declaring the wonders of God' (2:11).

[25] Cf. also similar uses of *pimplēmi* with the action of speaking in Luke 1:15–16, 41–42, 67.

Jesus is proclaimed or defended. In this way the Lord Jesus himself enables all of his people to be witnesses of him to the ends of the earth in the inaugurated kingdom of God.

## A restored people of God

Although the purpose of the Spirit to enable God's people to point to Jesus is an obvious feature of Luke's portrait (esp. in the light of 1:8), it should also be noted that this is not all Luke has to say about the work of the Spirit in Acts. As we have already observed (in ch. 3 and in this chapter on Acts 1 – 2), the pouring out of the Spirit is integrally related to the restoration of Israel anticipated in Isaiah. In this sense, as Turner has particularly shown, the Spirit is also involved in the transformation of God's people.[26]

This transforming work of the Spirit is also apparent in Acts 2. Thus after Peter's explanation that the events of Pentecost must be understood as the arrival of the last days and that Jesus (the suffering Messiah and reigning Lord) has poured out the promised Holy Spirit, Luke tells us that about three thousand respond to Peter's warnings and call to 'be saved' (2:40–41).[27] Thus God's people are those who have responded in repentance, embraced the risen Jesus as the suffering Messiah and reigning Lord, and have received the new-covenant blessings of forgiveness and the Holy Spirit. The summary passage that follows in 2:42–47 then provides a portrait of this restored community who have received the Spirit.[28] This portrait of a people devoted to God's word (apostolic teaching about Jesus) and expressing unity and devotion to one another through sharing food, possessions and meeting needs and praising God is also reminiscent of the hope of the prophets. Repentance, or a 'return' to God, is a feature of the hoped-for restoration in Isaiah[29]

[26] Turner (1996: 402) argues that the Spirit is *the* means of 'God's saving/ transforming presence for Israel (and through her to the nations)'. Turner (344) thinks that 'the gift of inward transformation by the Spirit (as in Ezek. 36)' is not in view here. The allusions to Ezek. 37 in Acts 2, however, weaken Turner's argument at this point. See also the discussion in ch.1 about the kingdom's 'not yet' aspect.

[27] The passive voice of *sōthēte* (be saved) recalls the promise of 2:21 that 'everyone who calls on the name of the Lord will be saved (*sōthēsetai*)'; i.e. by the Lord.

[28] The terminology of a 'portrait of a restored people' is used by L. T. Johnson 1992: 56.

[29] Cf. Pao 2000: 118–120. Cf. esp. Isa. 45:22, '*Turn* to me and be saved, / all you ends of the earth; / for I am God, and there is no other'; 55:6–7, 'Seek the LORD while he may be found; / call on him while he is near. / Let the wicked forsake his way / and

and a characteristic message of the prophets in general.[30] Warnings against idolatry and failure to care for the needy were frequently at the heart of the prophetic message.[31] At the very beginning of Luke's Gospel, John the Baptist declares that sharing with those in need is the 'fruit' of repentance (Luke 3:7–14). It should also be noted that the call to repent characterized Jesus' ministry. He came 'to call sinners to repentance' (Luke 5:32).[32] In the context of Acts 2 this portrait of a restored people is meant to be seen as a result of the new-covenant blessing of the Holy Spirit sent by Jesus himself.[33]

A similar portrait of the unity of the Christian community is found in Acts 4:32. Like Acts 2, this is placed immediately after a reference to the activity of the Holy Spirit among the believers in 4:31. It seems unlikely that the two portraits of the Christian community (2:42–47; 4:32–37), which highlight most the selfless activity of the believers in caring for one another and which are placed immediately after references to the 'filling of the Holy Spirit', are meant to be read in isolation from that activity of the Spirit. This is especially highlighted in the deliberate contrast Luke makes between the 'filling' that takes place for the believers in 4:31–32, and the 'filling' that takes place with Ananias in 5:3. Similarities between 4:32–37 and 5:1–4 clearly indicate that Luke intends the two sections to be read together. Both sections deal with the selling of property (4:32, 34, 37 and 5:1), the

the evil man his thoughts. / Let him *turn* to the LORD, and he will have mercy on him, / and to our God, for he will freely pardon.'

[30] Cf. Robertson 2004: 184–186. Cf. e.g. Ezek. 18:30–31, 'Therefore, O house of Israel . . . *Repent*! *Turn* away from all your offences . . . get a new heart and a new spirit. Why will you die, O house of Israel?' Cf. also Joel 2:11–13, 'The day of the LORD is great; / it is dreadful. Who can endure it? / "Even now," declares the LORD, "*return* to me with all your heart . . ." / Rend your heart / and not your garments. / *Return* to the LORD your God . . .'

[31] Cf. Isa. 58:6–7. Cf. Robertson 2004: 161–168 for numerous references to the prophetic charge to love God and people (e.g. idolatrous loves in Isa. 57:8–9; Jer. 2:25, 33; Ezek. 8:1–18; Hos. 3:1; 9:10; Amos 4:4–5; and failure to care for the needy among them in Isa. 1:17; Jer. 5:28–29; 7:5–7; Mic. 6:7–8; Zech. 7:9–10; Mal. 3:5; cf. also Deut. 24:17–22).

[32] Cf. also Luke 13:2–5; 15:7; 16:30–31. Peterson (2009: 154) notes the link made in the preaching of Jesus between repentance and the kingdom of heaven ('repent for the kingdom of heaven is at hand'). Though this specific connection is not made in the wording of Luke's Gospel, Peterson is correct to note that repentance 'involves a change of mind about Jesus and his role in God's kingdom purposes' as well as a 'radical reorientation of life with respect to Jesus, expressing sorrow for having rejected the one accredited by God as Lord and Christ'.

[33] Cf. Ezek. 36:25–27; 37:24. Cf. also Jer. 31:33. Note that in Acts 5:31 Jesus is the one who gives 'repentance and forgiveness of sins to Israel', and in 11:18 God is said to have given repentance to the Gentiles. Cf. also 3:26.

placement of proceeds 'at the apostles' feet' (4:35, 37 and 5:2) and the voluntary nature of this action of meeting needs (4:34–35 and 5:4). In 4:31 the believers are described as 'all filled with the Spirit' and speaking 'the word of God'. Immediately following this 'filling with the Spirit', the believers are described in 4:32 as being 'one in heart', a unity that finds expression in selflessly giving up what they have to meet the needs of others. Peter's declaration to Ananias in 5:3 that Satan has 'filled your heart' (cf. also 5:4; lit. 'this deed in your heart') seems to be a deliberate contrast therefore to the believers in 4:31–37. The result of this 'filling' is seen in Ananias' deceitful speech. Rather than being filled with the Holy Spirit and speaking the word of God, Ananias is filled with Satan and speaks, not the word of God, but lies, specifically a lie to the Holy Spirit (5:3). Thus it is likely that the work of the Spirit is meant to be seen here as more than enabling proclamation. The Spirit here also transforms hearts in the Christian community, enabling love for others and freedom from the master of money (Luke 16:13).

It is possible that in Acts the noun *plērēs* (full) is used to highlight this 'ethical' aspect of the Spirit's work in the character of those described.[34] In Acts 6:3 the seven who were chosen to participate in the ministry of 'tables' so that the apostles could continue in prayer and the 'ministry of the word' were to be 'full of the Spirit and wisdom'. Similarly, a few verses later, one of the seven, Stephen, is described as 'full of faith and of the Holy Spirit' (6:5).[35] In 11:24 Barnabas is described as 'full of the Holy Spirit and faith'. Finally, in 13:52 the disciples are full 'with joy and with the Holy Spirit'.[36] In contrast to this use of the noun *plērēs* with the Holy Spirit, in 13:10 the noun is used to describe Elymas the magician as full of 'deceit and trickery'. Thus in these instances of being 'full of the Holy Spirit and . . .' it seems as though some character trait is associated with the person who has the Holy Spirit (i.e. wisdom, grace, faith and joy).

Therefore, we have seen that the Holy Spirit in Acts is particularly associated with the restoration purposes of God. In fulfilment of the prophetic hopes for a restored people in which God will fulfil his saving promises we find that Jesus himself brings this restoration as the disciples correctly understood he would (1:6). His death and resurrection have inaugurated a new age and he rules from

---

[34] Cole 2007: 114.

[35] In 6:8 Stephen is described as 'full of grace and power'.

[36] In 13:52 the cognate verb *plēroō* is used.

the throne of David as anticipated. The means by which the risen Lord Jesus brings about this restored people, however, is through his sending of the Holy Spirit. He grants repentance, forgiveness of sins (5:31) and the gift of the Holy Spirit (Luke 24:49; Acts 2:33, 38; 16:7). The Holy Spirit then enables Jesus' people to be his witnesses (Luke 24:48–49; Acts 1:8), to 'prophesy' or tell forth the fulfilment of God's plans in Jesus (Acts 2:14–36) and to speak with appropriate boldness in difficult settings (4:8, 13, 29, 31). The Holy Spirit also brings about the new-covenant change of heart that leads the restored people of God to display their love for one another in tangible expressions of giving as the 'fruit' of repentance (2:42–47; 4:32–37) and a new-covenant change of character such that wisdom, faith and joy characterize those 'full of the Holy Spirit'. Another significant feature of Luke's teaching on the role of the Holy Spirit in Acts is that all who believe in the Lord Jesus for the forgiveness of sins receive the same gift, the Holy Spirit. There is, therefore, only one people of God.

## One people of God

Luke explicitly emphasizes the fact that the giving of the Holy Spirit means that there is one people of God under the one Lord.[37] This is especially seen in the account of the inclusion of Gentiles among God's people in Acts 10 – 11.[38] The overwhelming emphasis of the passage is that these Gentile believers are part of the same people of God as the Jewish believers who received the Holy Spirit on the day of Pentecost. Numerous parallels are made with Pentecost as well as

[37] This feature of Luke's teaching on the work of the Holy Spirit has been neglected in studies of Lukan pneumatology. Thus Turner (1996: 349–350) lists five categories for the Spirit's role in Acts: the author of revelatory visions and dreams, gives revelatory words or instruction or guidance, grants charismatic wisdom or revelatory discernment, inspires praise, and inspires preaching or witness. Menzies (1991: 224–225) basically groups the Spirit's role in Acts under two categories: the Spirit is the agent of inspired speech; the Spirit gives special revelation to direct the mission of the church. Wenk (2000: 303–307) corrects this neglect (though his view that Acts 15 relates to conditions for Gentiles after entering the Christian community neglects the soteriological emphasis in Acts 15).

[38] As we have noted, the tangible expression of this unity ('fellowship' in 2:42, or 'one heart' in 4:32) was also displayed in 2:42–47 and 4:32–37. That is, from time to time, as people had need, they gave voluntarily to meet the needs of others (2:45; 4:34–35). This was not 'communal living' or an idealized 'community of goods' from a distant utopian age; it was the concrete expression of concern for others expressed in other ways elsewhere in Acts (cf. 9:39; 20:33–35). Cf. A. J. Thompson 2008a: 70–74, 88–93.

explicit statements that emphasize this unity. Thus (1) Peter declares that 'everyone' who believes in the name of Jesus receives the forgiveness of sins (10:43; cf. 2:38). (2) The Gentile believers are heard to be 'speaking in tongues and magnifying (*megalynontōn*) God' (10:46; cf. 2:11). (3) The Holy Spirit is described as God's 'gift' (*dōrea*, 10:45; 11:17; cf. 2:38). (4) Peter's recollection of 'what the Lord had said' refers to his promise to baptize with the Holy Spirit (11:16; cf. 1:5). (5) Peter explicitly states that 'they have received the Holy Spirit *just as we have*' (*hōs kai hēmeis*, 10:47), the Holy Spirit came on them '*as he had come on us*' (*hōsper kai eph hēmas*, 11:15) and God gave them '*the same gift as he gave us*' (*tēn isēn dōrean . . . hōs kai hēmin*, 11:17).

If we missed those narrative clues to the unity of God's people through the gift of the same Holy Spirit to those who believe in the Lord Jesus (11:17), then Luke highlights it again in his summary of Peter's speech to the Jerusalem Council in 15:8–9. Peter, looking back to the inclusion of the Gentiles through faith in the Lord Jesus, states that God gave 'the Holy Spirit to them, *just as he did to us* (*kathōs kai hēmin*). He made no distinction between us and them*, for he purified their hearts by faith.' It might also be noted that in the narrative of Acts between these two accounts of the inclusion of the Gentiles into the one people of God, it is the continuing 'work' (Acts 13:2) of the inclusion of the Gentiles that is the focus of Paul's first 'missionary journey' (Acts 13 – 14). The account of this first journey opens with an emphasis on the calling and sending by the Holy Spirit for his 'work' (13:2, 4) and concludes with the completion of this 'work' (14:26), marking out this Spirit-initiated journey as a narrative unit. The summarizing conclusion of this 'work' specifically highlights the inclusion of the Gentiles (14:27; cf. also 13:46–48, 52), which, of course, also prepares the reader for the issues raised in Acts 15.

Thus, on the one hand, this unity comes about because all equally receive forgiveness of sins through faith in Jesus. On the other hand, the Holy Spirit both works to bring messengers to proclaim that good news and is then the common gift to those who receive that good news. It is for this reason that, in Acts, to be a follower of Jesus is to have the gift of the Spirit and to be a full member of God's people. It is misreading Acts to think that some of God's people have the Spirit and others do not, or that the Spirit is merely an 'additional gift' given to God's people to empower them for proclamation.[39]

---

[39] As proposed e.g. by Menzies 1991.

Sometimes Acts 2, 8, 10 – 11 and 19 are said to provide a pattern for individual believers who, after coming to faith, must seek an additional empowering of the Spirit for proclamation and that the reception of this empowerment is evidenced in the ability to speak in ecstatic tongues. Although space prevents a full treatment here, the overall framework of inaugurated eschatology in Acts helps to evaluate these claims. Luke's focus in these texts is on the fulfilment of prophecy, salvation history, and the beginning of the last days rather than paradigms for individual experiences. In each of these chapters Luke emphasizes 'corporate experience'.[40] Thus Acts 2 highlights the unique salvation-historical time frame (1:5; 2:1) for the sending of the Holy Spirit from the ascended Lord Jesus for Jesus' disciples among the people of Israel (2:14, 22, 36) as the setting for the day of Pentecost. Acts 8 highlights the inclusion of Samaria as a whole.[41] The wording of 8:14 ('Samaria had accepted the word of God') is almost identical to that of 11:1 ('the Gentiles also had received the word of God').[42] The emphasis, therefore, in Acts 8 and 10 – 11 is on the Samaritans as a group and Gentiles as a group.[43]

The 'disciples' in Acts 19 are no exception as they do not appear to have been believers in Jesus.[44] In 19:3 it appears that they are a group who for some reason have been caught out of sequence. They appear to have been followers of John the Baptist who missed out on transitioning to faith in Jesus. In a sense they are caught in a salvation-historically unique time warp. Thus, after they state that they have not heard that the Holy Spirit has come,[45] Paul's response is not to tell them about the Holy Spirit but to tell them that they

[40] Carson 1987: 137–158.

[41] I have referred to Acts 2 and 8 in terms of the restoration of Israel and the northern kingdom. Even if that discussion is not accepted, however, the point here is simply that the emphasis in Acts 2 and 8 is still on Jewish believers as a group and Samaritans as a group.

[42] *Dedektai (dechomai) hē Samareia ton logon tou theou* (8:14); *kai ta ethnē edexanto (dechomai) ton logon tou theou* (11:1).

[43] Note the numerous accounts of conversions in Acts that occur without a so-called additional empowering paradigm (cf. 2:41, 47; 4:4; 5:14; 6:7; 8:36–38; 9:35, 42; 11:21, 24; 13:12, 48; 14:1; 16:14–15, 31–34; 17:4, 12, 34; 18:8, 27; 28:24).

[44] Contra Bock 2007: 599. Note that the term 'disciples' was used for disciples of John the Baptist (Luke 5:33; 7:18; 11:1).

[45] This appears to be the point of their answer (cf. the similar wording in John 7:39, that the Holy Spirit is 'not yet') rather than the suggestion that they have not heard that there is a Holy Spirit. As followers of John the Baptist they would have heard that there is a Holy Spirit. However, as those who had not seen the arrival of Jesus and subsequent events they would not yet have heard that the Holy Spirit had come.

ought to believe in the one coming after John; that is, Jesus. They then demonstrate their newfound allegiance to Jesus in baptism (as in 2:38) – the missing link for them was Jesus.[46] As with the Gentile Cornelius and his household, the followers of John the Baptist in Acts 19 are told about the Lord Jesus and receive the Holy Spirit. The laying on of hands and similarities with Pentecost (19:6) are specifically designed to demonstrate the inclusion of these transitional John-the-Baptist believers into the new-covenant people of God.[47] Thus, after the salvation-historical event of Pentecost, the only occasion in which there is a delay for believers in Jesus to receive the Spirit is with the Samaritans in Acts 8. As we observed in the introductory chapter, when we want to discern the difference between what is prescribed as normative or what might be described, a helpful hint is to look for what is repeated. This unique situation in Acts 8 does not constitute a pattern for individuals today. In addition to the 'corporate' emphasis on 'Samaria accepting the word of God' noted above, the traditional antagonism with the northern kingdom seems to lie behind this emphasis on their equal inclusion among the people of God.[48] Peter's declaration in Acts 2:38 that allegiance to Jesus results in the reception of the Holy Spirit (and the forgiveness of sins), and his statement in 11:17 that God gives the gift of the Holy Spirit to those who believe in the Lord Jesus, express what is normative in Acts.[49] This is why Paul asks the disciples in 19:6 if they received the Holy Spirit when they believed. He assumes that if they had genuinely believed in Jesus they would have received the Holy Spirit. Their ignorance about the Spirit leads Paul to speak about faith in Jesus.

---

[46] Twelftree 2009: 93–94.

[47] As the parallels to Pentecost in the account in Acts 10 – 11 also indicated. Peterson (2009: 328) is probably correct to suggest that Cornelius is presented as a faithful believer (who is relying on OT promises) transitioning to faith in Jesus. This faith in Jesus (as Peterson notes) is nevertheless essential for Cornelius to 'be saved' (11:14).

[48] It might also be noted that given the deliberate links between Acts 10 – 11 and 19 to Pentecost, the references to tongues speaking in Acts 10 and 19, since they are the only references to tongues in Acts apart from Acts 2, are most likely meant to be understood in the way tongues are described in Acts 2 (i.e. speaking in other human languages). There does not appear to be any indication in Acts that the 'tongues' of Acts 10 and 19 are different to Acts 2 (cf. Schreiner 2008: 722). The question of their cessation does not appear to be directly addressed in Acts. The disciples in Acts 19, however, are presented as a kind of last remaining group caught in this 'time warp' of hearing John the Baptist but without transitioning to faith in Jesus.

[49] Cf. Twelftree 2009: 85–86.

Overall then, Acts 2, 8, 10 – 11 and 19 contribute to this broad point about the role of the Holy Spirit in Acts. The giving of the Holy Spirit in Acts highlights the oneness of the people of God. These particular stages along the way accentuate that unity as Jew, Samaritan, Gentile and transitional John-the-Baptist-followers caught out of sequence are brought into the one people of God through faith in the one Lord Jesus and are given the same eschatological gift, the promised Holy Spirit.

# Faith, repentance, baptism and the reception of the Spirit in Acts

Something should also be said in this context about the relationship between the responses of faith/repentance and baptism and the promises of forgiveness of sins and the Holy Spirit.[50] Although Luke does refer to God's initiative and prior work of grace,[51] our focus here is on the reception of the gift of the Holy Spirit as a mark of being a believer in the Lord Jesus. Throughout this chapter we have examined Luke's theology of the Holy Spirit within the broad framework of the inauguration of the last days. Here, however, we will briefly note the relationship of this gift (along with forgiveness) to the required responses of faith/repentance and baptism. First, it must be observed that there are a number of passages where belief only is highlighted as the required response, there are a number of passages where repentance only is highlighted, and there are some passages where repentance and faith are grouped together.[52] In this regard, occasionally the reception of the Holy Spirit is linked to belief only and occasionally the reception of the Holy Spirit is linked to repentance only.[53] These passages indicate that repentance and

[50] For this section I must acknowledge indebtedness to Stein's very helpful essay (2006: 35–66).

[51] Cf. Acts 3:16 ('faith that comes through him'); 10:1 – 11:18 (God's initiative throughout); 13:48 ('appointed for eternal life'); 16:14 ('opened her heart'); 18:27 ('by grace had believed'); cf. also perhaps 2:37 ('were cut to the heart').

[52] Belief: 2:44; 4:4; 5:14; 6:7; 9:42; 10:43; 11:17; 13:12, 39, 48; 14:1, 27; 15:7, 9; 16:15, 31–34; 17:12; 18:8, 27; 19:2, 9, 18; 24:24; 26:18; 28:24. Repentance: 2:38; 3:19; 5:31; 8:22; 9:35; 11:18; 17:30; 26:18, 20. Repentance and Faith: note 2:38 (repent) and 2:44 (believers); 9:35 (turned) and 9:42 (many believed); 10:43 (believe) and 11:18 (repentance); 17:30 (repent) and 17:34 (a few believed); but see esp. 11:21; 19:4; 20:21; 26:18 and 20. Stein 2006: 36–41.

[53] Repentance and the Spirit: 2:38; 11:16–18. Faith and the Spirit: 10:43–46; 19:2 (cf. also 5:32).

faith are two sides of the one coin: they are not identical, but where one is mentioned by itself the other may be presupposed.[54]

In a number of places throughout Acts baptism is also seen to be part of the expected response towards Jesus.[55] Thus it is true to say that baptism in Acts is part of the 'conversion-initiation' experience.[56] The idea of unbaptized believers is foreign to the book of Acts. Furthermore, as the exception of the Samaritans in Acts 8 indicates, the idea of a long separation between baptism/conversion and reception of the Holy Spirit is also unusual (nearly foreign!) in the book of Acts. It should be noted, however, that baptism is not a means of receiving the Spirit *ex opere operato* (from the work performed). Although Simon 'believed' and was baptized (8:13), the subsequent narrative makes clear that this 'belief' was spurious. Just as Simon had 'amazed' the people of Samaria for a long time with his magic, so also he was 'amazed' at the miracles performed by Philip (8:11, 13).[57] Peter's response to Simon's attempt to purchase the Holy Spirit so that he could do his own amazing feats is essentially 'To hell with you and your money!' (8:20).[58] Furthermore, things do not look good for Simon when Peter says that he has 'no part or share in this ministry (*logos*, 'word')', his 'heart is not right before God', he must 'repent of this wickedness', 'perhaps' the Lord will forgive him and, finally, he is 'full of bitterness and captive to sin' (8:20–23)! Clearly Simon's baptism did him no good! It should also be noted that in Acts 10:47–48 the reception of the Holy Spirit is given as the basis for baptism. It is *because* these Gentiles have received the Holy Spirit through faith in the Lord Jesus that Peter says they *ought* to be baptized.[59] Thus in Acts the norm is that the Holy Spirit is received by all believers at conversion and that baptism is associated with the response of conversion as an outward display of an allegiance (trust and repentance) to the Lord Jesus.[60]

[54] Stein 2006: 40–41.
[55] Cf. 2:38, 41; 8:12–13 (13, Simon), 37–38; 9:17–18 (cf. also 22:14–16); 10:43–47; 16:14–15, 31–34; 18:8; 19:4–6.
[56] Dunn 1970: 90.
[57] The same Greek term *existēmi* (amazed) is used in both instances.
[58] *To argyrion sou syn soi eiē eis apōleian* ('May your money perish with you' NIV).
[59] Cf. also Acts 9:17–18 and 22:13–16.
[60] In this regard it should also be noted that 'household baptism' in Acts is based on 'household belief'. Thus the emphasis in the account of the Philippian jailer is that if he believes he will be saved and the same goes for the rest of his household (probably including servants). Therefore, the word is preached to 'all the others in the house' (16:31–32). The implication is that they were all baptized because they all believed (16:33–34). The deliberate similarities of belief, household, baptism and

Faith and repentance are primary, however, as baptism, in and of itself, does not guarantee genuine conversion and the presence of the Spirit.

## Conclusion

Luke's teaching on the Holy Spirit in Acts is also best understood within his explanation of the inaugurated kingdom of God. The Lord Jesus has risen from the dead and is continuing to reign and administer God's saving promises. The Holy Spirit has been poured out in fulfilment of God's promises for the last days and Jesus is the one who has sent the promised Holy Spirit. As promised, therefore, all who turn to the Lord Jesus in repentance and faith receive God's Spirit, all are enabled by his Spirit to proclaim the good news of God's saving action in Christ, transformation is accomplished by his Spirit, and there is just one people of God under the Davidic King Jesus. Since the kingdom of God has been inaugurated in the death, resurrection and reign of Jesus, however, what happens to the old system and its authorities? The following two chapters will address the role that the temple, temple authorities and law play in the new era of the inaugurated kingdom of God in Acts.

---

hospitality between the Philippian jailer and Lydia indicate that the same is intended in her case. She is a believer and is baptized (16:15). However, what is implicit in the case of Lydia is made explicit in the case of Crispus, the synagogue ruler. Not only Crispus, but also 'his entire household believed in the Lord' (18:8; cf. also 11:14). The subsequent statement that many of the Corinthians believed and were baptized may indicate 'household baptism' followed 'household belief' in Crispus' house too.

Chapter Five

# The end of an era: the temple system and its leaders

So far we have seen that the inauguration of the kingdom of God provides cohesion to the emphases in Acts on the plan of God, the resurrection and reign of the Davidic King Jesus, the fulfilment of God's saving promises in the restoration of God's people, and the pouring out of the Holy Spirit. The introduction of this 'new era' of 'last days' fulfilment, however, also has implications for the 'old era'. We will see in this chapter that the ramifications of the Davidic kingship of Jesus and the arrival of the last days for the temple and temple authorities are especially highlighted in Acts 3 – 7. In the following chapter we will see that the role of the law as the authority for God's people has also undergone some change in Acts. Simply put, the book of Acts highlights the end of the old temple system and law and the inauguration of a new 'authority structure' in the inaugurated kingdom of God by virtue of Jesus' lordship and the authority of his 'authorized delegates', the apostles.[1] An outline of how we will proceed in the rest of this chapter will be provided following a summary of some of the debate concerning the role of the temple in Acts.

## The debate about the temple in Acts

Luke's interest in the temple is evident in the number of references he makes to the temple and in the strategic locations in the narrative of both Luke and Acts in which there is a focus on activity in the temple.[2] Debate has arisen in part because of two apparently

---

[1] Cf. pp. 63–67 for a brief discussion of the role elders play in strengthening local churches through teaching and modelling the apostolic message of God's grace. The phrase 'authorized delegates', used in this chapter and the next, is taken from Clark 1998: 190.

[2] Of the 71 occurrences of the term *hieron* (temple) in the NT 39 occur in Luke-Acts (though *naos*, 'shrine', is used only 5 times out of 45 in the NT). In Luke-Acts *hieron* refers more generally to the temple courts, whereas *naos* refers more specifically to the temple sanctuary (rather than the outer precincts). Cf. Head 2004: 106–109

conflicting types of evidence in the text of Acts.[3] First, the early believers appear to continue to be active in the temple even though NT teaching elsewhere points to the end of the temple as a place of sacrifice and God's dwelling. Secondly, there is debate over whether or not Stephen's speech criticizes the temple in the suggestion that David, rather than Solomon, found favour with God, the temple was a house 'made by men' (i.e. and not by God), and the declaration that the Most High does not dwell in such houses (Acts 7:46–50).

Although there are variations among the following views, some suggested solutions to this difficulty include the following three. First, some argue that Luke is inconsistent. This is stated in stark form by Barrett, who concludes:

> There are passages in Acts that assume the Jewish Christians will naturally continue to use the Temple as they did in their pre-Christian lives. Not only is the Temple a proper place in which to meet for religious discourse and for prayer, the old sacrificial system continues in use, and that even by Paul . . . There are also passages, or at least there is a passage, in which the most radical of all views is maintained. The Temple ought never to have existed at all. God did not intend it, and made the matter clear through his prophets.[4]

Secondly, some see Luke as essentially positive towards the temple. The difference between this view and the previous one is primarily that Stephen's speech is viewed more positively. According to Sylva, Stephen may be emphasizing the transcendence of God in Acts 7:48–50 but is not rejecting the temple.[5] According to some, although Luke may be criticizing the Jewish leaders in Acts 3 – 5,

---

for a discussion of the terms used by Luke. There is a focus on the temple at both the beginning and the end of Luke's Gospel; and although the word moves out from Jerusalem, there is a return to the themes of Jerusalem, temple and Jewish leadership in Acts 21 – 23 (on this latter point see A. J. Thompson 2008a: 159–170). References to the temple predominate in Acts 3 – 7 and do not reappear until Acts 21, where they again occur regularly.

[3] Cf. Walton's summary (2004: 135–149) of the debate over the role of the temple in Acts. I will discuss Luke's Gospel briefly below.

[4] Barrett 1991: 364. Barrett is referring, on the one hand, to practices in Acts 3 – 5, 21, and, on the other hand, to Stephen's speech in Acts 7.

[5] Sylva (1987: 261–275) argues for the 'transcendence' view against the 'rejection' view. He refers to a 'replacement' view but dismisses it in a footnote as having little to support it. Walton's survey (2004: 138) refers to three views but does not interact with the 'replacement' view.

this does not amount to a criticism of the temple itself.[6] Thus, J. Bradley Chance argues that 'Luke wants his readers to see that in the literal Jerusalem and at the literal temple, God fulfils his promises of salvation to Israel.'[7]

Thirdly, some resolve the difficulty in terms of the disciples' still coming to terms with the changes brought about by Christ. According to this view, accounts of temple activity among the early Christians are to be expected as they gradually work out the implications of Christ's death for the temple system.[8]

In this chapter I will argue that, although Luke does not criticize the actual building of the temple by Solomon, he views the role of the Jerusalem temple as having come to an end and its ultimate purpose is now found in the risen Lord Jesus, who not only replaces the temple but provides more for God's people than even the temple was able to provide. The two broad sections of (1) the temple activity in Acts 3 – 5 and (2) the account of Stephen's speech in Acts 6 – 7 are meant to be read together, and both sections are consistent in pointing beyond the temple to Jesus.[9] Thus, in contrast to the three views above, Luke's view of the temple is consistent, he points to its fulfilment and replacement in Jesus, and this view is also expressed by the earliest sermons of the apostles in Acts 3 – 5. We will especially focus on Acts 3 – 7 because these chapters particularly highlight the temple.[10] The rest of this chapter will proceed under three broad headings. First, under the heading 'The Davidic King, the last days and the temple (Acts 1 – 3)', we will see that the context of Acts 1 – 2 and the narrative links between Acts 2 and 3 prepare the reader for a focus on the temple in the chapters following Acts 2. Secondly, under the heading 'The temple, temple leadership and Jesus' universal authority (Acts 3 – 5)', we will focus on Acts 3 – 5

[6] Hurtado (2003: 195–196, 208–210) states that not only is Luke positive towards the temple and has no problem with the disciples continuing to take part in the temple system, but that neither Jesus nor Paul critiqued the temple. Thus there is no contradiction between Acts and the teachings of Jesus and Paul elsewhere in the NT: they were all positive towards the temple (though critical of the temple leadership)!

[7] Chance 1988: 85. Chance explicitly rejects any notion that there is a 'transferral of temple motifs to Jesus' (41–45). In this regard he sees Luke as contradictory to the other NT writers (35).

[8] Walton 2004: 149. Though Walton does argue for a 'transcendence' view of Stephen's speech, he also suggests that Jesus may be understood as the true temple in Acts.

[9] This view is closest to that of Franklin 1975: 99–108 (cf. also Perrin 2010: 63–65).

[10] As noted above, references to the temple predominate in Acts 3 – 7 and do not reappear until Acts 21 (Acts 21 will be treated briefly in ch. 6).

and observe that these chapters form one narrative unit which develops the implications of Acts 1 – 2, and that this narrative unit highlights the replacement of both the temple and the temple leadership. Thirdly, under the heading 'Stephen, the temple and Jesus (Acts 6 – 7)', we will see that Acts 6 – 7 continues the themes developed in Acts 3 – 5 and brings them to a dramatic conclusion as Stephen points to Christ.

# The Davidic King, the last days and the temple (Acts 1 – 3)

In this first main section we will see that, in drawing attention to both the Davidic kingship of Jesus and the arrival of the last days in Acts 2, and in deliberately linking the beginning of Acts 3 with the end of Acts 2, Luke is preparing his readers for why he will focus on the temple in Acts 3 – 7.[11] That is, Acts 3 – 7 is meant to be read in the light of Acts 1 – 2.

The account of David's rise to the throne in 2 Samuel demonstrates that the temple and the Davidic covenant have been associated from the very beginning.[12] It was, after all, the play on words between 'temple' and 'dynasty' in the term 'house' that gave rise to the promise that the Lord himself would establish the Davidic dynasty and a descendant of David would 'build a house for my Name', and therefore the Lord will 'establish the throne of his kingdom for ever' (2 Sam. 7:13). Solomon refers to this promise to David in his declaration of praise to the Lord following the filling of the temple with the glory of the Lord (1 Kgs 8:10–21). Furthermore, the hope for a restored temple was also central to the prophetic hope for a restored people of God under the rule of a future Davidic King. In Ezekiel 37 (a chapter already significant for Acts 2 in its discussion of the resurrection, God's Spirit and the restoration of 'all the house of Israel' under one king) the Lord promises a time when a new David will be king over God's people and says, 'I will put my sanctuary among them for ever. My dwelling-place will be with them ... Then the nations will know that I the LORD make

---

[11] Beale (2004: 201–216), in his discussion of the temple in Acts 2, though correctly highlighting the judgment upon the old temple, does not discuss the relationship between the Davidic kingship of Jesus in Acts 2 and the significance of this for the theme of the temple in Acts.

[12] Hahn 2005: 300. Hahn notes the wordplay on 'house' ('temple' or 'dynasty') in 2 Sam. 7:11–13. Cf. also 1 Kgs 8:17–19.

Israel holy, when my sanctuary is among them for ever' (Ezek. 37:26–28).[13]

As we have seen, Acts 1 – 2 particularly highlights the reign of the Davidic King Jesus in the inaugurated kingdom of God. Peter declares that the promise to David concerning the enthronement of one of his descendants has been fulfilled in the resurrection and exaltation of the Lord Jesus (Acts 2:30–33) and that Jesus is in fact David's Lord who reigns at the right hand of God (Acts 2:34–36). So already the strong Davidic emphasis in Acts 2, together with the biblical association between the Davidic King and the temple, prepares readers of Acts for the issue of the temple to be addressed.

Furthermore, expectations concerning the temple were associated more broadly with the arrival of the 'last days'. In Acts 2 the pouring out of the Holy Spirit is evidence for the reign of the Davidic King Jesus as Lord, and therefore the arrival of the last days. We have already noted that the phrase 'in the last days', which Peter adds to his citation from Joel (Acts 2:17), reflects the identical phrase from Isaiah 2.[14] It should also be noted that Isaiah goes on to say that

> In the last days
> the mountain of *the Lord's temple will be established*
> as chief among the mountains;
> it will be raised above the hills,
> and all nations will stream to it.
>
> (Isa. 2:2)

In the light of the biblical association between the Davidic King and the temple and between the 'last days' and the temple it is not surprising therefore that, following the announcement of the arrival of the 'last days' with the exaltation of Jesus to the throne of David in Acts 2, Luke then deals with the subject of the temple in the chapters that immediately follow.

---

[13] For the temple generally see Isa. 2:1–4; 56:6–8; 60:3–16; Ezek. 40 – 44; Joel 3:18; Mic. 4:1–4; Hag. 2:1–9; Zech. 6:12–15 (some of these are cited by Hahn 2005: 300).

[14] Isa. 2:2. As noted in ch. 4, the exact phrase 'in the last days' (*en tais eschatais hēmerais*), which Peter adds to his quotation from Joel in Acts 2:17, is found only in Isa. 2:2 in the LXX (though an explicit link with Isa. 2:2 is not crucial for the point here). The association of king and temple continued into Jewish hopes in the intertestamental period (cf. *Sib. Or.* 5.420–427 [414–432]; *1 En.* 53.6). Cf. Hahn 2005: 302.

That Luke intends Acts 3 – 7 to develop the expectations raised in Acts 1 – 2 is seen in the way Acts 3 begins by focusing on a specific example of what is found in his summary description of the restored 'last days' community in 2:42–47. Following references in 2:42–47 to *signs* being done through the *apostles*, the believers being devoted to *prayers*, and meeting *daily* in the *temple*, in Acts 3:1–2 Luke focuses on one sign accomplished through two apostles, at a particular time of prayer and at a specific temple site where a particular person is placed daily.[15] Thus it seems clear that Luke is being selective. He is highlighting a particular activity designed to be read in the light of the events of Acts 1 – 2, which flows directly out of his summary at the end of chapter 2.[16]

Furthermore, as indicated above, the miracle that is the focus of events in Acts 3:1 – 4:22 is called a 'sign' in 4:16 and 4:22, and this is the only specific event called a 'sign' in Acts.[17] Why is this particular 'sign' recounted in this narrative context? Furthermore, as a 'sign', what is this event 'pointing to' in this narrative context? In the next section we will see that Luke has selected this event to authenticate the apostolic preaching of Jesus as the fulfilment of all of God's promises, the means of receiving all of God's blessings, and therefore that Jesus is the one in whom believers find all they need. In doing this, the event in its narrative context also highlights the end of the old temple system and its authorities. We must now turn therefore to the narrative unit itself.

---

[15] Spencer 2004: 54. Though, as we will note below, this event is not specifically called a 'sign' until 4:16 and 22.

[16] Although Luke records the events in Acts 3 as taking place in the location of the temple courts because that is where the lame man was healed and that also is where crowds then came to see what had happened, the disciples were not at the temple all the time. In 2:42–47 Luke has referred to the occasional selling of possessions and helping those in need, meeting in homes and having meals together – none of which may have taken place in the temple. Luke is being selective and, given that he has made some obvious links to ch. 2, it is reasonable to suggest that he has chosen this one event in the temple to illustrate the role of the temple in the light of the momentous events of Acts 1 – 2.

[17] Cook 2007: 95. In 4:16, 22 the NIV translates *sēmeion* as 'miracle/miraculously'. General statements about 'signs' are given in 2:22 (Jesus); 2:43; 4:30; and 5:12 (apostles); 6:8 (Stephen); 7:36 (Moses); 8:6 and 13 (Philip); 14:3 and 15:12 (Paul and Barnabas). However, 4:16 and 22 are the only places where a particular event is called a 'sign' in Acts. It should also be noted that 4:22 is the concluding statement regarding this healing and its explanation in 3:1 – 4:22.

# The temple, temple leadership and Jesus' universal authority (Acts 3 – 5)

In this section we will observe that in Acts 3 – 5, as one narrative unit, Luke is focusing on the implications of Acts 1 – 2 for both the temple and the temple leadership, and the foundation for Stephen's speech in Acts 7 is already being laid here in Acts 3 – 5.[18] That is, Luke is not here just offering a critique of the Jewish leadership; he is developing his argument that both temple and leadership have come to an end.

As Spencer helpfully observes, the reference to the believers' 'daily' (*kath hēmeran*) meeting 'in the temple' (*en tō hierō*) and 'from house to house' (*kat oikon*) in 2:46 is virtually identical to the reference to the proclamation about Jesus 'every day in the temple and from house to house' at the conclusion of Acts 5 (*pasan te hēmeran en tō hierō kai kat oikon*, 5:42).[19] These two references to 'daily temple and house' activity then 'frame' chapters 3 and 5. Within these two temple-house framing references is a focus on public temple activity in 3:1 – 4:22 and again in 5:12–41, with an 'interlude' in-between (4:23 – 5:11) that focuses on the believers. Thus, visually, the structure may be set out as follows:[20]

Temple-house frame (2:46) ['daily in the temple . . . house to house']
Temple and temple authorities (3:1 – 4:22)
Interlude: the true people of God and their leaders (4:23 – 5:11)
Temple and temple authorities (5:12–41)
Temple-house frame (5:42) ['every day in the temple and house to house']

---

[18] Beale (2004: 201–244) in his discussion of the new temple in the book of Acts lacks any reference to Acts 3 – 5, except for a brief mention of Acts 3:25–26 and 4:11, as he moves from a discussion of Acts 2 to focus on Acts 7.

[19] Spencer 2004: 51 (my tr. slightly modified from Spencer's observations).

[20] Adapted in modified form from ibid. In Luke's Gospel there is also a 'frame' between Luke 19:47 – 20:1 and 21:37–38, which refers to Jesus' activity of daily teaching in the temple. Within this 'frame' of teaching activity in the temple there is (as in Acts 3 – 5) an emphasis on the judgment and end of the temple leadership (20:17–18; Ps. 118:22 is cited, as in Acts 4:11) and the temple itself (19:44, 45–46; 21:6), as well as a stress on the authority and lordship of Jesus (20:1–44; Ps. 110:1 is cited, as in Acts 2:34–35), which follows a focus on the kingship of Jesus as he arrives in Jerusalem (19:11–12, 14–15, 27, 38). At the conclusion of Luke's Gospel Jesus' name is declared to be the means of forgiveness (24:47) and the disciples *worship* the ascended Lord Jesus (24:52, near Bethany, and therefore not in the temple!).

Although the focus of 3:1 – 4:22 and 5:12–41 is on the temple and temple authorities, the first section begins with more of an emphasis on the temple itself (3:1–26) followed by an emphasis on the temple authorities in particular (4:1–22), whereas the second section (5:12–41) focuses primarily on the temple authorities.[21] Thus, under this broad heading of the temple and temple leadership in Acts 3 – 5, we will focus primarily on these two 'temple' sections (3:1 – 4:22 and 5:12–42) in the following subdivisions: first, 3:1–10 ('Leaping over temple boundaries'); secondly, 3:11–26 ('The explanation'); thirdly, 4:1–22 ('The end of the old temple leadership'); and finally, 4:23 – 5:11 and 5:12–42 ('The leadership of the new Israel').

## Leaping over temple boundaries (Acts 3:1–10)

### Activity in the temple

Those who argue that Luke demonstrates a so-called positive view of the temple refer to the activity of the apostles in the temple in 2:46 and 3:1.[22] It is assumed that these are references to participation in the temple sacrifices and rituals because Luke says that Peter and John went up to the temple 'at the time of prayer – at three in the afternoon' (3:1). Before we focus on 3:1–10 we should observe, however, what Luke does and does not say about the believers and the temple.[23] Although the 'time of prayer' at 'three in the afternoon' would have been the time for afternoon sacrifices at the temple,[24] Luke makes no mention of sacrifices in his summary of the activity of the believers in the temple. In 2:46 he merely states that they 'continued together' ('continued to meet together' NIV) in the temple as well as sharing meals together in their homes, and in 3:1 a particular time is all that is mentioned. It is of course quite possible that they did go and pray in the temple.[25] It should be noted, however, that the *only* activity Luke records the believers doing in the temple in

---

[21] The repetition in Acts 3:1 – 4:22 and in 5:12–42 of a pattern of healing activity, followed by proclamation, arrest, trial and release is also indicative of the parallel nature of these two sections. Cf. C. Green 2005: 54–57.

[22] Chance 1988: 82–85; Barrett 1991: 347–350; Fitzmyer 1998: 277.

[23] As mentioned earlier, the term Luke uses for temple, *hieron*, more accurately refers to the temple courts and this is clarified with references to Solomon's Colonnade later (3:11; 5:12).

[24] Bock 2007: 159; Walton 2004: 136.

[25] However, they also 'continued together in prayer' in an upper room in 1:14 (cf. also 1:24–25). The same terms *proskarterountes homothymadon* (continue together) are found together only in 1:14 and 2:46. Cf. also 22:17.

this context is proclaiming Jesus (4:2; 5:20, 25, 42).[26] Thus it must be acknowledged that to see anything more in Luke's references to the believers' activity in the temple courts in Acts 2 – 5 is to read more into Acts than Luke himself has said. It would be more fruitful to examine the narrative itself to see what Luke is emphasizing in this context. In this section we will first examine the account of the miracle in 3:1–10 and observe the hints that this account provides for the significance of the temple in this literary context. Then we will examine Peter's explanation of this miracle in 3:11–26 in the light of this emphasis on the temple in 3:1–10.

### A healing that overcomes temple boundaries

The details in verse 2 of the man being 'lame from his mother's womb' (i.e. from birth), being carried, begging and being placed at the door of the temple all highlight the man's helplessness.[27] This emphasis on the man's helplessness, however, further highlights the transformation that will follow. In contrast to the language in verse 2 of crippled, carried, placed and begging, the man 'leaps', 'stands', 'walks', 'goes into' and again 'walks', 'leaps' and 'praises God' in verses 8–9. The contrast could not be more dramatic!

Repeated references to the temple, however, surround the healing in verses 4–7:

| | |
|---|---|
| v. 1 | Peter and John were going up *into* the temple (*eis to hieron*) |
| v. 2 | The man was carried *to* the (Beautiful) gate of the temple (*pros tēn thyran tou hierou*) |
| v. 2 | The man used to beg from those going *into* the temple (*eis to hieron*) |
| v. 3 | Peter and John were about to enter *into* the temple (*eis to hieron*) |
| vv. 4–7 | The man is healed |
| v. 8 | The man went *with them into* the temple (*syn autois eis to hieron*) |
| v. 10 | He used to sit begging *at* the (Beautiful) gate of the temple (*epi tē . . . pylē tou hierou*) |

---

[26] Paul's activity in Acts 21 will be discussed in the next chapter.
[27] The name of the gate is, perhaps ironically, 'beautiful'. Translations throughout this section are my own.

153

References to locations with respect to the temple are particularly emphasized with the use of the prepositions 'into' (*eis*) and 'to/at' (*pros*, *epi*).[28] Thus the man's position 'at the door of the temple' (v. 2) is stated in contrast to Peter and John and everyone else who are repeatedly said to be going 'into the temple' (vv. 1–3). This contrast between the man *outside* the temple and everyone else going *into* the temple is again highlighted in the verses following the man's healing. Not only was the man leaping, standing and walking (i.e. dramatically healed); we are specifically told that he entered '*with them into the temple*', walking, leaping and praising God (v. 8). The significance of this entry 'into the temple' is again highlighted in the concluding statement of this healing account in verse 10, where, in a deliberate recollection of verse 2, we are told that the people recognized him as the one who used to sit 'at the Beautiful Gate of the temple'.[29]

One of the themes being highlighted here in this man's healing is this overcoming of the man's desperate situation and placement outside 'the gate of the temple' with the man's healing leading to his entry 'into the temple'.[30] Spencer notes that the law's prohibition of offering lame (and blemished) animals as sacrifices and the prohibition of lame (and disabled) priests in the temple (Lev. 21:16–24; Deut. 15:21; cf. Mal. 1:8, 13) were used to develop the stereotype in Israelite society of the lame as despised creatures (cf. also 2 Sam. 5:6–8; 9:8).[31] Although these original prohibitions related to sacrifices and priests, the repeated references to these contrasting locations with respect to the temple in this context indicate that it is the inadequacy of the temple system together with the overcoming of that old-system inadequacy through Jesus that is being highlighted here.[32] In the wider context of Luke's Gospel it should also be noted

[28] Cf. Spencer 2004: 55.

[29] Though a different term is used in v. 10 (*pylē*, 'gate') than v. 2 (*thyran*, 'door'), the references to the name 'beautiful' with respect to this 'gate of the temple' and the request for 'alms' all indicate that v. 10 is deliberately recalling v. 2. Peterson (2009: 168) leans towards the view that the gate is the Nicanor (or Corinthian) Gate, which led from the 'eastern part of the outer Court of the Gentiles into the first of the inner courts of the temple (the Court of the Women)'.

[30] It may also be said, of course, that these references to 'the temple' are here because that is where the incident took place. However, since we have observed that Luke has selected this particular incident, we are enquiring into the significance of this selection in this narrative context.

[31] Spencer 2004: 55.

[32] Peterson (2009: 168) does not think that the lame man was 'prevented from entering the temple because of his condition'. Bock (2007: 162), however, states that

that (1) the lame are often associated with the blind, deaf, lepers and poor as 'typical social and religious outcasts' (Luke 7:22; 14:13, 22);[33] (2) Jesus drives out of the temple 'those who were selling' and declares that the temple system is not a 'house of prayer' but rather a 'den of robbers' (Luke 19:45–46); and (3) Jesus condemns the temple leadership as those who 'devour widows' houses' (Luke 20:47 – 21:4).[34] When these broader Lukan themes are kept in mind together with the narrative context that will lead to Stephen's speech concerning the temple, it seems likely that, as Spencer observes, the repeated references to the temple in this healing account are meant to highlight the lame beggar's leap over temple boundaries through Jesus.[35]

### Walking and leaping and praising God

A further indication as to the significance of this healing is the description of the man's healing in 3:8–9. Given the emphasis already in Acts 1 – 2 on the fulfilment of the promises in Isaiah concerning the pouring out of the Holy Spirit and the restoration of God's people as witnesses to the ends of the earth (1:6–8) and the arrival of the 'last days' (2:17) with the resurrection and exaltation of the Davidic King (2:30–33), readers of Luke's Gospel who now read about the lame 'leaping' and walking and praising God would be reminded of something else familiar to them from Isaiah. Just as some today might read this account and immediately recall a well-known children's Sunday school song,[36] it is likely that Luke expects readers of Luke and Acts to be familiar with Isaiah and therefore also to recognize in this description the words of Isaiah 35:3–6.[37] In Luke 7:20–23 Jesus already alluded to Isaiah 35:5–6 when he described his ministry as one in which 'the blind receive sight, the lame walk, those who have leprosy are cured, the deaf

---

the healing 'allows the man to walk into the temple proper for the first time' (citing Lev. 21:17–20; 2 Sam. 5:8).

[33] Spencer 2004: 55.

[34] The narrative location of Luke 21:1–4 makes the 'widow' of Luke 21:1–4 an example of what is described in Luke 20:47. J. B. Green 1997: 725, 728–729.

[35] Spencer 2004: 55.

[36] 'He went walking and leaping and praising God, walking and leaping and praising God. "In the name of Jesus Christ of Nazareth, rise up and walk!"' The lyrics to 'Silver and Gold Have I None' are in the public domain.

[37] In ch. 3 I referred to the pervasiveness of Isaiah in Acts and the likelihood that Luke expected his readers to know Isaiah in order to understand what was taking place in Acts.

hear, the dead are raised, and the good news is preached to the poor' (NIV). In Acts 3:8 the double reference to the lame man 'leaping' and walking and praising God recalls the specific wording of Isaiah 35:6, where it is anticipated that in the coming day of salvation and restoration of creation there will be shouting for joy in Zion and 'the lame' will 'leap like a deer'.[38] In the context of Acts 1 – 2, therefore, this account is a further indication, or sign (4:16, 22), of the authenticity of the apostolic message concerning the arrival of the last days with the resurrection and exaltation of Jesus and the promised restoration of all things that will culminate in the return of Christ (3:21). The reason why these temple boundaries are able to be overcome through 'the name of Jesus' (3:6), however, is developed further in the apostle Peter's explanation in the rest of Acts 3.

## The explanation: God's 'last days' blessings are found only in Jesus (Acts 3:11–26)

The account of the healing in 3:1–10 has particularly drawn attention to the overcoming of temple boundaries through Jesus. The 'significance' of the miracle is then explained by Peter in 3:11–26. In this comprehensive yet compact sermon, Peter explains that Jesus fulfils all of God's saving promises in Scripture. In this context, therefore, the inadequacy of the temple system is now contrasted with Peter's message about the all sufficiency of Jesus. Thus there is a shift in focus in 3:11–12 as attention turns away from both the lame man and the apostles Peter and John to the true source of the miracle: the name of Jesus (3:12, 16).

### Jesus fulfils all of God's saving promises found in all of Scripture

Peter employs a particularly rich and varied range of terms to speak of Jesus in such a short amount of space. Jesus is God's exalted 'servant' (vv. 13 and 26),[39] the 'Holy and Righteous One' (v. 14),[40]

---

[38] The same terminology for 'lame' (*chōlos*) and 'leaping' (*hallomai*) is found in Isa. 35 and Acts 3 (*exallomai, hallomai*).

[39] The terms *pais* (servant) together with the language of *doxazō* (glorify) in 3:13 alludes to Isa. 52:13, the introductory verse to the song about the 'Suffering Servant' in Isa. 52:13 – 53:12. The reference to the servant blessing Israel 'first' in Acts 3:26 alludes to the sequence found in Isa. 49:5–6.

[40] 'Righteous One' is probably also an allusion to the 'righteous Servant' of Isa. 53 (Isa. 53:11). Though 'righteous' was a common designation in the prophets for the Messiah (cf. Isa. 32:1; Jer. 23:5; Zech. 9:9). The term 'Holy' here perhaps adds to the picture of Jesus as 'set apart' (Bock 2007: 170), though the combination of 'holy and

the 'author of life' (v. 15),[41] the (suffering) Messiah (vv. 18, 20), the prophet like Moses who must be listened to (vv. 22–23),[42] the Davidic King (v. 24)[43] and the 'seed of Abraham' who will bring blessing to Israel first as well as to all nations (vv. 25–26).[44] Thus from verse 13 through to verse 26 Peter refers to Jesus in seven or eight different ways, ranging from the seed of Abraham, to the prophet like Moses, the Davidic Messiah and the Suffering Servant of Isaiah.[45] Furthermore, the blessings of the Abrahamic covenant (vv. 25–26), the Davidic covenant (the reference to Samuel in v. 24, the title 'Christ' in vv. 18, 20) and the new covenant ('forgiveness of sins' and the 'times of refreshing' in v. 19 parallel promises of forgiveness and the Holy Spirit in 2:38) are all fulfilled in the Lord Jesus. Peter also draws attention to comprehensive fulfilment here with repeated references to 'all the prophets' (vv. 18, 21, 24). Peter is emphasizing the fulfilment of all of God's purposes anticipated throughout the whole of Scripture in Jesus alone.[46] All that one needs from God is now to be found in Jesus: forgiveness of sins and refreshing (v. 19), restoration (v. 21), God's final authoritative revelation (vv. 22–23), the blessing of God (vv. 25–26) and repentance (v. 26).[47]

## *The 'name' of Jesus*

This emphasis on the fulfilment of all of God's blessings in the person of Jesus is particularly brought out in 3:16, which draws attention to 'the name' of Jesus (developing the point raised by

righteous' with one article probably indicates that the terms are synonymous here (Peterson 2009: 175).

[41] Given the contrast with murder here (i.e. taking life), the phrase 'author of life' probably means that Jesus is the one who grants life, as evidenced in this healing (cf. also 5:20). Bock 2007: 171.

[42] Cf. Deut. 18:15, 19; Lev. 23:29.

[43] The reference to Samuel as one of the prophets who 'foretold these days' indicates that Peter is referring to Samuel's involvement with David. Samuel anointed David (1 Sam. 16:13) and spoke of the granting of the kingdom to David (1 Sam. 28:17).

[44] Cf. Gen. 12:3; 22:18 ('offspring' NIV).

[45] Whether the number is seven or eight depends on whether 'holy and righteous' in 3:14 is one designation or two.

[46] Thus, contra Bock 1987: 197–198, it is not quite accurate to say that this sermon has a 'Pentateuchal emphasis'.

[47] Just over a hundred years ago Warfield (1907: 198–199) observed that this 'composite portrait' which Peter 'presents of Jesus the Messiah as he passes freely from one of these designations to another is a complex and very lofty one; what is most apparent is that he conceives Him as the focus upon which all the rays of OT prophecy converge, and as exalted above all earthly limitations'.

Peter in 3:6). A rather wooden translation of this grammatically complex sentence reads, 'by faith in his name this man ... was made strong, his name, and the faith through him gave him this wholeness ...' The general structure of the verse ('faith ... his name ... his name ... faith') highlights the centrality of 'the name' of Jesus.[48]

In this context this reference to 'the name' as the means of bringing about this 'wholeness' is reminiscent of references in the OT to 'the name' of Yahweh as the means by which God's people were delivered.[49] The 'name' of Yahweh was especially associated with the temple of Solomon, where it was used with reference to the presence of God among his people. In 1 Kings 8:17–20 Solomon praised the Lord before the people of Israel saying:

> My father David had it in his heart to build a temple for the Name of the LORD, the God of Israel. But the LORD said to my father David, 'Because it was in your heart to build a temple for my Name, you did well to have this in your heart. Nevertheless, you are not the one to build the temple, but your son, who is your own flesh and blood – he is the one who will build the temple for my Name.' The LORD has kept the promise he made: I have succeeded David my father and now I sit on the throne of Israel, just as the LORD promised, and I have built the temple for the Name of the LORD, the God of Israel.

Then, in Solomon's prayer of dedication, he asks in 8:29–30 that the eyes of the Lord

> be open toward this temple night and day, this place of which you said, 'My Name shall be there,' so that you will hear the prayer your servant prays toward this place. Hear the supplication of your servant and of your people Israel when they pray toward this place. Hear from heaven, your dwelling place, and when you hear, forgive.[50]

---

[48] Spencer 2004: 57.

[49] Cf. Pss 20:1–7 (esp. v. 7, 'we trust in the name of the Lord our God'); 44:4–8; 54:1–7.

[50] For a summary of the issues related to 'Name theology' in OT scholarship see I. Wilson 1995: 3–11.

For Solomon 'the name' was the active presence of Yahweh (in the fullness of his character), the God who would keep his promises to David, forgive and restore Israel.[51] Solomon himself recognized, however, that even the temple could not ultimately serve as a dwelling that could contain God. Now, in *Solomon's* (!) Colonnade (3:11) of the (second) temple, Peter declares that it is the 'name' of the exalted Jesus, who sits on David's throne as the Lord in fulfilment of God's promises (to David), who must be called upon, who answers prayer and who brings forgiveness, wholeness and the restoration hoped for by Solomon and anticipated by the prophets. In this context the temple and its now corrupt system contributed to the exclusion of the lame man. Now all that the temple pointed to may be found perfectly in 'the name of Jesus'.

The 'name of Jesus', therefore, is perhaps best understood in this context not simply as 'Jesus' nor even the titles 'Lord and Christ' (though it is of course not less than any of these) but the active presence of Jesus in the fullness of his character as the means of receiving God's blessings.[52] This 'fullness of character as the means of God's blessing' is what Peter highlights when he emphasizes that Jesus is the fulfilment of everything from the seed of Abraham to the suffering and exalted Servant of Isaiah.

It is in this light that we may understand why Luke has drawn attention to 'leaping over *temple* boundaries' in the miracle recounted in 3:1–10. It was a 'sign' authenticating the apostolic message that God's promised restoration of the last days is found only in the exalted Lord Jesus. As Franklin correctly observes, 'The miracle in the temple points to the fulfilment of its life in Jesus so that now the "name" of Jesus brings that salvation to which the manifestation of the divine name in the Temple had been a pointer.'[53] In 4:1–22 Luke highlights the ramifications of the authority of the name of Jesus for the authority of the temple leadership.

---

[51] Though varying emphases may be found in different contexts, the 'name' as a reference to the presence of God in the fullness of his character may be suggested by 1 Kgs 8:11, 28; 9:3. Cf. also Exod. 20:24; 34:5–7, 14; Deut. 16:11. Cf. House 1998: 254–255.

[52] O'Reilly (1987: 100) refers to the titles 'Lord' and 'Christ' (cited by Peterson 2009: 169). The 'name' of Jesus as a reference to the power and authority of Jesus is noted e.g. in Calvin 1965: 94; Barrett 1994: 183; Peterson 2009: 169.

[53] Franklin 1975: 100. Cf. also Peterson 1998: 377.

## *The end of the old temple leadership (Acts 4:1–22)*

If the 'name' of Jesus was the turning point in the account of the miracle (3:6) and the focal point in Peter's explanation (3:16), it rises to be the dominant point in this section as references to 'the name' of Jesus occur in 4:7, 10, 12, 17–18.[54] This emphasis on 'the name of Jesus', however, comes in the context of claims for authority from the temple leadership.

### *The temple authorities*

The immediate focus of attention in Acts 4 becomes clear in verses 1, 5–6. The chapter begins with reference to the 'priests and the captain of the temple guard and the Sadducees' (v. 1), all of whom are closely aligned with the temple system and have a vested interest in the operations of the temple. After recounting the imprisonment of Peter and John and the unstoppable spread of the word despite the efforts of these leaders (vv. 1–4), Luke focuses again on the rulers of the people with a full description in verses 5–6: 'the rulers, elders and teachers of the law ... Annas the high priest ... Caiaphas, John, Alexander and the other men of the high priest's family'.[55] These are, as Peter calls them, the 'rulers ... of the people' (4:8) whom Luke later specifies as the ruling council of the Sanhedrin (4:15). The issue of most concern to these 'rulers' becomes clear in 4:7 when they ask Peter and John, 'By what power or what name did you do this?' The issue being raised in this section then is the current status of the power and authority of the temple leadership.

### *Jesus' universal authority*

Peter then declares that it is by 'the name of Jesus Christ' that this man stands healed. He adds a point, however, that would be sure to disturb these temple authorities in this temple setting and it is applied with special emphasis to this audience. 'He is the stone *you* builders rejected, which has become the cornerstone.'[56] The implication here is that Jesus is 'the cornerstone of the true temple'.[57] In Luke 20:19 Luke specified that when Jesus quoted this same psalm

---

[54] Cf. also 4:30; 5:28, 40–41 (5:41 concludes these references in Acts 3 – 5 with the absolute use of 'the name').

[55] Cf. also Luke 22:52–53.

[56] In both Ps. 118:22 and in Luke 20:17 the verse simply refers to 'the builders'. Cf. Head (2004: 116) and Beale (2004: 184) for the use of this psalm in Luke 20:17.

[57] Beale 2004: 216.

he spoke about the end of the Jewish leadership (20:16). In Acts 4 Peter moves directly to a declaration of Jesus' universal authority. Salvation is found in him alone, he has universal authority as there is not another name (1) 'under heaven' and (2) given among all people (i.e. in contrast to the limited 'authority' of these rulers) that brings salvation. Thus Luke highlights the contrast between these Jewish 'rulers' and the Lord Jesus, who has universal authority not only over Israel but over all creation.[58]

Overall then, Luke's account of public temple activity in 3:1 – 4:22 draws attention to the fulfilment of God's restoration purposes in 'the name of Jesus'. The Lord Jesus culminates the hopes of Scripture and the promises of God from Abraham to Moses, David, Isaiah and 'all the prophets'. His reign as the Lord who sends the Holy Spirit and in whom forgiveness is found (Acts 1 – 2) means that believers find all they need in him. There is now no need for the old temple system and its leadership, as both have come to an end for the true people of God. The following sections (the 'interlude' in 4:23 – 5:11 and the return to public temple activity in 5:12–42) especially develop the role of the apostles as leaders of the new people of God.

## The leadership of the new Israel (Acts 4:23 – 5:11; 5:12–42)

In 4:23 – 5:11 the focus shifts as Peter and John return to 'their own people' (4:23).[59] The gathering of believers is a place of prayer (4:24–31), generosity (4:32–37) and the holy presence of God's Spirit (5:1–11). Furthermore, following the citation of Psalm 2 in their prayer in 4:24–30, the believers associate the Jewish leaders who are opposing the apostles with those who oppose God and his anointed one, the Lord Jesus,[60] and they associate the suffering apostles with

---

[58] The rest of 4:1–22 shows that the leaders are powerless in the face of this obvious 'sign' (vv. 14, 16, 18–21). The concluding verse of this section highlights again the remarkable transformation of this man (i.e. the power of the Lord Jesus) with even more force, as we are told for the first time that he had been lame for more than forty years (v. 22).

[59] *Pros tous idious* (to their own). The heading for this section ('Leadership of the new Israel') is taken from Peterson 2009: 185. Peterson, however, uses this heading with reference to 4:1–22 only. Although these themes run throughout the entire section of Acts 3 – 5, in 4:1–22 the emphasis is more on the (universal) authority of 'the name of Jesus'. The leadership of the apostles over the new people of God becomes more prominent in 4:23 – 5:42.

[60] The verb 'threaten' (*apeileō*) is used in 4:17, 'threaten further' (*prosapeileō*) is used in 4:21 and the noun 'threat' (*apeilē*) is used in 4:29. Cf. also 3:23 ('anyone who does not listen to him will be completely cut off from among his people'), 4:10–11 ('the

the Lord's Suffering Servant, the Lord Jesus.[61] Believers in Jesus, therefore, are seen here as the true people of God, and the suffering apostles, as representatives of the Lord Jesus, are the true leaders of God's people.

The leadership of the apostles over the Christian community is then illustrated in the summary passage of 4:32–37 and the incident with Ananias and Sapphira in 5:1–11.[62] Although the voluntary and occasional nature of the giving continues (4:34–35; 5:4),[63] an emphasis on the role of the apostles in the sharing of possessions is added to this picture as the placement of money at the apostles' feet is mentioned three times (4:35, 37; 5:2). Following the judgment on Ananias and Sapphira for their lie to the Holy Spirit (5:1–11), the third summary passage in these early chapters of Acts focuses especially on the public activity of the apostles (5:12, 15–16). This then leads into another clash with the temple hierarchy in 5:17–42.

### The temple authorities

Although the focus returns again to the temple in 5:17–42 (5:20–21, 24–25), in this context, following the emphasis on the leadership of the apostles over the new people of God in 4:23 – 5:11, the focus in 5:17–42 is more specifically on the apostles as the leaders of the true people of God in contrast to the temple leadership. In 5:17–24 (as with 4:1–22) the authority of the temple leadership is again noted. In 5:17, 21, 24 full descriptions of the leadership are given: 'the high priest and all his associates, who were members of the party of the Sadducees' (v. 17), 'the high priest and his associates . . . the Sanhedrin – the full assembly of the elders of Israel' (v. 21) and 'the captain of the temple guard and the chief priests' (v. 24). The rising intensity of their opposition is seen in the move from 'threats' (4:21) to imprisonment (5:18) to flogging and wanting to put them

stone you builders rejected') and 4:19 (judge whether it is right 'to obey you rather than God').

[61] This has already been indicated in 4:13 ('they took note that these men had been with Jesus'), not least because the apostles are quoting the same passage of Scripture (Ps. 118:22) that Jesus quoted to them in Luke 20:17!

[62] Cf. A. J. Thompson 2008a: 71–74, 89–90 for a comparison of these summary passages in their narrative contexts.

[63] Note that the selling and giving was 'from time to time' (as the imperfect tense in the context of 4:34 indicates), it was distributed to anyone 'as he had need' (4:35) and Ananias' property belonged to him before it was sold, and after it was sold the money was still at his 'disposal' (5:4). Thus this is not a 'community of goods' (contra Capper 1998: 499–518) but a 'community of unity', a unity expressed in concern for the needs of others.

to death (5:33, 41). This increasing hostility is also highlighted in the move from the arrest of just Peter and John (4:7) to the arrest of the apostles as a group (5:18, 21). Nevertheless, the inability of this 'full assembly of the elders of Israel' to put a stop to the apostles is evident again in the apostles' rescue from prison and the confusion of the leaders in the face of a securely locked, well-guarded, but empty, jail (vv. 23–24)!

## The teaching of the apostles

The opposition of the temple authorities to God is now emphatically contrasted with 'the apostles' (cf. vv. 18, 29, 40) or, more specifically, the *teaching* of the apostles. Thus the purpose of the apostles' miraculous release from prison is so that they will go to the temple and 'tell the people the full message of this new life' (5:19–20). Early the next morning the apostles enter the temple and 'they began to teach' (5:21). In 5:25 news comes to the temple leadership that the apostles are 'in the temple courts teaching the people'. In 5:28 the high priest declares that they were charged not 'to teach in this name' and yet the apostles have 'filled Jerusalem' with their 'teaching'. The final verse in this section declares that every day they never stopped 'teaching and preaching the good news that the Messiah is Jesus' (5:42).[64] The apostles' teaching is again (cf. 4:19–20) stated to be in obedience to God (5:29–32). In this context, given the example of apostolic preaching in 3:11–26 and the more succinct summaries in 4:8–12 and 5:29–32, it is likely that the emphasis on the 'teaching' of the apostles is the teaching that all of God's blessings (repentance, forgiveness, the Holy Spirit, restoration) are now to be found only in the name of Jesus. Thus the statement of Gamaliel (a 'teacher of the law', 5:34) that if this plan is of God 'you will not be able to stop these men; you will only find yourselves fighting against God' (5:39) becomes a commentary on the unstoppable apostolic proclamation in this section of the Lord Jesus as the only means of receiving God's blessings.[65]

In summary: Acts 3 – 5 develops the implications of Acts 1 – 2 for the old temple system and leadership in the last days. The arrival of the last days with the death, resurrection and ascension of the Lord Jesus (Acts 1 – 2) means that the temple system and leadership of

---

[64] My tr.

[65] Note the contrasts between 4:3 and 4:4, 5:18 and 5:19–21, which highlight the unstoppable word.

the old era have come to an end (Acts 3 – 5). The fulfilment of all of God's promises of blessing in the name of Jesus points to the end of the inadequate temple system (esp. 3:1–26), and the universal authority of Jesus points to the end of the Jewish leadership (4:1–22). As Jesus' authorized delegates, the apostles are the new leaders over the true people of God (4:23 – 5:42). More specifically, the apostolic teaching that Jesus has fulfilled all of God's saving promises, including all that the temple pointed to, should be followed rather than the teaching of the temple leadership. The foundation is now laid for Stephen's sermon as the climax of Acts 3 – 7.

## Stephen, the temple and Jesus (Acts 6 – 7)

Although Acts 5:42 forms an inclusio with 2:46 and helps to highlight the temple focus of chapters 3 – 5, that temple focus is intensified dramatically in chapters 6 and 7. Acts 6:1–7 then is best viewed as a transition passage that leads into the following section. It continues the previous development of the leadership of the apostles over the new people of God.[66] It also introduces Stephen, whose speech is the central feature of Acts 6:8 – 7:60.[67] The account of Stephen's speech and death then culminates two main themes which have been running throughout Acts 3 – 5: (1) Stephen's death brings to a climax the opposition that has been intensifying throughout Acts 3 – 5. Thus opposition has moved from threats to Peter and John (4:21) to the arrest and imprisonment of all the apostles (5:18),

---

[66] The threats against the church throughout Acts 3 – 7 alternate between external opposition (Acts 3 – 4), internal conflict (5:1–11), external opposition (5:12–42), back to internal conflict (6:1–7) and again to external opposition (6:8 – 7:60). In 6:1–7 the apostles demonstrate wise and godly leadership. The interplay between the initiative taken by the apostles in gathering 'all the disciples' and proposing a solution (6:2–4), followed by the involvement of 'the whole group' in choosing seven men (6:5), and finally the presentation of the chosen helpers to the apostles again who ratified the decision (6:6) is a model of harmonious cooperation. The 'frame' of 6:1 and 7 shows not only that God is preserving his people and enabling their growth despite the threat of internal conflict and external opposition, but also that the leadership of the apostles over the people of God is crucial to their continued survival. Furthermore, it is the apostles, rather than the Jewish leadership, who, like Jesus, care for widows as God has commanded (cf. Luke 18:1–8; 20:45 – 21:4; see further in ch. 6). See A. J. Thompson 2008a: 93–96 for discussion concerning the emphasis on the unity of the Christian community in this narrative context and a response to suggestions that Acts 6:1–7 conceals a so-called theological divide between 'Hellenists' and 'Hebrews'.

[67] Acts 6:7 notes that 'a large number of priests became obedient to the faith'. These priests are perhaps (like Barnabas in 4:36) contrasted with the priestly (i.e. temple leadership) opposition that has been escalating in Acts 3 – 5.

to flogging as well as desires to put all the apostles to death (5:33, 40), and now to the first death of a Christian for his proclamation of the Lord Jesus (7:59–60).[68] Despite this opposition, however, the message about the Lord Jesus has continued to spread (4:4; 5:20, 28, 39, 42). (2) Stephen's speech focuses primarily on the significance of the temple and concludes by directing attention to the reigning Lord Jesus.

In addition to culminating themes that have run throughout Acts 3 – 5, Acts 6 – 7 is also crucial for the developments that follow: (1) Stephen's death is associated with the persecution that leads to this spread of the gospel outside Jerusalem (8:1; 11:19). (2) The theological view expressed in Stephen's speech (developed below) concerning the relativization and replacement of the temple in Jesus (and God's involvement outside the temple and the land of Israel) prepares the way for the spread of the gospel outside Jerusalem and the inclusion of Samaritans and outcasts. Thus, rather than place a significant break in the narrative at Acts 6:7 (as in the outlines of Acts that follow the exact location of the summary statements), it is better to see the summary statement of the spread of the word (6:7) as located in the midst of this transition that leads to the climax of Acts 3 – 7 and a new section that begins in Acts 8. The importance of Acts 7 as a transitional chapter may be illustrated in the following diagram:

———————————————→ Acts 7 ——————————————→

| Acts 3 – 5 | Acts 8 → |
|---|---|
| (1) Gospel spreads despite rising opposition | (1) Gospel spreads beyond Jerusalem |
| (2) God's blessing is found in Jesus, not in the temple | (2) Samaritans and outcasts included |

Acts 7
(1) Stephen's death
(2) God has never been
limited to the temple:
look to Jesus

## *The charges against Stephen*

The charges brought against Stephen are particularly important for understanding the significance of his speech. These charges are repeated with slight variations in three pairs (6:11, 13, 14). In 6:11 Stephen is charged with 'blasphemy against Moses and against

[68] Cf. Cunningham 1997: 204.

God'. In verse 13 the charge is that he never stops speaking 'against this holy place and against the law', and then in support of that charge they accuse Stephen of saying that 'Jesus of Nazareth will destroy this place and change the customs Moses handed down to us' (6:14). The repetition here indicates that the two charges in 6:11 of blasphemy against Moses and against God are further developed in 6:13–14 such that 'to speak blasphemous words against Moses is to speak against the law and the customs handed down from Moses. To speak blasphemous words against God is to speak against the temple ("this holy place"; v. 13).'[69]

## Stephen's response

A major theme of Stephen's speech, therefore, is his response to the charges that he is against the law of Moses and the temple, God's dwelling place ('this holy place', 6:13). Regarding Stephen's attitude to the temple in his speech, Stephen is often viewed as either critical of the actual original building of the temple in the first place,[70] or as critical only of the limitation of God to the temple (rather than critical of the temple itself).[71] It should be noted that Luke twice indicates that these charges are not true. In 6:11 Luke notes that the opposition to Stephen 'secretly persuaded some men' to make these accusations, and then in verse 13 Luke states that they are 'false witnesses' and hence are bringing false charges. According to Luke, therefore, Stephen is neither blaspheming the law (Moses) nor the temple (God). Thus the following narrative as an account of Stephen's response to these charges indicates that the second view mentioned above has more in its favour. However, this does not mean that Stephen must then be viewed as offering unqualified endorsement of the temple (or the law) in its current form. The narrative flow of Stephen's speech indicates that he is doing more than making an abstract point about God's omnipresence. Not only is he *relativizing* the temple, but he is also pointing *beyond* the temple to Jesus, the One who supersedes the temple.[72] This is seen first in

[69] Peterson 2009: 241.

[70] Haenchen 1971: 285; Barrett 1991: 350–352; and Matthews 2010: 69.

[71] Walton 2004: 138–143; Bock 2007: 302–303.

[72] Schreiner 2008: 633–634. Schreiner states that Stephen 'suggested a change in the status of the temple in light of the fulfillment of salvation history with the coming of Jesus but he did not explicitly argue that the law and temple were no longer in force' (634). This may depend on the force of 'explicitly'. We will see below that at the conclusion of Stephen's speech he points to the fulfilment of the temple in Jesus (which therefore ends the need for the temple).

the way he shows that he is not against Moses by proclaiming the one Moses pointed to, and secondly in the way his references to the presence of God throughout his speech culminate in Jesus.

## Moses and Jesus

After the high priest's brief question 'Are these charges true?' (his only contribution to this discussion!), Stephen launches into an extended discourse, the longest in Acts, providing a history of Israel with an emphasis on certain patterns in God's plan. Stephen's history of Israel focuses on the characters of Abraham (vv. 2–8), Joseph (vv. 9–16), Moses (vv. 17–44), Joshua (v. 45), David (vv. 45–46) and Solomon (v. 47).[73] For obvious reasons Stephen's section on Moses is the longest, with three forty-year blocks (vv. 23, 30, 36).

A recurring theme that runs through Stephen's speech is the continued rejection of God's messengers. This is particularly emphasized in regard to Moses, as the rejection of Moses is highlighted three times (7:27, 35, 39).[74] That allusions are being made to Jesus here is indicated most clearly in Stephen's clarification that 'this is that Moses who told the Israelites, "God will send you a prophet like me from your own people"' (v. 37). Within the narrative of Acts in this context, however, there are also other indications that we are meant to read Stephen's account of Moses in the light of the one Moses pointed to. The terminology of Moses as 'ruler and redeemer' (*archonta kai lytrōtēn*, v. 35) reflects the language of Peter that the exalted Jesus is 'Ruler and Saviour' (*archēgon kai sōtēra*, 5:31) and the 'denial' (or 'rejection') of Moses (7:35) is also the same terminology that has been used of the Israelites' 'denial' (or 'rejection') of Jesus, 'the Holy and Righteous One' (*arneomai*, 'deny/reject', is used in 3:13–14 and 7:35).[75] Thus when Stephen reaches his conclusion in verses 51–53 and turns with intensity to a series of second-person plural pronouns to offer prophet-like judgments concerning his audience, he is only making more explicit what he has developed

---

[73] This telling of Israel's history by focusing on significant characters to recount God's dealings with his people is also reflected in Paul's speech in Acts 13:20–25 and reflects the way Luke himself is recounting the history of the church in Acts as the fulfilment of God's purposes in Jesus and his people.

[74] In addition to these references, the patriarchs were earlier 'jealous' of Joseph (v. 9), and in vv. 42–43 this pattern (of turning to idols and Egypt and rejecting the pattern given by God to Moses, vv. 39–41) is what led to the exile.

[75] Tannehill 1990: 91 (my translations, adapted from Tannehill's observations). Cf. also Luke 18:14.

throughout his speech.[76] In murdering 'the Righteous One' they are continuing this pattern of opposition to God's purposes and messengers, 'like fathers, like sons'. In rejecting Jesus, therefore, it is Stephen's accusers, rather than Stephen, who are the ones guilty of being 'against Moses'. They have rejected the one to whom Moses and the law pointed.

The rage of Stephen's accusers in 7:54 proves Stephen's point and thus they continue the pattern of their reaction to Jesus and 'their fathers' treatment of the prophets.[77] In contrast to their angry rage Stephen utters two dying prayers (vv. 59–60) that mark him out as a follower of Jesus. First Stephen commits his spirit to the Lord Jesus (as Jesus committed his to the Father in Luke 23:46). Secondly, he 'yells' a prayer of forgiveness over the crowd's 'yells' of anger (as Jesus prayed in Luke 23:34).[78] However, Stephen does so as one who now points to Jesus (v. 56) and who prays to Jesus (vv. 59–60), rather than as someone who merely follows the pattern or example of Jesus. Jesus is clearly not just a 'prophet like Moses'; he is the one who receives prayer and provides forgiveness for sin.

## *The temple and Jesus*

One of the points Stephen makes in his response to the charge that he is against the temple is that God's presence has never been limited to the temple or even to the land of Israel. Stephen gives a kind of 'theological geography' lesson from Israel's history to his audience.[79] Thus in verse 2, at the very outset of Stephen's speech, he states that 'the God of glory' appeared to Abraham in Mesopotamia (God's glory, of course was regularly associated with the temple).[80] The exodus that leads to worshipping God in 'this place' (*topos*, v.

[76] The language of stiff-necked (Exod. 33:3, 5; Neh. 9:16–17), uncircumcised hearts and ears (Jer. 6:10; 9:26), resisting the Spirit (Isa. 63:10; cf. also Acts 5:3, 9; though cf. also Acts 6:10!), killers of prophets (Neh. 9:26) and lawbreakers, reflects OT (prophetic) denunciations. Tannehill 1990: 87; Peterson 2009: 264–265.

[77] Spencer (2004: 91) notes that 'gnashing of teeth' recalls the response that Jesus said would come from those excluded from the kingdom (Luke 13:27–28).

[78] The idea that Stephen 'yells' his prayer for forgiveness over 'yelling' of the crowd is indicated by the repetition of the verb *krazō* (cried out) in 7:57 and 60 ('with a loud voice'). Cf. Bock 1996: 1867–1868 for a discussion of the text-critical issues in Luke 23:34.

[79] The tables in C. Green 2005: 64–68 helpfully point out what Green calls 'theological geography'.

[80] The 'glory of God' was associated with Solomon and the priests at the temple dedication (1 Kgs 8:10–13), Isaiah in the temple (Isa. 6:1–3) and Ezekiel in exile (Ezek. 1:4–28; 8:1–4; 10:1–22).

7) probably refers to Mount Horeb (Exod. 3:12), but the use of the term 'place' here is an allusion to the complaint in 6:13 that Stephen speaks against 'this holy place' (*tou topou tou hagiou*). Stephen is drawing attention to God's presence at Sinai (i.e. God is not limited to a temple). In verse 9 God was with Joseph in Egypt. In verses 30–33 God meets Moses in the flames of the burning bush in the desert near Mount Sinai. Once again Stephen quotes the Lord as saying that this 'place' is 'holy ground' (*ho topos . . . gē hagia*, 7:33) – another allusion to the charge in 6:13 regarding 'this holy place'. This time a 'holy place' is 'in the desert' (7:30). Finally, in verses 48–50 the words of God himself from Isaiah 66:1–2 declare the universal and uncontainable presence of God, who cannot be limited to a house. Stephen declares that God cannot be contained in the temple and therefore also relativizes the temple as the only location for God's presence.

As Stephen draws his history of Israel to a close in verses 48–50 he appears to charge his audience with turning the temple into an idol. The reference to the Most High not living in 'handmade' houses (v. 48) repeats the language used of idolatry in verse 41 as the worship of what their 'hands had made'.[81] The fact that every occurrence of the term *cheiropoiētos* (handmade) in the LXX refers to idols especially strengthens the idea that Stephen is charging his audience with idolatry here.[82] Thus Stephen indicates that the idolatry characteristic of Israel's history of rejecting God is still present in the generation of those who have rejected the Lord Jesus. As Stephen will go on to demonstrate in 7:51–53, his criticism at this point is with the attitudes and responses of the people rather than with the temple itself.[83]

Although it is unlikely that Stephen is criticizing the actual building of the temple,[84] he has relativized the temple as the location for God's presence as well as declared that God is greater than the temple. However, Stephen also points beyond the temple to

---

[81] *Ergois tōn cheirōn autōn* ('works of their hands', v. 41); *cheiropoiētois* ('handmade', v. 48).

[82] Pao (2000: 195) refers to Isa. 10:11; 16:12; 19:1; 21:9; 31:7; 46:6; Lev. 26:1, 30. Cf. also Acts 17:24.

[83] Pao 2000: 195.

[84] Just as Solomon's praise to God for the temple notes God's approval of David's desire to build a temple (1 Kgs 8:18), so Stephen associates David's finding favour with God with his request to build a dwelling place for God (Acts 7:46). Furthermore, the quotation from Isa. 66:1–2 concerning God's uncontainable presence is the same point made by Solomon in his prayer of dedication (1 Kgs 8:27).

Jesus. It is possible that, just as the promise that a descendant of David would be placed on his throne was not ultimately fulfilled in Solomon (Acts 2:29–31), so also Stephen sees the promise that David's son would build a 'dwelling place' for God as ultimately unable to be fulfilled in the temple built by Solomon.[85] It is also important, however, to read Stephen's final word that tips his accusers over the edge in verses 55–56 in the context of his whole speech.[86] It is Stephen's claims in verses 55–56 that are the immediate cause of his death and that bring to a climax the rising opposition in Acts 3 – 7. In these verses immediately before Stephen's accusers block their ears and rush towards him to drag him out and stone him, Luke states that Stephen, full of the Holy Spirit (cf. 6:3, 10), sees 'the glory of God, and Jesus standing at the right hand of God' (vv. 55–56).[87] This reference to the glory of God and the presence of God is a deliberate reference to themes found in Stephen's speech. The glory of God, which Stephen said had appeared to Abraham in Mesopotamia at the very beginning of his speech (v. 2), is now associated with Jesus. Stephen then points ('Look') and declares that heaven (the place of God's throne, v. 49) is open and Jesus is in God's presence now in a position of power and universal authority in glory as the risen and reigning 'Son of Man' (cf. Dan. 7:13). In pointing to Jesus, therefore, Stephen points away from the temple, not just because God is bigger than the temple but because in the kingdom of God, which Jesus inaugurated, Jesus is the one who fulfils the goals of the temple. Just as Stephen's death brings to a climax the rising opposition of Acts 3 – 7, so his final prayers bring to a climax the focus on the temple in Acts 3 – 7. Not only is Jesus associated with the glory of God, the presence of God and the rule of God (vv. 55–56), but in verses 59–60 Stephen also shows that Jesus is the one who receives prayer ('Stephen prayed, "Lord Jesus . . ."'), he is the one who brings access to God's presence ('receive

---

[85] Beale 2004: 217–218. Franklin (1975: 106–107) argues that the contrast between David and Solomon, though not a criticism of the actual building of the temple, is meant to highlight that the promise to David 'is realized not through the Temple, but through Jesus to whom the temple points'. Beale (2004: 219) notes that the context of Isa. 66 (esp. Isa. 63 – 66) refers to a new creation and the extension of God's heavenly temple.

[86] Sleeman (2009: 165–169) highlights the importance of this conclusion to Stephen's speech and the geographical locations for God's presence referred to throughout the speech.

[87] Note again the references to the association of God's glory with the temple (1 Kgs 8:10–13; Isa. 6:1–3; Ezek. 8:1–4; 10:1–22).

my spirit') and he is the one who grants forgiveness of sins ('do not hold this sin against them').

As indicated above, Stephen's 'theological geography' prepares the way, in this narrative context, for the spread of God's word beyond Jerusalem to the nations (as the rest of Acts will develop). In this context in which the fulfilment and replacement of the temple in Jesus are emphasized, it should also be noted that the following two accounts in the narrative of Acts refer to the inclusion of two groups who had difficulties with the temple: Samaritans and eunuchs. As we have already observed in chapter 3, the focus in 8:4–25 is on Samaria as a whole and it recalls OT references to the northern kingdom. This northern kingdom of course set up not only its own rival line of kings, but also its own rival temple and place of worship (Gerazim). It was the hope that the arrival of the long-expected Davidic King would unite the people of God under one king (Ezek. 37:15–24). It is the arrival of Jesus as the object of worship (Luke 24:52), the means of receiving forgiveness (Acts 2:38; 5:31; 7:60) and the place of God's presence (7:55–56, 59) that unites the worship of Samaria and Judea, north and south, in the kingdom of God (8:12, 14). Furthermore, as we saw in our discussion on pp. 116–118, the focus in Acts 8:26–40 is on the description of the Ethiopian as a 'eunuch'. This emphasis recalls Deuteronomy 23:1–4 and Isaiah 56:3–8. In Deuteronomy 23 eunuchs are described as those who are excluded from the assembly of the Lord.[88] In Isaiah 56:3–8, however, a day is anticipated when not only will eunuchs be accepted, but they will also have a place in God's temple, and will have joy in the Lord's 'house of prayer' (56:5, 7). Stephen's speech in Acts 7, therefore, not only brings to a climax the emphasis on the authority of Jesus in Acts 3 – 5 as the One who replaces both the temple as well as the temple leadership, but also prepares the way for the inclusion of rival northern temple builders, the Samaritans, and excluded temple outcasts such as eunuchs.[89]

Thus Stephen shows that he is not *against* Moses or the temple because (1) in proclaiming the suffering Lord Jesus, he proclaims the One whom God's suffering messengers, such as Moses, have always pointed to (and his accusers therefore belong to those who

---

[88] The term 'eunuch' is not used in Deut. 23. Note also that in Acts 8:27 the eunuch 'had gone to Jerusalem to worship'. His (disappointing) relationship with the temple is in view here.

[89] Though this has already been indicated in Acts 3:1–10.

have always been the cause of that suffering and are the ones who are opposed to Moses); and (2) in proclaiming the ascended Lord Jesus as the One with universal authority and the One who is in God's presence and who provides access to God's presence, he proclaims the culmination and fulfilment of the various locations for meeting God throughout Israel's history, including the temple (and his accusers belong to those who have been characterized by the idolatry of false worship in Israel's history). In this sense then Stephen is not critical of Solomon's building of the temple, but is also not *merely* saying that God is greater than the temple either. In response to both charges, Stephen points beyond Moses and the temple to Jesus, the One whom Moses and the temple anticipated.[90]

## Conclusion

Luke's emphasis in Acts 1 – 2 on the enthronement of Jesus as the Davidic King and the arrival of the last days anticipates clarification in Acts 3 – 7 regarding the role of the temple and temple leadership in God's kingdom under the reign of the Lord Jesus. The focus on the temple in Acts 3 – 7 is therefore deliberately chosen and linked to Acts 2. The flow of the narrative in Acts 3 – 5 and 6 – 7 indicates that both sections are to be seen together, so that there is no 'positive' (Acts 3 – 5) versus 'negative' (Acts 6 – 7) portrayal of the temple in these chapters; the two sections together provide a consistent portrait. More specifically, Acts 3 – 7 primarily highlights the apostolic proclamation of Jesus as the one with universal authority and therefore as the 'name' in whom all of God's blessings are now received. The Lord Jesus is therefore the fulfilment of and replacement for the temple and the one through whom previous temple boundaries may now be overcome. The inadequacy of the temple is contrasted with the all sufficiency of the Lord Jesus: all of God's blessings are found through faith in him alone. He is the Lord to whom all, including the temple leadership, must submit. For readers such as Theophilus, therefore, the apostolic proclamation of Jesus as the only means of receiving God's blessings must be listened to, and believers may be assured that this good news will continue to spread despite the most

---

[90] Thus, contra Barrett 1994: 338, it is unlikely that Stephen's speech contains two different responses to the temple and law (i.e. being critical of the temple but positive towards the law).

severe opposition. In the light of this emphasis on apostolic teaching and the leadership of the apostles, the role of the law in this new era has also undergone a change. It is to the role of the law, therefore, that we now turn.

## Chapter Six

# The end of an era: the law is no longer the direct authority for God's people

In the previous chapter we observed that Acts 3 – 7 shows the ramifications for the old-era institutions of temple and temple leadership in the light of the emphasis in Acts 1 – 2 on the reign of the Davidic King Jesus in the inaugurated kingdom of God. The pouring out of the Holy Spirit is evidence that the Lord Jesus reigns from the throne of David, the last days have arrived and God's last-days promises for the restoration of his people are being fulfilled. Since God's intentions for the temple have been fulfilled in Jesus and since Jesus now reigns as Lord and his chosen apostles are the new leaders of God's new people (those who have turned to Jesus in repentance and faith and have received God's blessings of forgiveness and the Holy Spirit), then what has become of the Mosaic law in this new age? This question is all the more pressing given Jesus' words that 'the Law and the Prophets were proclaimed until John. Since that time, the good news of the kingdom of God is being preached' (Luke 16:16).[1] What is the relationship between the law of Moses and the people of God now, in the inaugurated kingdom after Jesus' ascension? After a brief orientation to some of the debate about the law in Acts, this chapter will argue that Luke points to the authority of the Lord Jesus and the teaching of his apostles as the direct guiding authority for God's people now that the One to whom the Mosaic law pointed has come.[2] Thus although Luke is not against the Mosaic law, he emphasizes (1) that the proclamation of Jesus is a proclamation of the one to whom the law

---

[1] Luke 16:17–18 then shows that the law continues to point to the kingdom (v. 16) but that nevertheless Jesus is now the 'sovereign interpreter' of the law (v. 18). For a succinct summary of the role of the law in Luke-Acts see Schreiner 2010: 171–180 (the phrase 'sovereign interpreter' is Schreiner's, 175–176).
[2] In this sense we are focusing on the role of the law as the authority for how believers must conduct themselves. The phrase 'direct guiding authority' is borrowed from Moo's phrase 'direct and immediate source of guidance' (1993: 375 [319–376]).

pointed; (2) the authority and teaching of the apostles is now the guiding authority for believers in Jesus; and (3) even though, under the direct authority of the Lord Jesus and his apostles, aspects of the law are no longer required, this shift does not mandate insensitivity to Jews.

## The debate about the law in Acts

Some have argued that Lukan theology is 'fundamentally Mosaic'.[3] Vielhauer's famous essay 'On the "Paulinism" of Acts' asserted that Paul is portrayed as 'a Jewish Christian who is utterly loyal to the law'.[4] Jervell has become particularly influential since his essay 'The Law in Luke-Acts', where he argued that 'the Law is not invalidated, abridged or outmoded'.[5] Others, however, have dissented from the conclusion that Luke is 'fundamentally Mosaic'.[6] Inevitably, much of this discussion revolves around certain practices of Paul in Acts (i.e. circumcision in 16:3; participation in vows in 18:18; 21:22–26) and the nature of the decree at the Jerusalem Council (15:20, 29; 21:25). Those who see more of a consistency between Acts and Paul's letters on the view of the law correctly note that (1) such practices in Acts do not contradict Paul's teaching elsewhere that circumcision is a matter of indifference (Gal. 5:6; 6:15); (2) as long as the matter is not made a requirement for salvation (Gal. 2:3–5), Paul is willing to 'become like a Jew' (i.e. to follow the law) when there is opportunity 'to win those under the law' (1 Cor. 9:19–23); and (3) the law is nevertheless 'fulfilled' by Christians, as they are

---

[3] Catchpole (1977: 428) used this phrase in his summary of Lukan scholarship on the law. Cf. also the evaluation in Blomberg 1998: 398–399. Some of the following discussion on Luke's view of the Mosaic law is adapted from A. J. Thompson 2008a: 79–81, 89–104. The focus there was on Luke's view of the law in the wider literary context of ancient discussions of unity.

[4] Vielhauer 1966: 33. Vielhauer even claimed that Luke advocates a doctrine of salvation by works (42).

[5] The essay appears in Jervell 1972: 133–151 (the citation here is from p. 143). Cf. also Jervell's defence of this view in 1996: 54–61; and 1998: 100–103. Tyson (2001: 140, 142) notes the influence of F. C. Baur (that the Lukan Paul is essentially Jewish in his adherence to the Mosaic law) in the work of John Knox, Gerd Lüdemann, Jervell, Goulder and Barrett. Indeed, Tyson speaks of a 'Tübingen revival'.

[6] Representatives of this view are Bruce 1975–6: 282–305; Turner 1982: 99–158; Seifrid 1987: 39–57; Blomberg 1984: 53–80; 1998: 397–416. S. G. Wilson (1983: 58) criticizes several of Jervell's arguments (see below on Acts 15) yet argues that, on balance, in Acts 'the criticism of the law is generally implicit and has to be read between the lines, whereas the affirmation of the law is generally explicit'.

under 'the law of Christ' (Gal. 5:14; 6:2; Rom. 13:10).[7] When these perspectives from Paul's letters are kept in mind, the accounts of his practices in the book of Acts do not require the conclusion that the Paul of Acts is more 'Mosaic' than the Paul of the letters. We will focus, however, on Luke's view of the law in Acts.

## Jesus: the one to whom the law pointed has now come

Luke emphasizes that believers in Jesus are not opposed to the Mosaic law because the law is 'fulfilled' in Jesus. The frequent charge of Jewish opponents in Acts that Christians are opposed to Moses and the law indicates that this is a major feature in Luke's view of the law (Acts 6:11, 13–14; 18:13; 21:21, 28). The defences against these charges by Stephen and Paul in particular, however, as well as Luke's statement that the charges against Stephen are false charges, indicate that Luke's view is that believers are obviously *not* opposed to the law. As observed above, Stephen's defence in Acts 7 draws to a conclusion with his own charge that it is not he but his accusers who have disobeyed the law (7:53). Specifically, in his proclamation of the rejected and risen Lord Jesus, Stephen proclaims the one to whom Moses pointed. A similar point is made by Peter in Acts 3. Peter, like Stephen, proclaims the one Moses spoke about. More than that, Moses said that 'you must listen to everything he tells you. Anyone who does not listen to him will be completely cut off from among his people' (3:22–23). Thus failure to listen to Jesus is disobedience to Moses and will incur the judgment of God.

The final chapters of Acts are devoted to defending Paul and the gospel in a similar way. Paul repeatedly declares in Acts 21 – 28 that he believes 'everything that agrees with the Law and that is written in the prophets' (24:14); he has 'done nothing wrong against the law of the Jews or against the temple or against Caesar' (25:8, 10); he is 'saying nothing beyond what the prophets and Moses said would happen' (26:22); and he has 'done nothing against our

---

[7] That Paul does not view himself as directly under the law may be seen e.g. in 1 Cor. 9:20–21; Rom. 14:5; Col. 2:16; Gal. 2:3–5. That Paul views the law as being able to be 'fulfilled' by Christians may be seen e.g. in Rom. 13:8, 10; Gal. 5:14; 6:2; 1 Cor. 9:21. On 'fulfilling the law' in Pauline theology see Westerholm 2004: 433–439 and Moo 1993: 319–376.

people or against the customs of our ancestors' (28:17).[8] As we saw in chapter 2, it is the death and resurrection of Jesus that Paul repeatedly claims to be the fulfilment of the hopes of Moses and the prophets (23:6; 24:15, 21; 26:8, 23). Thus Paul declares that his proclamation of the resurrection is the fulfilment of the same hope that his fellow Jews have (23:6; 24:15; 26:6–7) and is therefore 'the hope of Israel' (28:20).[9] In this sense then, Jesus' followers are not *against* the law and the prophets, the One they proclaim as risen Lord was *anticipated* by the law and the prophets!

# Apostolic leadership and authority

## Apostolic authority and teaching

As we observed in chapter 5, the opening chapters of Acts indicate that a shift has taken place regarding who the leaders of the new people of God are. The direct authority now for believers is found primarily in the teaching of the apostles. In Acts 1 the apostles are described in close association with the Lord Jesus as his 'authorized delegates'. Thus they are chosen by the Lord Jesus (1:2), taught by him (1:2) and commissioned by the Lord Jesus to bear witness to him (1:8). The account of the appointment of the twelfth apostle in the final verses of Acts 1 emphasizes this close relationship even more. The one who will take over this 'apostolic ministry' (1:25) and be 'added to the eleven apostles' (1:26) must be one who was with the apostles throughout the whole of Jesus' ministry (1:21), which is then further clarified as 'beginning from John's baptism to the time when the Lord Jesus was taken up' (1:22). Like the other eleven apostles, therefore, the replacement for Judas must have been taught by Jesus, must have seen the risen Lord Jesus so as to bear witness to Jesus (1:23), and must also be personally chosen by the Lord Jesus

---

[8] In these same contexts Paul is portrayed in contrast to his accusers who really are lawbreakers. Paul speaks with prophetic judgment against the High Priest for commanding that Paul be struck in violation of the law (23:2–3) and in this same context the chief priests, elders and Sanhedrin are involved in a plot to murder Paul: an obvious violation of the law (23:14–15; cf. also 7:52–53, 57–58).

[9] A focus merely on the first set of statements that Paul is in agreement with the law and the prophets to the neglect of these clarifications by Paul as to why he is in agreement with the law and the prophets (i.e. he proclaims their fulfilment in Jesus' resurrection) leads to a more one-sided emphasis on the continuity of the Mosaic law in the recent study of Butticaz (2009: 128).

(1:24).[10] The status of the apostles as the 'authorized delegates' of the risen Lord Jesus is clearly established in Acts 1.

The focus then turns to the *message* of the apostles in Acts 2. Peter stands 'with the Eleven' when he raises his voice and addresses the crowd (2:14). Likewise, in 2:37 the people respond 'to Peter *and the other apostles*'. Those who accept this apostolic message to call on the name of the Lord Jesus for salvation (2:21, 36–41) then devote themselves to 'the apostles' teaching' (2:42). In the light of the Jewish commitment to the teaching of Moses elsewhere in Acts (e.g. 6:14; 15:21; 21:21, 28) this description of devotion to the teaching, not of Moses, but of the apostles, is a striking early indication that a new authority is in place for God's people.

As we noted in chapter 5, the narrative flow of Acts 3 – 7 shows that the Davidic King Jesus who reigns as Lord on the throne of David fulfils and replaces the temple in the inaugurated kingdom of God – Jesus is now the only means by which all of God's blessings are received. We also saw that, along with this emphasis on the temple, Luke highlights the end of the temple leadership in Acts 3 – 5. The authority of the temple leadership is contrasted with the universal authority of the Lord Jesus (4:7, 12) and there is a growing emphasis on the leadership and teaching of the apostles (who are closely associated with the Lord Jesus, 4:13, 27–30) for the new people of God (4:33, 35, 37; 5:2, 12). The emphasis in 5:17–42 is especially on the *teaching* of the apostles about the Lord Jesus (5:20–21, 25, 28–32, 40). Thus Acts 3 – 5 culminates in the statement that the apostles 'day after day in the temple courts and from house to house never stopped teaching and proclaiming the good news that Jesus is the Christ' (5:42). It is especially noteworthy then that in this context Gamaliel, a 'teacher of the law', declares that the Jewish leaders should 'Leave these men alone! Let them go! For if their purpose or activity is of human origin, it will fail. But if it is from God, you will not be able to stop these men; you will only find yourselves fighting against God' (5:38–39). The reign of the Lord Jesus, who enables the message of the apostles concerning Jesus to spread despite opposition, is the theme of Acts 3 – 7 (cf. 6:7). Because the apostles are the authorized delegates of the reigning Lord Jesus, it is their teaching that must now be listened to (5:17–42); it is response to their teaching about faith in the Lord Jesus that brings salvation

---

[10] The uniqueness of this appointment is indicated by these qualifications and the fact that no replacement was necessary following James's death in Acts 12.

and a place among the true people of God (2:41; 4:4; 5:14); it is their leadership that enables the people of God to continue to grow as one people under the Lord Jesus (6:1–7); and it is therefore the message they proclaim about the Lord Jesus that will continue to spread despite opposition (5:38–39, 41–42; 6:7; 8:4).

## Apostolic authority where aspects of the law are fulfilled

In this section we will examine two passages where aspects of the law are fulfilled in the life of the early Christian community (Acts 4:32–37; 6:1–7). First, the general statement in the second summary passage that 'there were no needy persons among them' (Acts 4:34) reflects the wording of Deuteronomy 15:4.[11] In the context of Deuteronomy 15 God's people are promised that there will be 'no needy persons' among them when they experience God's blessing in the land he is giving them, if they follow the law (15:5).[12] Secondly, the provision for widows in Acts 6 is in keeping with the law's injunctions to provide for widows.[13] The command to provide for widows is especially emphasized in Deuteronomy, where it is often linked with the Lord's blessing 'in all the work of your hands' (cf. Deut. 14:29; 24:19 [17–22]; 26:12–15; cf. also 10:18). In Deuteronomy 27 one of the curses to which 'all the people' respond with 'Amen' is the curse on 'the man who withholds justice from the alien, the fatherless or the widow' (27:19). Thus the provision for the widows in Acts 6 fulfils the injunctions of Deuteronomy in the Christian community.

In both of these contexts in Acts, however, the emphasis is on the authority of the apostles. In Acts 4:34, for example, the fulfilment of Deuteronomy is found in a context that particularly emphasizes the

[11] Barrett 1994: 254; Fitzmyer 1998: 314; Witherington 1998: 207; Bock 2007: 214–215; Peterson 2009: 205.

[12] *Oude gar endeēs tis ēn en autois* ('there was not a needy person among them', Acts 4:34); *ouk estai en soi endeēs* ('there will be no needy person among you', Deut. 15:4).

[13] This is often neglected in studies of Acts 6. C. C. Hill (1992) in his response to Baur has no discussion of widows in his study. Similarly, Conzelmann (1987: 44–46) discusses 'the disciples', 'the twelve' and 'the seven' but not 'the widows'; Blomberg's discussions of Acts 6 – 7, in 1984: 63–64 and 1998: 403–404, also have no mention of the widows. Spencer (1994: 715–733) draws attention to the neglect of the widows in this passage. He, however, blames the apostles for their condescending response in comparison to Peter's treatment of the widows in Acts 9:41 (728–733). For further discussion see A. J. Thompson 2008a: 93–96. In addition to the texts cited above, see Deut. 16:11, 14; Isa. 1:17, 23; 10:2; 47:8; Jer. 5:28 (LXX); 7:6; 22:3; Ezek. 22:7; Mal. 3:5; Zech. 7:10.

authority of the apostles. There is 'no needy person' (4:34) because the grace of God brings about this new situation (4:33) and, as the repeated references to the placement of proceeds at 'the apostles' feet' indicates (4:35; 4:37; 5:2), because the apostles are responsible for administering these voluntary donations.[14] Similarly, the provision for widows in Acts 6 is accomplished by the initiative and leadership of the apostles (6:2–4). They overcome this need through men 'full of . . . the Holy Spirit' (6:3), and the result is a continued spread of the word and increase in disciples (6:1, 7). Thus, although the injunctions of Deuteronomy concerning the needy and widows among God's people are being 'fulfilled', the emphasis in Acts is not so much on specific laws cited and then obeyed in these contexts, but on the enablement of God through the apostolic leadership which brings about provision for the needy and widows among the people of God.[15]

## Apostolic authority where aspects of the law are abrogated

The abrogation of aspects of the law in Acts is also evidence that the guiding authority for believers in the Lord Jesus is now the leadership and teaching of the apostles, as authorized delegates of the Lord Jesus, rather than the Mosaic law.

### The conversion of Cornelius

The abrogation of certain laws is explicit in the account of Cornelius' conversion in Acts 10 – 11.[16] Among other things this passage emphasizes (1) the abrogation of the food laws, (2) the acceptance of Gentiles without circumcision, and (3) the impartiality of God.[17] Jervell argues that Luke's view of the law as continuing without abrogation is seen in his omission (in Luke's Gospel) of Jesus' statement that all foods have been made clean (from Mark

---

[14] Peterson (2009: 205) notes that the Greek text of Acts 4:34 indicates that this is evidence of the grace of God at work among them with the conjunction *gar* (for). Thus 4:33–34 should read, 'much grace was upon them all for there was no needy person among them' (brought out more clearly in the TNIV).

[15] Contra Fitzmyer 1998: 314, who states that the ideal of Deut. 15 was 'actually governing the life of Jewish Christians in Jerusalem'.

[16] Abrogation of aspects of the Mosaic law is hinted at already in the inclusion of the eunuch in Acts 8. As indicated in ch. 3, the demands of Deut. 23:1–4 appear to be overcome in the inclusion of the eunuch as a full member of God's people in fulfilment of Isa. 56:3–8. Cf. A. J. Thompson 2008a: 96–99.

[17] Cf. Acts 10:34.

7:17–23). This is countered, however, by the Lord's statement at the climax of the vision in Acts 10:10–15: 'What God has cleansed, you must not call common' (Acts 10:15 RSV).[18] In the narrative of Acts, Peter has clearly made the connection between the vision concerning the abrogation of food laws (Acts 10:15) and the association with and acceptance of Cornelius (10:28; 11:12; 15:9).[19] It also should be noted that in the vision of verses 10–15 Peter is not encouraged to break God's laws. Rather, it is the Lord himself who determines in his sovereignty that he has made these things clean and therefore Peter is not to call them unclean.[20] The overall emphasis of the passage, therefore, is that a salvation-historical shift has taken place. God has taken the sovereign initiative in declaring a change to the food laws and in including Gentiles like Cornelius. It is by faith in the Lord Jesus for forgiveness of sins that one is cleansed (10:43; 15:9). As Peter had already emphasized in his messages to Jewish audiences earlier in Acts, God's blessings are now found through the Lord Jesus alone (10:36, 42–43, 48; 11:17). Thus clearly a shift has taken place in the role of the direct authority of the law. The reference to the apostles in 11:1 followed by a speech by (the apostle) Peter highlights again the role of the new leadership in leading God's people even as aspects of the law are abrogated.

## The council on circumcision

Similar themes are found in the account of the Jerusalem Council in Acts 15.[21] The issue is clearly stated in 15:1 where some from Judea

---

[18] Jervell 1972: 139–140, 149. Jervell's argument that the law is not abrogated here because Peter enters the house only after God had cleansed him is countered by Peter's statement that he would be transgressing Jewish standards (*athemiton*) after entering the house and that the cleansing took place after the gospel was heard (Acts 15:7–9). Cf. the criticism of Jervell in Turner 1982: 116. Contra Klinghardt 1988: 212–213, who argues that the reference to food is merely symbolic and that the focus is on the Gentiles as not unclean. Salo (1991: 208–210) claims that Luke is deliberately ambiguous.

[19] Cf. S. G. Wilson 1983: 68–70; Bovon 1970: 22–45, cited by Pao 2000: 236. The emphasis of the passage on the acceptance of and 'table fellowship' with *Gentiles* is seen in 10:45; 11:1, 18; 15:7. Cf. J. T. Sanders 1991: 434–455; contra Jervell 1988: 11–20.

[20] Spencer 2004: 121.

[21] It is often suggested that Acts 15 is a 'Lukan' view of the events described from a Pauline view in Gal. 2:1–10 (cf. most recently Marguerat 2009: 106–107, 109–110). More persuasive, however, is the view that these accounts refer to two different events addressing different concerns with different settings and that Gal. 2:1–10 fits better with Paul's visit to Jerusalem in Acts 11:27–30 (Witherington 1998: 440–449; Schnabel 2004, 2: 987–992).

had come to Antioch and declared that 'unless you are circumcised, according to the custom taught by Moses, you cannot be saved'. Then at the Council itself the issue is stated again in such a way as to highlight the implications of this requirement of circumcision for the role of the Mosaic law more generally: 'The Gentiles must be circumcised and required to obey the law of Moses' (15:5).[22] After Luke's statement that 'the apostles and elders met to consider this question' (15:6), Peter's opening response clarifies that salvation is by God's gracious initiative and is through faith (15:7), that the gift of the Holy Spirit is evidence of inclusion among God's people (15:8), that faith in the Lord Jesus brings cleansing (15:9) and, in an interesting turn of phrase, that it is Jews who by the grace of the Lord Jesus are saved through faith just as Gentiles are (15:11).[23] The implication of this is that circumcision is not even required for Jews, let alone Gentiles, in order to belong to the people of God. In fact this statement of salvation by grace through faith is stated in sharp contrast (highlighted in 15:11 by the strong adversative *alla*, 'but') to the law, which is described as a 'yoke' in 15:10, a yoke neither Peter and his fellow Jews nor their fathers have been able to bear![24] Following this emphasis on 'faith alone', Barnabas, Paul and James continue to emphasize God's initiative in including the Gentiles. Paul and Barnabas do so by highlighting God's work among the Gentiles through them; and James does so by highlighting the fulfilment of God's promises in the prophets.[25] Up to this point then the

---

[22] Contra Butticaz 2009: 120–121, 15:1 indicates that the issue of circumcision here has to do with soteriology, how one is saved, rather than merely social identity. Furthermore, the restatement of the issue in 15:5 indicates that circumcision is mentioned not merely as an 'identity marker' but as part of adherence to the law of Moses more broadly.

[23] As noted earlier, this translation ('through the grace of the Lord Jesus we believe in order to be saved') of 15:11 better reflects the structure of the Greek text (*pisteuomen sōthēnai*) than that of the NIV ('we believe it is through the grace of our Lord Jesus that we are saved'). Nolland 1980–1: 112–113; Tannehill 1990: 185.

[24] Blomberg 1984: 64; Turner 1982: 118–119; Pao 2000: 239–240. Salo (1991: 237–243) thinks that Acts 15:10 is inconsistent with Luke's view, expressed in James's speech. The view of Peter here is consistent with that expressed by Paul in 13:38–39 that 'it is faith in Christ, not Law, that grants forgiveness of sins' (Marguerat 2009: 103). Contra Marguerat, however, in view of Rom. 4:4–8, the close association between justification by faith and forgiveness of sins in Acts 13:38–39 is certainly faithful to Paul's presentation of justification (Marguerat cites only Col. 1:14 and Eph. 1:7 as 'deutero-Pauline').

[25] See ch. 3 regarding James's reference to Amos, the restoration of Israel and the inclusion of the Gentiles.

Council establishes that salvation is by God's grace through faith in the Lord Jesus.

Questions remain regarding the role of the law, however, when at the conclusion of the Council James adds certain 'requirements' for Gentiles (15:20; cf. also 15:29; 21:25). These requirements seem, on the face of it, to indicate the ongoing validity of the Mosaic law for the Gentiles after all. The injunctions to abstain from strangled animals (*pniktos*), blood (*haima*), the 'food polluted by idols' (*alisgymata tōn eidōlōn*, 15:20) or 'food sacrificed to idols' (*eidōlothyta*, 15:29), and sexual immorality (*porneia*) seem to impose a strange collection of moral and ceremonial laws.[26] If these are drawn from the Mosaic law it is difficult to know, however, why just these four laws are selected out of all of the laws commanded by Moses. According to Jervell, the apostolic decree 'enjoins Gentiles to keep the Law, and they keep that part of the Law required for them to live together with Jews'.[27] Specifically, Jervell argues that the apostolic decree in Acts 15 refers to Leviticus 17 – 18 and the requirements for 'strangers' among Israelites.[28] In his critique of this view, however, Wilson correctly argues that it is difficult to link *pniktos* (strangled animals) with Leviticus 17 – 18 (the term is not found anywhere in the LXX) and the term *porneia* (immorality) is unlikely to be limited to the forms of incest listed in Leviticus 18.[29] It should also be noted that there were numerous other laws, in addition to these, for the 'sojourner' in the land of Israel.[30] In this context it is remarkable that when these injunctions are sent to the churches, these four restrictions are presented as the *sole* requirements and no link is made to the Mosaic law as the basis for these requirements. The letter to these Gentile believers states, 'It seemed good to the Holy Spirit and to us *not to burden you with anything beyond*

---

[26] Contra Polhill 1992: 331–332, the inclusion of *porneia* in this list indicates that the requirements are more than just ceremonial laws. The manuscript evidence is against the Western text with its three prohibitions (omitting *pniktos*) and the addition of the golden rule in its negative form. Cf. Metzger 1994: 379–383.

[27] Jervell 1972: 144.

[28] Jervell 1998: 396–398. Cf. also Polhill 1992: 331–332; Bauckham 1995: 459–480; Schnabel 2004, 2: 1016–1018; Pervo 2009: 376–378.

[29] S. G. Wilson 1983: 84–94.

[30] Cf. Exod. 23:12; Lev. 16:29; 20:2; 22:10, 18; Num. 15:30; Deut. 16:11, 14; 26:11. Blomberg (1998: 409) cites these references and observes that Deut. 31:12 even implies that 'the sojourner was expected to obey all the law'. Pao (2000: 241–242) notes that the laws in Lev. 17 – 18 are intended for 'foreigners living among the Jews in the land of Israel' and that residence in the land of Israel is obviously not the context of Acts 15. Cf. also Witherington 1998: 464–465.

*the following requirements*' (15:28). The obvious question remains: if immorality is ruled out, then why not stealing, lying and other 'moral laws'?[31]

Thus some have argued in opposition to this view that these are essentially ad hoc requirements just for this situation out of concern for the sensitivities of Jews.[32] So, these are just a collection of laws that reflect the kinds of things most offensive to Jewish sensibilities. In contrast to those such as Jervell who see this as the imposition of the Mosaic law, advocates of this view highlight (1) the 'occasional' nature of these requirements as the letter is specifically addressed to Gentile believers in Antioch, Syria and Cilicia (the areas where the problems arose),[33] and (2) the lack of any 'legislative' force to these requirements as they are presented as what 'seemed good', there are *no other requirements,* and these believers would 'do well' to avoid these things (15:28–29).[34] Thus, in this view, the Jerusalem Council essentially concludes that although salvation is by grace through faith in the Lord Jesus, and although circumcision or observance of the law is not required in order to be saved, nevertheless, Gentiles should be sensitive to Jews when they live in their midst and avoid immorality and the kinds of food most offensive to them.

Although this view is more likely than the view that associates these requirements with Leviticus, it seems that this second view nevertheless overlooks the general applicability of these requirements to all Gentiles in 15:19 and 21:25 (cf. also 16:4) and downplays the repeated emphasis on the authority of the apostles and elders throughout this account (15:2, 4, 6, 22–23, 28; 16:4). The references to 'requirements' (*epanankes,* 'necessary things', 15:28), and especially 'the decisions' of the apostles and elders (*ta dogmata,* 'rules, regulations', 16:4),[35] indicate that there is more 'force' to these requirements than advocates of the ad hoc view suggest. What must be noted about these 'decrees', therefore, is that (even if they were based on Lev. 17 – 18) they have been 'filtered'

---

[31] Seifrid 1987: 50.

[32] Blomberg 1998: 408–410. Cf. also Seifrid 1987: 44, 47; Turner 1982: 118–119. Schreiner (2008: 638; 2010: 183–184) also sees the issue here as sensitivity to Jews.

[33] Blomberg 1998: 408.

[34] Ibid.

[35] As many have noted, this term is 'widely used for official declarations and laws'. L. T. Johnson 1992: 284. Cf. also Witherington 1998: 477; Barrett 1998: 763. Haenchen (1971: 479) notes the similarity to imperial edicts.

through the leadership[36] of the new community. The emphasis on the nature of the four 'requirements' is that they are the decrees of 'the apostles and elders', not the direct imposition of the 'laws of Moses'.[37] The Mosaic law has been displaced as the direct governing authority for the people of God.[38] Nevertheless, the issue of the source of these regulations requires explanation. In this regard the best explanation is still Witherington's argument that these requirements relate primarily to pagan practices associated with temple idolatry.[39]

Among Witherington's detailed and helpful arguments, he particularly notes the following: (1) the reason why the four restrictions against idol food, blood, strangled animals and immorality are grouped together is because they were all associated with pagan temple practices;[40] (2) the language of Gentiles 'turning to God' in Acts 15:19 is similar to the language in 1 Thessalonians 1:9, where the Thessalonian believers are described as those who 'turned to God *from idols*';[41] and (3) an association of food and immorality with idolatry is also found in 1 Corinthians 10 (cf. vv. 6–8, 14–22). In that context Paul declares, 'Therefore, my dear friends, flee from idolatry' (1 Cor. 10:14). The Jerusalem decree then forms part of a wider polemic against idolatry in (1) the narrative of Acts,[42] (2) Paul's own preaching where he critiques

---

[36] Contra Tyson 2001: 105–124, the transition from Peter to James and the appearance of 'elders' together with the apostles is not evidence of underlying conflict. Cf. Bauckham 1995: 427–441.

[37] Note also that the basis for James's decision in v. 19 ('therefore') appears to be the new salvation-historical situation brought about by the Davidic King and the restoration of the Davidic kingdom (vv. 16–18).

[38] S. G. Wilson (1983: 107) emphasizes the apostolic authority of the Council. Contra Jervell 1996: 59, who disputes the apostolic authority of the decree in favour of Mosaic authority. Marguerat (2009: 109–112) likewise claims that Mosaic authority is being upheld in the Jerusalem Council (he briefly describes the decree as an 'apostolic *didache* legitimated by the Holy Spirit' [111], but this is overshadowed by his insistence that they are merely mandating Mosaic prescriptions).

[39] Witherington 1993: 237–254; 1998: 459–467. A view entirely overlooked in the recent discussions of the decree by Marguerat (2009: 109–112) and Butticaz (2009: 124–129), but taken up by Steffeck in the same volume (2009: 133–140).

[40] Cf. 2 Macc. 6.4–5 (RSV), 'the temple was filled with debauchery and revelling by the Gentiles, who dallied with harlots and had intercourse with women within the sacred precincts, and besides brought in things for sacrifice that were unfit'. Cf. also Mal. 1:7 (LXX), where *alisgeō* refers to food offered on altars.

[41] Pao 2000: 242. *Epistrephousin epi ton theon* (Acts 15:19); *epestrepsate pros ton theon* (1 Thess. 1:9).

[42] Ibid. 181–216.

idolatry in Acts 14:16; 17:24–31; 19:26;[43] and (3) the wider context of early Christianity.[44]

The Jerusalem Council therefore clarifies two issues involved in how Gentiles may be saved: (1) Gentiles do not have to become Jews; salvation for Jew and Gentile alike is by grace alone through faith in the Lord Jesus alone. (2) However, Gentiles cannot remain pagan idolaters either; they must turn from their pagan idolatrous past.[45] Essentially then, the Jerusalem Council applies the way for pagan idolatrous Gentiles to be saved: faith (in the Lord Jesus) and repentance (turning from idolatry). In the context of 15:1 and 5, which urge the imposition of the law of Moses, 15:10, which highlights the difficulty the Jews have had in observing the law,[46] 15:11, which then indicates a rejection of the imposition of the law, and the statement of James that 'we should not make it difficult for the Gentiles who are turning to God' (15:19), it is likely that the reference in 15:21 to Moses being preached and read everywhere on every Sabbath is a further reference to the difficulty being imposed on Gentiles outside the Christian community. Thus James essentially states, 'We should not make it difficult for the Gentiles turning to God . . . (we should, of course, urge them to repent from their pagan idolatry) . . . for it is made difficult enough in the synagogues every Sabbath.'[47] This view of the decree, therefore, makes most sense of the reason why (1) these four requirements are grouped together; (2) there is an emphasis on the decisions of the apostles and elders rather than an appeal directly to the Mosaic law as the basis for Gentile behaviour;[48] (3) the decrees are applicable to pagan idolatry among Gentiles more generally; and (4) the decrees are not presented as options but as the 'requirements' or 'regulations' of the apostles and elders.[49]

---

[43] Thus putting an end to speculation as to whether or not Paul would agree with the supposed imposition of these 'Mosaic laws' upon Gentiles.

[44] In addition to 1 Thessalonians and 1 Corinthians, Witherington (1998: 466–467) refers to Rev. 2:14, 22 and the *Didache* (6:2).

[45] Contra Butticaz 2009: 128–129, the decree is not discussing cultural customs only. Note that as Peter's emphasis on salvation by grace through faith in the Lord Jesus has already indicated, it is the requirements for salvation in the message of the gospel that are being debated in this context.

[46] A view consistent with Stephen's assessment of Jewish inability to keep the law (Acts 7:53) and also Paul's assessment in Acts 13:39 and in his letters (Gal. 3:10–11; Rom. 3:19–20; 4:15; 5:20; 7:7–25).

[47] Contra Marguerat 2009: 111, 'the Mosaic antiquity of the demands of the decree' is not affirmed in 15:21.

[48] I.e. in contrast to the 'Lev. 17 – 18 view'.

[49] I.e. in contrast to the 'ad hoc view'.

# Sensitivity to Jewish beliefs about the law

In this chapter we have seen that, although Luke is not against the law, he nevertheless emphasizes (1) that the proclamation of Jesus is a proclamation of the one to whom the law pointed, and (2) the teaching of the apostles as the authorized delegates of the Lord Jesus is now the direct authority for believers in Jesus. We will now clarify that in Acts, even though believers are under the direct authority of the Lord Jesus and his apostles and the Mosaic law is no longer the direct authority for believers in Jesus, Luke also demonstrates that this shift does not mandate insensitivity to Jews.

## *Timothy and circumcision*

Although we have observed that compromise for the sake of Jewish sensibilities is not the point of the decrees at the Jerusalem Council, this issue is nevertheless taken up in the immediate context with Timothy's circumcision in 16:1–5. That the themes raised in Acts 15 are still on view in 16:1–5 is indicated by (1) the reference to circumcision again (of Timothy, whose father was a Gentile) and (2) the explicit reference to the decrees of the apostles and elders from Acts 15 which are now being delivered. Spencer helpfully outlines the flow of the narrative in 15:1 – 16:5 as (1) Dissension (15:1–5), (2) Discussion (15:6–18), (3) Decision (15:19–29), and (4) Dissemination (15:30 – 16:5)![50] The reference to Paul's circumcision of Timothy in the section immediately following an account in which circumcision was declared to be unnecessary is particularly striking. This narrative location together with the reference to the decrees of the Council in 16:4 indicates that Luke intends this to be read in the light of the account in Acts 15. At one level this indicates that the decision to be circumcised is now a matter of freedom.[51] Acts 15 did not introduce a new law that now mandates uncircumcision! The Council merely affirmed that repentance and faith *are* required for salvation and that circumcision is *not* required for salvation.

More specifically, in 16:3 Luke provides readers with the reason for this circumcision of Timothy: 'Paul wanted to take him along on the journey, so he circumcised him *because of the Jews who lived in that area*, for they all knew that his father was a Greek.' Timothy,

[50] Spencer 2004: 163. Thus in the narrative of Acts a major break does not take place at 15:36, as seen in the 'missionary journey' structures of Acts.

[51] C. Green 2005: 95.

therefore, is not circumcised by Paul here because of Paul's commitment to conform to the law of Moses, nor is he circumcised in order to be saved (as some from Judea were advocating in 15:1, 5).[52] The practice here is still consistent with the principle that circumcision is not required for salvation. Rather, the reason given is specific: it was because of the Jews in that area, who all knew Timothy's father was a Greek (his father had perhaps opposed his Jewish mother's desire to have him circumcised on the eighth day).[53] The best suggestion, in the light of Paul's desire to have Timothy accompany him on the journey, is that, being uncircumcised but with a Jewish mother, Timothy would have been viewed as an 'apostate Jew' and would not have gained a hearing among the Jews in the area.[54] Therefore Paul, freely, rather than out of Mosaic or soteriological necessity, has Timothy circumcised for the sake of taking him along on a mission that still included appeals to Jews in synagogues to believe in Jesus.[55]

## Paul and vows in Jerusalem

Finally, this circumcision of Timothy because of the Jews in the area of Lystra also prepares readers of Acts to understand better the incident surrounding Paul's arrival in Jerusalem in 21:17–26. The information that has apparently been passed on to Jews in Jerusalem that Paul teaches 'all the Jews who live among the Gentiles to turn away from Moses, telling them *not* to circumcise their children or live according to [the Jewish] customs' is therefore already seen to be another false charge in the light of 16:3. Clearly there is no basis for the charge that Paul tells Jews *not* to circumcise their children.[56] The

---

[52] Contra Jervell 1972: 145. In this sense, of course, this is not a contradiction of Paul's rejection of Titus' circumcision in Gal. 2:3–5, which, as a requirement, would have compromised 'the truth of the gospel' (2:5). It should also be noted that even in Paul's letters he did not oppose circumcision in itself. Circumcision was a matter of *indifference* to Paul: 'neither circumcision nor uncircumcision has any value' (Gal. 5:6; 6:15; 1 Cor. 7:19).

[53] L. T. Johnson 1992: 284.

[54] Bruce 1990: 352; Witherington 1998: 475–476; Peterson 2009: 450. Witherington correctly observes that the implication here is that the Jews thought Timothy should have been circumcised and therefore he was viewed as Jewish (though apostate) because of his Jewish mother.

[55] Note the references to Timothy in 17:14–15 and 18:5 in the context of Jewish evangelism. This freedom is also evident in Acts 18:18.

[56] As noted above (n. 52), this is also the case regarding Paul's references to circumcision in his letters. That these are false charges recalls the charges against Stephen in 6:11, 13–14.

subsequent action of Paul's participation in the 'purification rites' of four men in the temple is then given as an example that Paul is not opposed to Jewish customs and that he himself observes the law when entering the temple area (21:23–24, 26).[57]

Sometimes it is argued that there is some animosity here between the Jerusalem leaders and Paul. Porter states that 'Paul was in some way, if not directly lured into, at least not prevented from, stepping into a trap.'[58] Luke, however, emphasizes the harmony of this occasion by noting that 'the brothers' in Jerusalem received Paul and those travelling with him 'warmly' (21:17). Then, following Paul's greeting and account of what God had done among the Gentiles through his ministry, Luke notes that they (presumably James and 'all the elders') 'praised God' (21:20).[59] The following verses highlight the agreement between Paul and the Jerusalem elders, as the instructions in 21:24 to take the men, join in their purification rites and pay their expenses are followed exactly by Paul in 21:26.[60] The reference in 21:25 to the decree from the Jerusalem Council recalls the Council's agreement in Acts 15 and clarifies that the issue here does not concern Gentile adherence to the Mosaic law.[61]

As with the circumcision of Timothy in Acts 16, this action of Paul in the temple shows that he does not see the new salvation-historical change in the role of the law as mandating insensitivity to the Jews. Paul does not purposely enter the temple 'unclean' (21:26;

[57] It is likely that two actions are involved here. Paul (1) pays for the fulfilment of the Nazaritic vows of the four men and (2) undertakes another ritual of purification, perhaps for those who come from unclean lands. Witherington 1998: 649; Peterson 2009: 586–587.

[58] Porter 1999: 179. Porter follows Mattill 1970: 115–116. Dunn (1990: 256) states that the Jerusalem church leaders 'washed their hands of Paul, left him to stew in his own juice'. Bauckham (1995: 478) rightly criticizes the views of Mattill and Dunn by noting the likelihood that James and the church leaders would have had little influence in the situation anyway. Bauckham correctly observes that 'no doubt the elders recognized that Paul was in some danger in Jerusalem, but their advice was calculated to dispel the danger, not to increase it'.

[59] Porter (1999: 175), after noting the emphasis on the harmony between Paul and the Jerusalem leaders, then surprisingly states that 'the narrative does not make it clear that the leaders were convinced that the accusations [of 21:21] were false'.

[60] Tajra (1989: 63) notes that 'Luke stresses Paul's agreement to do exactly what James and the elders suggested', but does not draw attention to the parallelism of 21:24 and 26. Cf. Porter 1999: 180–182 for a summary of the main views concerning the nature of the purification rites in 21:24, 26.

[61] In the light of the emphasis on agreement in both Acts 15 and in this context (21:17–20a), this is a more plausible explanation for this reference to the decrees than the idea that Paul was not at the Council (Catchpole 1977: 431) or that it is a source-critical error (Conzelmann 1987: 180–181).

24:18), nor does he bring an 'unclean' Gentile into the temple (21:29) to demonstrate his 'freedom' from the law. He is not out to flout Jewish sensibilities. Paul's activity in the temple in this context is not another supposedly 'positive' example of continuing temple activity among the early Christians. In this context, Paul is participating in 'purification' rites as a mark of respect to Jewish sensitivities as to what is deemed appropriate in the temple (there is no requirement here to keep the law for salvation as suggested in 15:1).

Furthermore, as with the circumcision of Timothy, this action of Paul in the temple is another example that demonstrates his desire to appeal to his fellow Jews. Thus there is an emphasis here on the proclamation of Jesus as the one who fulfils and replaces the temple. This action presents Paul with an opportunity, like Stephen (cf. 22:20), to point to the Lord Jesus. Thus Paul, outside the temple (21:30), announces that Jesus is the Lord who reigns from heaven (22:6–10), the 'Righteous One' (22:14), 'the name' who must now be called upon for the forgiveness of sins (22:16) and the One who commissioned Paul to leave the temple, to bear witness to Jesus and to go 'far away' to the Gentiles (22:17–18, 21).

## Conclusion

The role of the law in Acts is best understood in the context of the new salvation-historical situation brought about by the inauguration of the kingdom of God. Although not all questions concerning teaching and guidance for believers and the role of the Mosaic law are answered in Acts, the broad salvation-historical shift is clear. The enthronement of Jesus as the promised Davidic King and Lord has brought about the promised last days and the restoration of God's people. Charges against the apostles, Stephen and Paul that they are against the law of Moses are clearly false. The apostles could not be *against* Moses, for this would be to oppose the one who pointed to Jesus. This new situation, however, indicates that the Lord Jesus is now the one in whom all of God's blessings are found and, as reigning Lord, he is also the one to whom God's people submit and the one they call upon. As the authorized delegates of the Lord Jesus, the apostles' authority and teaching about the Lord Jesus are now the direct guiding authority for God's people.

# Chapter Seven

# Concluding summary

Luke's 'biblical narrative', the book of Acts, highlights the continued outworking of God's saving purposes through the risen Lord Jesus. In chapter 1 we saw that the kingdom of God, inaugurated in the person of the Lord Jesus, is continuing to be administered through Jesus even though he, as the one who announced the arrival of the kingdom, has ascended to heaven. The book of Acts, therefore, is about 'the acts of the risen Lord Jesus'. The departure of the Lord Jesus does not mean the departure of the kingdom. In this period between the 'now' and the 'not yet' of the kingdom he is continuing to reign from the right hand of the Father, as seen in the pouring out of the Spirit and the spread of the good news about him. The suffering and opposition that believers continue to face is because the kingdom has 'not yet' come in fullness. Nevertheless, the risen Lord Jesus ensures that the word will continue to spread and, in this 'inaugurated kingdom', God's people are strengthened by his word of grace in the context of local churches.

Luke's emphasis on the inauguration of the kingdom by Jesus and his continuing rule is the reason why the resurrection of Jesus features so prominently in Acts. In chapter 2 we saw that the resurrection of Jesus especially highlights the arrival of the age to come as anticipated in the OT Scriptures. The resurrection is therefore integral to the outworking of God's saving promises and the inauguration of the kingdom of God: it is the fulfilment of Israel's hope. Luke had already drawn attention to the saving significance of the wrath-bearing and sacrificial death of Jesus in his Gospel. In Acts, therefore, he summarizes this aspect of apostolic preaching more succinctly in order to highlight the new event in God's saving purposes: the resurrection as supreme evidence of the achievement of God's saving purposes and the arrival of the age to come. It is therefore on the basis of the death and resurrection of Jesus that the blessings of the age to come may be offered to all who come to the risen Lord Jesus in repentance and faith.

In chapter 3 we saw that the close relationship between the nature of God's kingdom in this era (following Jesus' death, resurrection and ascension) and the prophetic hopes for the restoration of Israel and the inclusion of Gentiles is established in the first chapter of Acts. In response to the disciples' question concerning the kingdom, Jesus clarified that God's saving promises would indeed be fulfilled: Israel would be restored to God and salvation would come to the Gentiles. The narrative of Acts then shows the unfolding of those saving promises as thousands of Jews (including the southern kingdom of Judea) respond to the message of the saving reign of the Davidic King, Samaria (reminding us of the northern kingdom) hears and responds to the good news of the kingdom of God and the name of Jesus Christ, outsiders (as illustrated by the eunuch) joyfully respond to the good news about Jesus (as Isa. 56 anticipated), and Gentiles also receive salvation through faith in the Lord Jesus (according to God's promises in the prophets). All (Jew and Gentile) who receive the blessings of forgiveness and the Holy Spirit through faith in Jesus are God's people. God's saving kingdom through the reign of the Davidic King Jesus is continuing according to plan.

This framework of the inaugurated kingdom of God also helps to explain Luke's focus on the role of the Holy Spirit in Acts. In chapter 4 we saw that the pouring out of the Holy Spirit is evidence that the Lord Jesus reigns from the throne of David: the Lord Jesus is continuing to reign and administer God's saving promises. Peter declares in Acts 2 that, in the light of the promise found in Joel, the pouring out of the Holy Spirit shows that the last days have arrived, and God's last-days promises for the restoration of his people are being fulfilled. As promised, therefore, all who turn to the Lord Jesus in repentance and faith receive the Holy Spirit, all are enabled by the Spirit to proclaim the good news of God's saving action in Christ, God's people are transformed by the Holy Spirit and, therefore, there is just one people of God under the Davidic King Jesus.

The introduction of this 'new era' of 'last days' fulfilment, however, also has implications for the 'old era'. If the kingdom of God has been inaugurated in the death, resurrection and reign of Jesus as the Davidic King and Lord, what happens to the old system and its authorities? In chapter 5 we saw that Luke follows an emphasis in Acts 2 on the Davidic kingship of Jesus and the arrival of the last days with a focus on the temple and temple leadership in Acts 3 – 7. Luke especially draws attention to the replacement and fulfilment of the temple in the risen Lord Jesus by highlighting the all sufficiency of Jesus as the only one in whom all of God's blessings may now be found. Thus Stephen, in his dying words, points to Jesus as the One who reigns in the presence of God, receives prayer, brings access to God's presence and grants forgiveness of sins. Because of this, the temple authorities are not the leaders of the new people of God. Rather, God's people are formed and strengthened by the apostolic proclamation of Jesus as the one with universal authority and as the 'name' in whom all of God's blessings are now received.

Since Jesus now reigns as Lord and his chosen apostles are the leaders of God's new people, what is the relationship now between the law of Moses and the people of God, in the inaugurated kingdom after Jesus' ascension? In chapter 6 we saw that the role of the law in Acts is best understood in the context of the new salvation-historical situation brought about by the inauguration of the kingdom of God. The apostles are not *against* Moses, for this would be to oppose the one who pointed to Jesus. This new situation, however, indicates that, as reigning Lord, Jesus is the one to whom God's people submit and the one they call upon. As the authorized delegates of the Lord Jesus, the apostles' authority and teaching are now the direct guiding authority for God's people. The book of Acts highlights the end of the old temple system and law and the inauguration of a new 'authority structure' in the inaugurated kingdom of God by virtue of Jesus' lordship and the teaching of his authorized delegates, the apostles.

The inauguration of the kingdom of God therefore provides cohesion to the emphases in Acts on (1) the sovereign plan of God, (2) the reign of the Davidic King Jesus, (3) the spread of the word and the strengthening of local churches in the midst of opposition, (4) the resurrection of the Lord Jesus and the offer of God's end-time blessings on the basis of his death and resurrection, (5) the fulfilment of God's saving promises in the restoration of God's people, (6) the pouring out of the Holy Spirit from the risen and reigning Lord Jesus, (7) the replacement and fulfilment of the temple in Jesus, and (8) the salvation-historical shift to the teaching of the apostles as the guiding authority for God's people.

Thus, according to Luke, believers such as Theophilus may be assured that God's plan of salvation is being carried out according to his promises through the continuing reign of the risen Lord Jesus. The inaugurated kingdom of God continues to be administered by the Lord Jesus. In this era of the kingdom of God the Lord Jesus continues to add to his church, to enable the spread of the word, and to strengthen his people before the consummation of the kingdom at his return. His death and resurrection mean that the blessings of the age to come are found in him even now. All who turn to him receive the blessings of forgiveness of sins and the gift of the Holy Spirit. God's people may be assured that they will be enabled and transformed by the Spirit of Jesus. The Lord Jesus is the one who grants these gifts to Jew and Gentile alike. Thus Gentiles are receiving God's salvation by the grace of the Lord Jesus through hearing and believing the same good news of forgiveness of sins through faith in Jesus, not because God has failed to keep his word to Israel. God's people may be reassured, therefore, that God fulfils his promises through the acts of their Saviour, the risen and reigning Lord Jesus!

# Bibliography

Allen, O. W., Jr. (1997), *The Death of Herod: The Narrative and Theological Function of Retribution in Luke-Acts*, SBLDS 158, Atlanta: Scholars.

Allison, D. C. (1988), 'Was There a "Lukan Community"?', *IBS* 10: 62–70.

Anderson, K. L. (2006), *'But God Raised Him from the Dead': The Theology of Jesus' Resurrection in Luke-Acts*, Milton Keynes: Paternoster.

Barrett, C. K. (1991), 'Attitudes to the Temple in the Acts of the Apostles', in W. Horbury (ed.), *Templum Amicitiae: Essays on the Second Temple Presented to Ernst Bammel*, JSNTSup 48, Sheffield: Sheffield Academic Press, 345–367.

—— (1994), *A Critical and Exegetical Commentary on the Acts of the Apostles*, vol. 1: *Acts I–XIV*, ICC, Edinburgh: T. & T. Clark.

—— (1996), 'The First New Testament', *NovT* 38: 94–104.

—— (1998), *A Critical and Exegetical Commentary on the Acts of the Apostles*, vol. 2: *Acts XV–XXVIII*, ICC, Edinburgh: T. & T. Clark.

Barton, S. C. (1998), 'Can We Identify the Gospel Audiences?', in R. Bauckham (ed.) *The Gospels for All Christians: Rethinking the Gospel Audiences*, Grand Rapids: Eerdmans, 173–194.

Bauckham, R. (1995), 'James and the Jerusalem Church', in R. Bauckham (ed.), *The Book of Acts in Its First Century Setting*, vol. 4: *The Book of Acts in Its Palestinian Setting*, Grand Rapids: Eerdmans; Carlisle: Paternoster, 415–480.

—— (2001), 'The Restoration of Israel in Luke-Acts', in J. M. Scott (ed.), *Restoration: Old Testament, Jewish and Christian Perspectives*, JSJSup 72, Leiden: Brill, 435–487.

—— (2008), *The Jewish World Around the New Testament*, WUNT 233, Tübingen: Mohr Siebeck.

Beale, G. K. (2004), *The Temple and the Church's Mission: A Biblical*

*Theology of the Dwelling Place of God*, NSBT 17, Leicester: Apollos; Downers Grove: IVP.

Beasley-Murray, G. R. (1986), *Jesus and the Kingdom of God*, Grand Rapids: Eerdmans.

Bird, M. F. (2007), 'The Unity of Luke-Acts in Recent Discussion', *JSNT* 29: 425–448.

Blomberg, C. L. (1984), 'The Law in Luke-Acts', *JSNT* 22: 53–80.

—— (1998), 'The Christian and the Law of Moses', in Marshall and Peterson 1998: 397–416.

Bock, D. L. (1987), *Proclamation from Prophecy and Pattern: Lucan Old Testament Christology*, JSNTSup 12, Sheffield: Sheffield Academic Press.

—— (1992), 'The Reign of the Lord Christ', in C. A. Blaising and D. L. Bock (eds.), *Dispensationalism, Israel and the Church: The Search for Definition*, Grand Rapids: Zondervan, 37–67.

—— (1994), *Luke 1:1 – 9:50*, BECNT, Grand Rapids: Baker.

—— (1996), *Luke 9:51 – 24:53*, BECNT, Grand Rapids: Baker.

—— (1998), 'Scripture and the Realisation of God's Promises', in Marshall and Peterson 1998: 41–62.

—— (2007), *Acts*, BECNT, Grand Rapids: Baker.

Bolt, P. G. (2004), *The Cross from a Distance: Atonement in Mark's Gospel*, NSBT 18, Leicester: Apollos; Downers Grove: IVP.

Bovon, F. (1970), 'Tradition et redaction en Actes 10:1 – 11:18', *TZ* 26: 22–45.

—— (1995), 'The Holy Spirit, the Church and Human Relationships According to Acts 20:36 – 21:16', in *New Testament Traditions and Apocryphal Narratives*, PTMS 36, Allison Park: Pickwick, 27–42.

—— (2006), *Luke the Theologian: Fifty-Five Years of Research (1950–2005)*, Waco: Baylor University Press.

Bruce, F. F. (1975–6), 'Is the Paul of Acts the Real Paul?', *BJRL* 58: 282–305.

—— (1988), *The Book of Acts*, NICNT, Grand Rapids: Eerdmans.

—— (1990), *The Acts of the Apostles: The Greek Text with Introduction and Commentary*, Grand Rapids: Eerdmans.

Buckwalter, H. D. (1996), *The Character and Purpose of Luke's Christology*, SNTSMS 89, Cambridge: Cambridge University Press.

Butticaz, S. (2009), 'Acts 15 or the "Return of the Repressed"? The Church and the Law in Acts', in Tait and Oakes 2009: 118–132.

Cadbury, H. J. (1927), *The Making of Luke-Acts*, New York: Macmillan.

Calvin, J. (1965), *The Acts of the Apostles 1–13*, ed. D. W. Torrance and T. F. Torrance, Grand Rapids: Eerdmans.

Capper, B. J. (1998), 'Reciprocity and the Ethic of Acts', in Marshall and Peterson 1998: 499–518.

Carson, D. A. (1987), *Showing the Spirit: A Theological Exposition of 1 Corinthians 12 – 14*, Grand Rapids: Baker.

—— (2000), *The Difficult Doctrine of the Love of God*, Wheaton: Crossway; Leicester: IVP.

—— (2008), 'The *SBJT* Forum: What Are the Most Common Errors That People Make When it Comes to Understanding and Proclaiming the Kingdom?', *SBJT* 12: 104–107.

Carson, D. A., and D. J. Moo (2005), *An Introduction to the New Testament*, 2nd ed., Grand Rapids: Zondervan.

Cassidy, R. J. (1987), *Society and Politics in the Acts of the Apostles*, Maryknoll: Orbis.

Catchpole, D. (1977), 'Paul, James and the Apostolic Decree', *NTS* 23: 428–444.

Chance, J. B. (1988), *Jerusalem, the Temple, and the New Age in Luke-Acts*, Macon: Mercer University Press.

Childs, B. S. (2001), *Isaiah*, Louisville: Westminster John Knox.

Clark, A. C. (1998), 'The Role of the Apostles', in Marshall and Peterson 1998: 169–190.

Cole, G. A. (2007), *Engaging with the Holy Spirit: Six Crucial Questions*, Nottingham: Apollos.

Conzelmann, H. (1960), *The Theology of St. Luke*, New York: Harper & Row.

—— (1987), *Acts of the Apostles*, Philadelphia: Fortress.

Cook, D. (2007), *Teaching Acts: Unlocking the Book of Acts for the Bible Teacher*, Fearn: Christian Focus.

Cosgrove, C. H. (1984), 'The Divine *DEI* in Luke-Acts: Investigations into the Lukan Understanding of God's Providence', *NovT* 26: 168–190.

Cunningham, S. (1997), *'Through Many Tribulations': The Theology of Persecution in Luke-Acts*, JSNTSup 142, Sheffield: Sheffield Academic Press.

Doble, P. (1996), *The Paradox of Salvation: Luke's Theology of the Cross*, SNTSMS 87, Cambridge: Cambridge University Press.

Dodd, C. H. (1944), *The Apostolic Preaching and Its Developments*, London: Hodder & Stoughton.

Dunn, J. D. G. (1970), *Baptism in the Holy Spirit: A Re-examination of the New Testament Teaching on the Gift of the Spirit in Relation to Pentecostalism Today*, London: SCM.

—— (1990), *Unity and Diversity in the New Testament: An Inquiry into the Character of Earliest Christianity*, 2nd ed., Philadelphia: Trinity Press International.

Ehrman, B. D. (1991), 'The Cup, the Bread, and the Salvific Effect of Jesus' Death in Luke-Acts', in E. H. Lovering (ed.), *Society of Biblical Literature 1991 Seminar Papers*, Atlanta: Scholars, 576–591.

Esler, P. F. (1987), *Community and Gospel in Luke-Acts: The Social and Political Motivations of Lucan Theology*, SNTSMS 57, Cambridge: Cambridge University Press.

Fee, G. D. (1994), *God's Empowering Presence: The Holy Spirit in the Letters of Paul*, Peabody: Hendrickson.

Fee, G. D., and D. Stuart (2003), *How to Read the Bible for All Its Worth: A Guide to Understanding the Bible*, 3rd ed., Grand Rapids: Zondervan.

Ferguson, E. (1993), *Backgrounds of Early Christianity*, 2nd ed., Grand Rapids: Eerdmans.

Fitzmyer, J. A. (1981), *The Gospel According to Luke (i–ix)*, AB 28, New York: Doubleday.

—— (1998), *Acts of the Apostles: A New Translation with Introduction and Commentary*, AB 31, New York: Doubleday.

Fowler, A. (1982), *Kinds of Literature: An Introduction to the Theory of Genres and Modes*, Oxford: Clarendon.

France, R. T. (1990), *Divine Government: God's Kingship in the Gospel of Mark*, London: SPCK.

—— (2002), *The Gospel of Mark*, NIGTC, Grand Rapids: Eerdmans; Carlisle: Paternoster.

Franklin, E. R. (1975), *Christ the Lord: A Study in the Purpose and Theology of Luke-Acts*, London: SPCK.

Gasque, W. W. (1989), *A History of the Interpretation of the Acts of the Apostles*, Peabody: Hendrickson.

Gathercole, S. J. (2006), *The Preexistent Son: Recovering the Christologies of Matthew, Mark, and Luke*, Grand Rapids: Eerdmans.

Gaventa, B. R. (2003), *The Acts of the Apostles*, Nashville: Abingdon.

Green, C. (2005), *The Word of His Grace: A Guide to Teaching and Preaching from Acts*, Leicester: IVP.

Green, J. B. (1997), *The Gospel of Luke*, NICNT, Grand Rapids: Eerdmans.

—— (1998), '"Witnesses of His Resurrection": Resurrection, Salvation, Discipleship, and Mission in the Acts of the Apostles', in R. N. Longenecker (ed.), *Life in the Face of Death: The Resurrection Message of the New Testament*, Grand Rapids: Eerdmans, 227–246.

Haenchen, E. (1971), *The Acts of the Apostles*, Philadelphia: Fortress.

Hahn, S. W. (2005), 'Kingdom and Church in Luke-Acts: From Davidic Christology to Kingdom Ecclesiology', in C. G. Bartholomew, J. G. Green and A. C. Thiselton (eds.), *Reading Luke: Interpretation, Reflection, Formation*, Grand Rapids: Zondervan, 294–326.

Hamilton, J. M. (2006), *God's Indwelling Presence: The Holy Spirit in the Old and New Testaments*, Nashville: Broadman & Holman.

—— (2008), 'The Center of Biblical Theology in Acts: Deliverance and Damnation Display the Divine', *Them* 33: 34–47.

—— (2010), *God's Glory in Salvation Through Judgment*, Wheaton: Crossway.

Hays, C. (2010), *Luke's Wealth Ethics*, WUNT 2.275, Tübingen: Mohr Siebeck.

Hays, R. B. (1989), *Echoes of Scripture in the Letters of Paul*, New Haven: Yale University Press.

Head, P. M. (2004), 'The Temple in Luke's Gospel', in T. D. Alexander and S. Gathercole (eds.), *Heaven on Earth: The Temple in Biblical Theology*, Carlisle: Paternoster, 101–119.

Hemer, C. J. (1989), *The Book of Acts in the Setting of Hellenistic History*, WUNT 49, Tübingen: Mohr Siebeck.

Hengel, M. (1983), *Between Jesus and Paul: Studies in the Earliest History of Christianity*, Philadelphia: Fortress, 1983.

Hill, C. C. (1992), *Hellenists and Hebrews: Reappraising Division within the Earliest Church*, Minneapolis: Fortress.

Hill, D. (1984), 'The Spirit and the Church's Witness: Observations on Acts 1.6–8', *IBS* 6: 16–26.

House, P. R. (1990), 'Suffering and the Purpose of Acts', *JETS* 33: 317–330.

—— (1998), *Old Testament Theology*, Downers Grove: IVP.

—— (2005), 'Examining the Narratives of Old Testament Narrative: An Exploration In Biblical Theology', *WTJ* 67: 229–245.

Hur, J. (2001), *A Dynamic Reading of the Holy Spirit in Luke-Acts*, JSNTSup 211, Sheffield: Sheffield Academic Press.

Hurtado, L. W. (2003), *Lord Jesus Christ: Devotion to Jesus in Earliest Christianity*, Grand Rapids: Eerdmans.

Jervell, J. (1972), *Luke and the People of God: A New Look at Luke-Acts*, Minneapolis: Augsburg.

—— (1988), 'The Church of Jews and Godfearers', in J. B. Tyson (ed.), *Luke-Acts and the Jewish People: Eight Critical Perspectives*, Minneapolis: Augsburg, 11–20.

—— (1996), *The Theology of the Acts of the Apostles*, Cambridge: Cambridge University Press.

—— (1998), *Die Apostelgeschichte*, Göttingen: Vandenhoeck & Ruprecht.

Johnson, D. E. (1990), 'Jesus Against the Idols: The Use of Isaianic Servant Songs in the Missiology of Acts', *WTJ* 52: 343–353.

—— (1997), *The Message of Acts in the History of Redemption*, Phillipsburg: Presbyterian & Reformed.

Johnson, L. T. (1992), *The Acts of the Apostles*, SP 5, Collegeville: Liturgical.

Kepple, R. J. (1977), 'The Hope of Israel, the Resurrection of the Dead, and Jesus: A Study of their Relationship in Acts with Particular Regard to the Understanding of Paul's Trial Defense', *JETS* 20: 231–241.

Kern, P. H. (2003), 'Paul's Conversion and Luke's Portrayal of Character in Acts 8 – 10', *TynBul* 54: 63–80.

Kilgallen, J. J. (1994), 'Paul's Speech to the Ephesian Elders: Its Structure', *ETL* 70: 112–121.

Klinghardt, M. (1988), *Gesetz und Volk Gottes. Das lukanische Verständnis des Gesetzes nach Herkunft, Funktion und seinem Ort in der Geschichte des Urchristentums*, WUNT 2.32, Tübingen: Mohr Siebeck.

Kodell, J. (1974), '"The Word of God Grew": The Ecclesial Tendency of *Logos* in Acts 6:7; 12:24; 19:20', *Bib* 55: 505–519.

Koet, B. J. (1989), *Five Studies on Interpretation of Scripture in Luke-Acts*, Leuven: Leuven University Press.

Köstenberger, A. J., L. S. Kellum and C. L. Quarles (2009), *The Cradle, the Cross, and the Crown: An Introduction to the New Testament*, Nashville: Broadman & Holman.

Kurz, W. S. (1993), *Reading Luke-Acts: Dynamics of Biblical Narrative*, Louisville: Westminster John Knox.

Ladd, G. E. (1993), *A Theology of the New Testament*, rev. ed., Grand Rapids: Eerdmans.

Larkin, W. J. (1977), 'Luke's Use of the Old Testament as a Key to His Soteriology', *JETS* 20: 325–335.

Maddox, R. (1982), *The Purpose of Luke-Acts*, Edinburgh: T. & T. Clark.

Mallen, P. (2008), *The Reading and Transformation of Isaiah in Luke-Acts*, LNTS 367, London: T. & T. Clark.

Marguerat, D. (2002), *The First Christian Historian: Writing the 'Acts of the Apostles'*, SNTSMS 121, Cambridge: Cambridge University Press.

—— (2009), 'Paul and the Torah in the Acts of the Apostles', in Tait and Oakes 2009: 98–117.

Marshall, I. H. (1970), *Luke: Historian and Theologian*, Exeter: Paternoster.

—— (1978), *The Gospel of Luke*, NIGTC, Grand Rapids: Eerdmans.

—— (1993), 'Acts and the "Former Treatise"', in Winter and Clark 1993: 163–182.

—— (2007), 'Acts', in G. K. Beale and D. A. Carson (eds.), *Commentary on the New Testament Use of the Old Testament*, Grand Rapids: Baker, 513–606.

Marshall, I. H., and D. G. Peterson (eds.) (1998), *Witness to the Gospel: The Theology of Acts*, Grand Rapids: Eerdmans.

Matthews, S. (2010), *Perfect Martyr: The Stoning of Stephen and the Construction of Christian Identity*, Oxford: Oxford University Press.

Mattill, A. J. (1970), 'The Purpose of Acts: Schneckenburger Reconsidered', in W. W. Gasque and R. P. Martin (eds.), *Apostolic History and the Gospel: Biblical and Historical Essays Presented to F. F. Bruce on His 60th Birthday*, Grand Rapids: Eerdmans, 108–122.

Menzies, R. P. (1991), *The Development of Early Christian Pneumatology with Special Reference to Luke-Acts*, JSNTSup 54, Sheffield: Sheffield Academic Press.

Metzger, B. M. (1994), *A Textual Commentary on the Greek New Testament: A Companion Volume to the United Bible Society's Greek New Testament (Fourth Revised Edition)*, New York: United Bible Society.

Moessner, D. P. (1986), '"The Christ Must Suffer": New Light on the Jesus–Peter, Stephen, Paul Parallels in Luke-Acts', *NovT* 28: 220–256.

Moo, D. J. (1993), 'The Law of Christ as the Fulfillment of the Law of Moses: A Modified Lutheran View', in W. G. Strickland (ed.), *The Law, the Gospel, and the Modern Christian: Five Views*, Grand Rapids: Zondervan, 319–376.

Morgan, G. C. (1924), *The Acts of the Apostles*, New York: Fleming H. Revell.

Motyer, J. A. (1993), *The Prophecy of Isaiah: An Introduction and Commentary*, Leicester: IVP; Downers Grove: IVP.

Moule, C. F. D. (1966), 'The Christology of Acts', in L. E. Keck and J. L. Martyn (eds.), *Studies in Luke-Acts: Essays Presented in Honor of Paul Schubert*, Nashville: Abingdon, 159–185.

Moxnes, H. (1994), 'The Social Context of Luke's Community', *Int* 48: 379–389.

Nolland, J. (1980–1), 'A Fresh Look at Acts 15:10', *NTS* 27: 105–115.

—— (1993), *Luke 9:21 – 18:34*, WBC 35B, Dallas: Word.

O'Reilly, L. (1987), *Word and Sign in the Acts of the Apostles: A Study in Lucan Theology*, Rome: Editrice Pontificia Università Gregoriana.

Oswalt, J. N. (1998), *The Book of Isaiah: Chapters 40 – 66*, NICOT, Grand Rapids: Eerdmans.

O'Toole, R. F. (1987), 'The Kingdom of God in Luke-Acts', in W. Willis (ed.), *The Kingdom of God in Twentieth-Century Interpretation*, Peabody: Hendrickson, 147–162.

Padilla, O. (2008), *The Speeches of Outsiders in Acts: Poetics, Theology and Historiography*, SNTSMS 144, Cambridge: Cambridge University Press.

Pao, D. W. (2000), *Acts and the Isaianic New Exodus*, WUNT 2.130, Tübingen: Mohr Siebeck.

Pentecost, J. D. (2010), *New Wine: A Study of Transition in the Book of Acts*, Grand Rapids: Kregel.

Perrin, N. (2010), *Jesus the Temple*, Grand Rapids: Baker.

Pervo, R. I. (2009), *Acts: A Commentary*, Minneapolis: Fortress.

Peterson, D. G. (1993), 'The Motif of Fulfilment and the Purpose of Luke-Acts', in Winter and Clark 1993: 83–104.

—— (1998), 'The Worship of the New Community', in Marshall and Peterson 1998: 373–395.

—— (2009), *The Acts of the Apostles*, PNTC, Grand Rapids: Eerdmans; Nottingham: Apollos.

Polhill, J. B. (1992), *Acts*, NAC 26, Nashville: Broadman & Holman.

Porter, S. E. (1999), *The Paul of Acts: Essays in Literary Criticism, Rhetoric, and Theology*, WUNT 115, Tübingen: Mohr Siebeck.

Rapske, B. (1998), 'Opposition to the Plan of God and Persecution', in Marshall and Peterson 1998: 235–256.

Ravens, D. (1995), *Luke and the Restoration of Israel*, JSNTSup 119, Sheffield: Sheffield Academic Press.

Robertson, O. P. (2004), *The Christ of the Prophets*, Phillipsburg: Presbyterian & Reformed.

Rosner, B. S. (1993), 'Acts and Biblical History', in Winter and Clark 1993: 65–82.

—— (1998), 'The Progress of the Word', in Marshall and Peterson 1998: 215–233.

—— (2000), 'Biblical Theology', in T. D. Alexander and B. S. Rosner (eds.), *New Dictionary of Biblical Theology*, Leicester: IVP, 3–11.

Rowe, C. K. (2009), *World Upside Down: Reading Acts in the Graeco-Roman Age*, Oxford: Oxford University Press.

Salo, K. (1991), *Luke's Treatment of the Law: A Redaction-Critical Investigation*, Helsinki: Suomalainen Tiedeakatemia.

Sanders, J. A. (1982), 'Isaiah in Luke', *Int* 36: 144–155.

Sanders, J. T. (1987), *The Jews in Luke-Acts*, Philadelphia: Fortress.

—— (1991), 'Who Is a Jew and Who Is a Gentile in the Book of Acts?', *NTS* 37: 434–455.

Schnabel, E. J. (2004), *Early Christian Mission*, vol. 1: *Jesus and the Twelve*; vol. 2: *Paul and the Early Church*, Downers Grove: IVP.

Schreiner, T. R. (2008), *New Testament Theology: Magnifying God in Christ*, Grand Rapids: Baker; Nottingham: Apollos.

—— (2010), *40 Questions About Christians and Biblical Law*, Grand Rapids: Kregel.

Seccombe, D. (1981), 'Luke and Isaiah', *NTS* 27: 252–259.

—— (2002), *The King of God's Kingdom: A Solution to the Puzzle of Jesus*, Carlisle: Paternoster.

Seifrid, M. A. (1987), 'Jesus and the Law in Acts', *JSNT* 30: 39–57.

Sleeman, M. (2009), *Geography and the Ascension Narrative in Acts*, SNTSMS 146, Cambridge: Cambridge University Press.

Soards, M. L. (1994), *The Speeches in Acts: Their Content, Context, and Concerns*, Louisville: Westminster.

Spencer, F. S. (1993), 'Acts and Modern Literary Approaches', in Winter and Clark 1993: 381–414.

—— (2004), *Journeying Through Acts: A Literary-Cultural Reading*, Peabody: Hendrickson.

Squires, J. T. (1993), *The Plan of God in Luke-Acts*, Cambridge: Cambridge University Press.

—— (1998), 'The Plan of God in the Acts of the Apostles', in Marshall and Peterson 1998: 9–39.

Steffeck, E. (2009), 'Some Observations on the Apostolic Decree in Acts 15:20, 29 (and 21:25)', in Tait and Oakes 2009: 133–142.

Stein, R. H. (2006), 'Baptism in Luke-Acts', in T. R. Schreiner and S. D. Wright (eds.), *Believer's Baptism: Sign of the New Covenant in Christ*, Nashville: Broadman & Holman, 35–66.

Stenschke, C. (1998), 'The Need for Salvation', in Marshall and Peterson 1998: 125–144.

Sterling, G. E. (1992), *Historiography and Self Definition: Josephus, Luke-Acts and Apologetic Historiography*, Leiden: Brill.

Steyn, G. J. (1995), *Septuagint Quotations in the Context of the Petrine and Pauline Speeches of the Acta Apostolorum*, CBET 12, Kampen: Kok Pharos.

Stott, J. R. W. (1990), *The Message of Acts: To the Ends of the Earth*, BST, Leicester: IVP.

Strauss, M. L. (1995), *The Davidic Messiah in Luke-Acts: The Promise and Its Fulfillment in Lukan Christology*, JSNTSup 110, Sheffield: Sheffield Academic Press.

Sylva, D. (1987), 'The Meaning and Function of Acts 7:46–50', *JBL* 106: 261–275.

Tait, M., and P. Oakes (eds.) (2009), *Torah in the New Testament: Papers Delivered at the Manchester-Lausanne Seminar of June 2008*, LNTS 401, London: T. & T. Clark.

Tajra, H. W. (1989), *The Trial of St. Paul: A Juridical Exegesis of the Second Half of Acts*, WUNT 2.35, Tübingen: Mohr Siebeck.

Tannehill, R. C. (1990), *The Narrative Unity of Luke-Acts: A Literary Interpretation*, vol. 2: *The Acts of the Apostles*, Minneapolis: Fortress.

Thompson, A. J. (2004), 'The Unity of the Church in Acts in its Literary Setting', PhD diss., Trinity Evangelical Divinity School.

—— (2008a), *One Lord, One People: The Unity of the Church in Acts in Its Literary Setting*, LNTS 359, London: T. & T. Clark.

—— (2008b), 'Unity in Acts: Idealization or Reality?', *JETS* 51: 523–542.

Thompson, M. B. (forthcoming), 'Paul in the Book of Acts: Differences and Distance', *ExpTim*.

Tiede, D. L. (1986), 'The Exaltation of Jesus and the Restoration of Israel in Acts 1', *HTR* 79: 278–286.

Troftgruben, T. M. (2010), *A Conclusion Unhindered: A Study of the*

*Ending of Acts Within Its Literary Environment*, WUNT 2.280, Tübingen: Mohr Siebeck.

Turner, M. B. (1982), 'The Sabbath, Sunday, and the Law in Luke/ Acts', in *From Sabbath to Lord's Day: A Biblical, Historical, and Theological Investigation*, Grand Rapids: Zondervan, 100–157.

—— (1996), *Power from on High: The Spirit in Israel's Restoration and Witness in Luke-Acts*, JPTSup 9, Sheffield: Sheffield Academic Press.

Twelftree, G. H. (2009), *People of the Spirit: Exploring Luke's View of the Church*, Grand Rapids: Baker.

Tyson, J. B. (2001), 'The Legacy of F. C. Baur and Recent Studies of Acts', *Forum* 4: 125–144.

Vanhoozer, K. J. (1998), *Is There a Meaning in This Text? The Bible, the Reader, and the Morality of Literary Knowledge*, Grand Rapids: Zondervan; Leicester: Apollos.

Verheyden, J. (1999), *The Unity of Luke-Acts*, Leuven: Leuven University Press.

Vielhauer, P. (1966), 'On the "Paulinism" of Acts', in L. E. Keck and J. L. Martyn (eds.), *Studies in Luke-Acts: Essays Presented in Honor of Paul Schubert*, Nashville: Abingdon, 33–50.

Wagner, R. (2004), *Tongues Aflame: Learning to Preach from the Apostles*, Fearn: Mentor.

Walaskay, P. W. (1983), *'And So We Came to Rome': The Political Perspective of St. Luke*, SNTSMS 49, Cambridge: Cambridge University Press.

Walton, S. (2004), 'A Tale of Two Perspectives? The Place of the Temple in Acts', in T. D. Alexander and S. Gathercole (eds.), *Heaven on Earth: The Temple in Biblical Theology*, Carlisle: Paternoster, 135–149.

—— (2008), 'The Acts – of God? What Is the "Acts of the Apostles" All About?', *EQ* 80: 291–306.

Warfield, B. B. (1907), *The Lord of Glory: A Study of the Designations of Our Lord with Especial Reference to His Deity*, New York: American Tract Society.

Webb, B. (1996), *The Message of Isaiah*, BST, Leicester: IVP; Downers Grove: IVP.

Wenk, M. (2000), *Community-Forming Power: The Socio-Ethical Role of the Spirit in Luke-Acts*, JPTSup 19, Sheffield: Sheffield Academic Press.

Westerholm, S. (2004), *Perspectives Old and New: The 'Lutheran' Paul and His Critics*, Grand Rapids: Eerdmans.

Wiarda, T. (2003), 'The Jerusalem Council and the Theological Task', *JETS* 46: 233–248.

Wilson, I. (1995), *Out of the Midst of the Fire: Divine Presence in Deuteronomy*, SBLDS, Atlanta: Scholars.

Wilson, S. G. (1983), *Luke and the Law*, SNTSMS 50, Cambridge: Cambridge University Press.

Winter, B. W., and A. D. Clark (eds.) (1993), *The Book of Acts in Its First Century Setting*, vol. 1: *The Book of Acts in Its Ancient Literary Setting*, Grand Rapids: Eerdmans; Carlisle: Paternoster.

Witherington, B. (1993), 'Not So Idle Thoughts About *EIDOLOTHUTON*', *TynBul* 44: 237–254.

—— (1998), *The Acts of the Apostles: A Socio-Rhetorical Commentary*, Grand Rapids: Eerdmans.

Wright, N. T. (1996), *Jesus and the Victory of God*, London: SPCK.

—— (2003), *The Resurrection of the Son of God*, London: SPCK.

Younger, K. L. (2004), 'The Repopulation of Samaria (2 Kings 17:24, 27–31) in Light of Recent Study', in J. K. Hoffmeier and A. Millard (eds.), *The Future of Biblical Archaeology: Reassessing Methodologies and Assumptions*, Grand Rapids: Eerdmans, 254–280.

Ziccardi, C. (2008), *The Relationship of Jesus and the Kingdom of God According to Luke-Acts*, Rome: Editrice Pontifica Università Gregoriana.

Zwiep, A. W. (1997), *The Ascension of the Messiah in Lukan Christology*, Leiden: Brill.

# Index of authors

# Index of Scripture references

212

**NEW TESTAMENT**

**Matthew**
2:15 *39*
2:18 *39*
5:21–48 *24*
10:5–6 *114*
13 *40*
13:41 *39*
14:14 *40*
21:33–46 *31*
25:14 *42*
25:14–30 *42*
27:5–8 *34*

**Mark**
1:38 *40*
4 *40*
6:34 *40*
7:17–23 *181, 182*
10:45 *84*
12:1–12 *31*
14:32–42 *85*

**Luke**
1:1 *19, 21, 24*
1:1–4 *61*
1:2 *24, 33*
1:4 *19*
1:5 *75*
1:6–7 *75*
1:9 *34*
1:15–16 *133*
1:20 *19*
1:32–33 *114, 123*
1:33 *76*
1:41–42 *133*
1:57 *19*
1:67 *133*
1:68 *43, 76*
1:68–69 *123*
1:77 *86*
1:79 *120*
2:1–12 *114*

2:6 *19*
2:11 *52*
2:21–22 *19*
2:25 *43, 76, 119*
2:25–27 *75*
2:30–32 *119*
2:32 *43, 119, 120*
2:36–38 *75*
2:37 *75*
2:38 *43, 76*
2:49 *30*
3 – 5 *26*
3:3 *86*
3:7–14 *135*
3:8–14 *41*
3:22 *120*
4:18–19 *120*
4:21 *19*
4:32 *19*
4:43 *30, 39, 40*
5:20–21 *86*
5:23–24 *86*
5:32 *135*
5:33 *139*
6:13 *50*
6:37 *86*
6:47 *19*
7:17 *19*
7:18 *139*
7:20–23 *155*
7:22 *120, 155*
7:28 *40, 132*
7:42–43 *86*
7:47–49 *86*
8:1 *39, 40*
8:10 *40*
9 – 19 *41*
9:2 *39*
9:11 *39, 40*
9:22 *30, 33, 42*
9:27 *40*
9:31 *19*
9:35 *85, 120*
9:44 *42*

# Index of ancient sources